W9-AVR-557

THE SECRET PLOT
TO MAKE
TED KENNEDY PRESIDENT

THE SECRET PLOT
TO MAKE
TED KENNEDY PRESIDENT

Inside the Real *Watergate Conspiracy*

Geoff Shepard

SENTINEL

SENTINEL
Published by the Penguin Group
Penguin Group (USA) Inc., 375 Hudson Street,
New York, New York 10014, U.S.A.
Penguin Group (Canada), 90 Eglinton Avenue East, Suite 700,
Toronto, Ontario, Canada M4P 2Y3
(a division of Pearson Penguin Canada Inc.)
Penguin Books Ltd, 80 Strand, London WC2R 0RL, England
Penguin Ireland, 25 St. Stephen's Green, Dublin 2, Ireland
(a division of Penguin Books Ltd)
Penguin Books Australia Ltd, 250 Camberwell Road, Camberwell,
Victoria 3124, Australia
(a division of Pearson Australia Group Pty Ltd)
Penguin Books India Pvt Ltd, 11 Community Centre, Panchsheel Park,
New Delhi—110 017, India
Penguin Group (NZ), 67 Apollo Drive, Rosedale, North Shore 0632,
New Zealand (a division of Pearson New Zealand Ltd)
Penguin Books (South Africa) (Pty) Ltd, 24 Sturdee Avenue,
Rosebank, Johannesburg 2196, South Africa

Penguin Books Ltd, Registered Offices:
80 Strand, London WC2R 0RL, England

First published in 2008 by Sentinel,
a member of Penguin Group (USA) Inc.

10 9 8 7 6 5 4 3 2 1

Copyright © Geoffrey C. Shepard, 2008
All rights reserved.

ISBN: 978-1-59523-048-5

Printed in the United States of America
Set in Garamond
Designed by Spring Hoteling

DEDICATION

The Watergate Special Prosecution Force was established with the appointment of Archibald Cox on May 25, 1973. Nixon resigned on August 9, 1974, but the savage onslaught did not finally end until June of 1977—well after the Democrats had regained control of the White House and vastly increased their majorities in both houses of Congress.

Charles Ruff, the fourth special prosecutor (and later counsel to President Bill Clinton), observed in a farewell interview with Bob Woodward that he expected his work on Watergate to be questioned someday, saying "there are judgment calls that were made that people can legitimately question."

Ruff assured Woodward that, should he be called to testify at such an inquiry, "I'd say, 'Gee, I just don't remember what happened back then,' and they won't be able to indict me for perjury and that, maybe, that's the principal thing that I've learned in four years. . . . I just intend to rely on that failure of memory."

This book marks the beginning of that inquiry, and is dedicated to the thousands of Republicans—candidates, supporters, contributors, and all of their families—whose aspirations were thwarted, whose careers were ended, and whose lives were ruined in the single-minded effort to destroy them and the GOP—to the end that Ted Kennedy might become president and the restoration of Camelot finally be achieved.

CONTENTS

PREFACE

xi

ACKNOWLEDGMENTS

xix

INTRODUCTION

1

CHAPTER 1

Two Summer Nights:

The Bridge at Chappaquiddick and the Watergate Break-in

8

CHAPTER 2

Watergate: What Really Happened—And Why

19

CHAPTER 3

The Hidden Hand of Edward Kennedy

31

CHAPTER 4

Kennedy Politics: Long Memories and Sharp Knives

36

CHAPTER 5

John Dean's Cover-up Collapses

52

CHAPTER 6

The Camelot Conspiracy Commences

69

CHAPTER 7

Obstructing Justice: Postponing Dean's Indictment

78

CHAPTER 8

The Pious Fraud of the Ervin Committee

91

CHAPTER 9

First Blood: John Dean Testifies

100

CHAPTER 10

The Ervin Committee Pioneers
the Politics of Personal Destruction

111

CHAPTER 11

The Watergate Special Prosecutor
and the Terrors of Prosecutorial Abuse

122

CHAPTER 12

Cox's Army of Ivy Leaguers

135

CHAPTER 13

Friends in High Places: The Strange and
Unusual Handling of William O. Bittman, Esq.

147

CHAPTER 14

The Denny/Rient Memo:
The Special Prosecutor's Own "Smoking Gun"

158

CHAPTER 15

The Media Invents a "Massacre"

164

CHAPTER 16

Impeaching a President:
The House Judiciary Committee Joins the Camelot Conspiracy

171

CHAPTER 17

The Liberal Media:
Long-term Enablers of the Kennedy Clan

177

CHAPTER 18

Stage One of the Camelot Conspiracy:
Destroying the President

185

CHAPTER 19

Stage Two of the Camelot Conspiracy:

Crippling the Republican Money Machine

193

CHAPTER 20

Stage Three of the Camelot Conspiracy:

Eviscerating Potential Opponents

202

CHAPTER 21

The Weakest Link: Teddy Kennedy Self-Destructs

209

CHAPTER 22

The Camelot Conspirators Today:

From Edward M. Kennedy to Hillary R. Clinton

216

LIST OF APPENDICES

233

APPENDICES

237

NOTES

305

BIBLIOGRAPHY

313

INDEX

319

PREFACE

After graduating from both Whittier College in 1966 and Harvard Law
School in 1969, I took a job with a law firm in Seattle. At the same
time I applied for a White House Fellowship—although I knew that the
odds of winning one of those highly competitive slots were slim at best.

Richard Nixon himself coincidentally had been responsible for my interest in the Fellows program. In 1965, shortly after being elected student
body president at Whittier, also Nixon's alma mater, I was informed that
I had been selected to receive that year's annual Nixon scholarship ($250,
which at that time was not an insubstantial amount) from the Whittier
Republican Women's Club.

It turned out that Nixon had agreed to present the award in person,
and I was seated at the head table next to the former vice president. When
he rose to speak, he didn't talk about politics or national affairs. Instead, he
set about comparing his experiences at Whittier with mine. We had both,
he said, won student body elections. We both had been on the college debate team and active in the societies (the Quaker equivalent of on-campus
fraternities). He then reviewed his life in politics, but kept bringing everything back to his years at Whittier. He finished on a graceful note, saying
that, having gotten to know me during lunch, he hoped I might go even
further than he had. I left with quite a swollen head in addition to the very
welcome boost in financial aid.

About a week later, I was called to the dean's office for an even greater surprise. Nixon apparently had thought so much of our lunch together that when he got back to New York he wrote a personal check for another $250—thus doubling my scholarship. There was no press release or public acclaim to be had; he simply thought I would benefit from the additional help. Years later this personal act of kindness was the determining factor in my decision to apply for a White House Fellowship in his administration.

The Fellows program was proposed by Secretary of Health, Education and Welfare John Gardner and established by President Johnson in 1964. The idea was to select a few young men and women in the early stages of promising careers and bring them to Washington. Each would be assigned either to the White House staff or to a cabinet member for a year of concentrated study and high-level government experience. They would return to their jobs and their communities with an enhanced understanding of (and possibly an increased desire someday to serve in) the federal government.

Each year's class of Fellows is chosen by a national selection process, which typically begins with a thousand applicants. After national, regional, and local interview panels winnow the numbers, some thirty finalists spend a weekend being grilled and evaluated by the members of the presidentially appointed Commission on White House Fellowships. In the end, an average of fifteen is selected.

I was among those chosen for the class of 1969–70. Not yet twenty-five years old, I was among the youngest ever selected for the program—before or since. I asked to be assigned to the Treasury Department, where I had the privilege of working with Undersecretary Paul A. Volcker. At the end of the Fellowship year, I was invited to join John Ehrlichman's Domestic Council staff, and made the short move from the Treasury building on the west side of the White House to the Old Executive Office building on the east side. In both places the grandeur of my surroundings (the high vaulted ceilings, the heavy carved doors, the patterned parquet floors) reflected the excellence of nineteenth-century craftsmanship rather than my entry-level position on the power grid.

It was very apparent that White House chief of staff H. R. (Bob) Haldeman ran a very tight ship. There were certain expectations of all the young professionals, especially those in policy-making positions on Ehrlichman's

Domestic Council staff, and they were made quite clear from the outset. Nixon didn't like face-to-face discussions of policy issues with anyone except his three direct reports: Haldeman, Ehrlichman, and Henry Kissinger. With these three alone, he frequently thought out loud in wide-ranging discussions that included a great deal of venting and anger and frustration— much to his later disgrace when the White House tapes became known and were made public.

Haldeman was the doorkeeper who enforced the requirement that all issues reach the president's desk in writing and via one-page cover memos on top of however much backup material was considered necessary. Very few staff members could draft papers to Nixon's satisfaction. Slowly at first, I became the drafter of choice for papers on many domestic issues. In retrospect, I don't think that my success was because I wrote like a lawyer (since a good many of us were lawyers); it had to do with a shared experience at Whittier.

More than thirty years apart, both Nixon and I had taken Dr. Albert Upton's semantics course. Upton, a demanding and charismatic teacher, explored the ambiguity of words and stressed the importance of the proper use of language as the adjunct of logical thought. I think that Nixon, however unconsciously, recognized and appreciated the Uptonian influence on my writing.

In reviewing my files from those days, I discovered that in five years on the Domestic Council staff I prepared almost a thousand memos analyzing myriad domestic issues involving the Departments of Justice, Treasury, State, and Defense. Only a hundred or so were directly addressed to the president, but a lot of my other work was included in discussions or papers that did reach him.

I was a member of Richard Nixon's staff for over five of the six years he was president. Ultimately, I became associate director of the Domestic Council. I knew all of the White House people who became involved with Watergate. I had worked with most of them; I was friends with many of them. I remember some with particular clarity. For example, I had a meeting with G. Gordon Liddy when he came back (as I learned much later) from reconnoitering the office of Daniel Ellsberg's psychiatrist for the break-in he conducted a week later. I asked him why his hand was heavily bandaged. He said it was because, while trying to light his pipe, he had become distracted by a pretty girl and inadvertently set the book of matches on fire. It turned out he had really burned his hand by placing it over a candle in order to demonstrate to his fellow burglars how much pain he could endure.

Workdays for those of us in policy-planning positions in the Nixon White House began around 7:00 A.M. By nine o'clock everyone had studied the president's daily news summary and attended or been briefed on the series of staff meetings that set the priorities for the day. When I started on the staff, I was given a parking permit for the Ellipse, the circular roadway that lies between the South Lawn and the Washington Monument. I can remember returning from meetings in the West Wing about mid-morning and seeing a sleek burgundy Porsche glide into one of the highly coveted reserved parking slots on West Executive Avenue—the gated street that divides the White House from the Old Executive Office building. That car, and the lifestyle it represented (and the late hours the lifestyle required), belonged to John W. Dean.

Both Gordon Liddy and John Dean will play important roles in this book; indeed, their actions lie at the very heart of the Watergate story. The one—whose capacity to endure pain wasn't limited to holding his hand over an open flame—refused to implicate anyone else and spent the longest time in prison of all the Watergate figures. The other—whose story about his involvement with Watergate changed as he tried to obtain immunity from prosecution—ended up with what amounted to a slap on the wrist and a brief confinement (the shortest jail time of any Watergate convict) in a country club–like holding facility.

During President Nixon's last year in the White House, I also worked as J. Fred Buzhardt's principal deputy. Fred, who had been general counsel of the Department of Defense, was appointed White House counsel for Watergate matters when Al Haig arrived in April 1973 to replace Bob Haldeman as chief of staff.

For a young man (I had just turned twenty-nine) working with Fred Buzhardt in crafting the president's Watergate defense was an incredible experience that left an indelible impression. We spent hours reviewing presidential documents and White House tapes, as well as preparing transcripts of many of them for publication. You may have heard about the phrase "expletive deleted" that was inserted in place of President Nixon's less polite language. Well, I was the deleter of those expletives.

At the time, along with everyone else in the White House, I was overwhelmed by the daily barrage of demands and subpoenas and leaks. On August 9, 1974, when President Nixon resigned, I was in the East Room for his farewell speech, and on the South Lawn when he boarded Marine One for the final time. Several months later I left the White House to join a prominent D.C. law firm.

Over the years, as I thought about what had happened to Nixon and to America in 1973 and 1974, I began to see patterns emerge that had previously eluded me—and, apparently, everyone else—during those hectic and frantic times inside the White House. As books about Watergate and memoirs of its many participants started to roll off the presses, the patterns began to take clearer shape, and to point in some unexpected directions.

In addition to my own knowledge and experience from being a principal member of Nixon's defense team, I ultimately bought and reviewed virtually all the books written by or about Watergate figures. This dubious collection eventually comprised over four dozen volumes. When I had exhausted the research I could do with my own records and published accounts, I began to dig further.

All internal records of both the Ervin Committee and the House Judiciary Committee were sealed for fifty years (until 2024). Nonetheless, some papers of the period, particularly from the Watergate Special Prosecution Force (WSPF), have survived and are not sealed. I spent many hours at the National Archives in Washington, filed dozens of Freedom of Information Act (FOIA) requests, and reviewed hundreds of pages of internal memos and investigatory documents. I was also able to trace some WSPF papers to special collections at the Harvard Law School and the Library of Congress. I was among the first to read many of these documents in the more than three decades since they were written—and certainly the first to appreciate their significance.

I began taking notes. Then I made charts. Slowly but surely the connections between ostensibly independent events and individuals began to emerge from the chaos that had surrounded them. Gradually I recognized what had, all the time, been hiding in plain sight: The staffs of all three major Watergate investigations had something in common. Seven of the top eight officials in the Watergate Special Prosecution Force had worked in Robert Kennedy's Department of Justice, as had the most aggressive investigators on the Senate Watergate Committee staff; and the House Judiciary impeachment inquiry staff had apparently been largely directed by Yale Law School professor Burke Marshall, another RFK alumnus, the longtime Kennedy family counsel who had advised Teddy Kennedy about Chappaquiddick, and who was generally expected to be named attorney general in Teddy Kennedy's impending presidential administration.

Many of these same people—as well as a significant number of others who took an active hand in bringing about Nixon's resignation—had shared experiences in connection with Robert Kennedy's unrelenting pursuit of Teamster president James Hoffa. In fact, a special unit of some twenty lawyers and other Justice Department staff, reporting directly to the attorney general, was known as the Get Hoffa Squad.

Far from being a group randomly assembled in the period 1972–74, many of the people who brought down Richard Nixon had worked together before. And their most common denominator was a connection with the Kennedys, as the Get Hoffa Squad of the early 1960s was transformed into a Get Nixon Squad in the early 1970s.

While never before fully disclosed to the American public in the way I can, because of the documents I have uncovered, it is clear that John Dean played the central role throughout the Watergate scandal. First, he hired G. Gordon Liddy, and helped set in motion the events that culminated in the Watergate break-ins. Then he orchestrated the entire cover-up without, I believe, ever informing his White House superiors or the president about his own risk of prosecution for the criminal acts he was committing in their names.

When his guilt was about to be uncovered by Congress and the federal prosecutors, Dean switched sides and retained a key Kennedy confidant as his criminal defense counsel. Even while still employed as counsel to the president, John Dean removed legal files from his White House office and facilitated disclosures to Kennedy insiders that enabled them to make allegations and spread leaks about totally non-Watergate-related aspects of the Nixon presidency.

John Dean's disclosures to Kennedy insiders also seem to have enabled Kennedy cohorts on the Senate Judiciary Committee to extend the special prosecutor's guidelines beyond Watergate to cover virtually all activities of the Nixon White House. This allowed an intensely partisan fishing expedition to masquerade as an independent inquiry about known criminal activities.

Dean soon showed that he was even willing to alter his initial version of events to place Nixon and his top two White House lieutenants at the center of the Watergate cover-up. The whole Kennedy campaign support team swung into action in Dean's defense—to enhance his reputation and establish his personal credibility—and his imminent indictment by federal prosecutors was quickly and effectively halted.

Dean's devastating testimony before the Ervin Committee was largely drafted in a series of secret meetings between its chief counsel, Dean, and his own lawyer. What was made to look like a regular congressional investigation was in fact a highly stage-managed and scripted performance. Media coverage bordered on reverent, as it accepted Dean's story of a serious young staffer who had found himself trapped in a situation not of his own making, and who had been forced to do things he knew were wrong. Dean's sober demeanor and chastened tone added weight to his charges. His apparently incredibly detailed memory of events (later substantially undermined by White House tape transcripts) was accepted as, no pun intended, unimpeachable.

I also made another startling, and not, I think, unconnected discovery. Contrary to today's conventional wisdom that honors Judge John Sirica, Senator Sam Ervin, Special Prosecutor Archibald Cox, and House Judiciary Committee chairman Peter Rodino, I believe the individual who launched the first investigation and really nurtured Watergate into a national issue was Senator Edward Kennedy.

Based on exhaustive research, and the discovery of many important original documents that long lay buried in the National Archives and other libraries, I can present a new interpretation of events that many Americans have long considered settled and familiar. My burden of proof was recently made much easier when former FBI deputy director Mark Felt revealed that he was Deep Throat—reporter Bob Woodward's famously anonymous source for many of the most important Watergate stories. Guessing the identity of Deep Throat had been a Washington parlor game for more than three decades.

The conventional wisdom was that Deep Throat had been a genuine whistle-blower—a high-level member of Nixon's White House staff upset by the wrongdoing around him, and determined to provide leads the reporters could follow lest the guilty escape detection and punishment. In fact, Deep Throat was not a whistle-blower with a conscience. He was a bitter bureaucrat, seeking revenge because he didn't get the promotion he thought he deserved (to replace J. Edgar Hoover as FBI director), and leaking information about the ongoing investigations by career prosecutors that were already well under way.

This book is not an attempt to change the reader's mind about Richard Nixon but to correct history and show that Watergate was, at its most fundamental level, a highly partisan political maneuver led by, and for the benefit of, Teddy Kennedy. While the documents and factual information presented in these pages are objective and undeniable, the interpretations I give them and the conclusions I draw from them are entirely my own.

For example, I use the term Kennedy Clan Democrats to describe participants in and supporters of a political dynasty founded and initially funded by Joseph Kennedy with the hope and expectation that his sons would someday rule America. They succeeded with JFK's 1960 defeat of Richard Nixon—but the fruits of their victory were cut all too short by Lee Harvey Oswald's bullet. Similarly, I use the term Camelot Conspiracy to describe their efforts to regain control of the White House; for only if a Kennedy could be returned to power, by fair means or foul, would Kennedy Clan Democrats be assured of their own return to glory—and all the power and prestige that would accompany Camelot's restoration.

If I do my job well, by the last page the reader will see Watergate as no more than partisan political theater. If I don't, I believe I will at least have provided some provocative food for thought. I will have made readers aware of a series of dots—incontrovertible facts—even if I can't persuade them to connect them in the same ways I do.

Either way, I am confident that after reading this book, people will never think about Watergate the same way again.

ACKNOWLEDGMENTS

This book was a long time in the making, both because of the complete devastation of Nixon supporters and the skill with which his Kennedy clan opponents covered their tracks. The burden of proof was materially lightened in the last several years with Mark Felt's confirmation as Deep Throat and William Bittman's death (which opened the twenty-two WSPF file boxes at the National Archives for review).

Nonetheless, my story would never have been published without the assistance and support of a number of people. Bill Safire and Ed Klein, experienced authors in their own right, encouraged me and took the time and effort to guide me in the right direction. My agent, Daniel Strone of Trident Media Group, consistently provided sage insight and advice regarding publication interests and priorities. David Paynter and Martha Murphy, archivists on the Special Access and FOIA staffs at the National Archives, responded willingly to my endless series of document requests over a five-year period. Wally Johnson and Ken Khachigian, colleagues from my government service, were kind enough to review a succession of drafts and provide insights and advice throughout the process. Bernadette Malone Serton and Jillian Gray, my Penguin Group editors, were determined taskmasters, asking all the right questions and requiring nothing less than perfection in my submissions. Other extraordinarily helpful people at Penguin included Will Weisser, Courtney Nobile, and Noirin Lucas. I also benefitted from excellent research by David Freddoso and a most thorough legal review by Gary Hailman.

Singled out for a special attention is Frank Gannon, former White House colleague and friend of thirty years' standing, who rose to the challenge of making my dense legal brief more readable and understandable. He is a talented and creative writer. He also brought insight and information about Richard Nixon and the his career that materially improved my story.

To all of the above, I owe a debt of gratitude. They each helped bring my effort to fruition and to them belongs much of the credit. Any shortcomings, errors, or misstatements are, of course, entirely my responsibility.

THE SECRET PLOT
TO MAKE
TED KENNEDY PRESIDENT

Introduction

For Edward M. Kennedy, the senior senator from Massachusetts, election night 1972 brought no surprises. It had been clear for weeks that Richard Nixon was going to be reelected president of the United States. The only question was how big his victory would turn out to be. As the results rolled in from across the country the answer became clear: very big indeed.

Nixon racked up the second biggest landslide in presidential history, winning 61 percent of the vote. How did Nixon, who was essentially a controversial and not particularly popular president, win so big? To Kennedy Clan Democrats, his victory was largely—if not entirely—the result of a one-night screwup three years earlier, when Teddy Kennedy drove his mother's big Oldsmobile Delmont 88 off a small bridge on Chappaquiddick Island, and his female passenger drowned. Until that night the conventional wisdom shared by everyone (including Richard Nixon) was that in 1972 Edward Moore Kennedy would likely become the thirty-eighth president of the United States.

For most people today, it is almost impossible to appreciate the unique phenomenon of the Kennedys, and of the Democrats who supported them, and the way they shaped and dominated American politics for most of the two decades following JFK's election in 1960.

For all those who didn't live through the early 1960s, there is no way of appreciating exactly what those years meant to those who did, and particularly to those who came of age in that era. Today it all seems somewhat blurry and dated; the best to be said for it is that some of the music wasn't that bad.

But for those experiencing it firsthand from 1960 to 1963, everything was promising and thrilling in a completely new way. Of course, the cynics now point out that this Kennedy Camelot was really the ersatz creation of a corrupt patriarch with a bottomless bank account and a calculating widow with an eye for the main chance. Joseph P. Kennedy, Sr., from his earliest days as a movie mogul in Hollywood, understood the potential for media to mold opinion, and the power that it could convey. As this rather dicey presidential paterfamilias once put it: "It's not what you are but what people think you are that counts."

The shock of President Kennedy's assassination on November 22, 1963, was unlike anything America had ever experienced before. The only modern approximation of its impact would be the reaction in England to the death of Diana, princess of Wales. The sudden death of a young man with everything to live for seemed doubly sad. Because of the newly ubiquitous medium of television—and because of his instinctive understanding of it—JFK had become personalized to Americans in a way no president or politician had before. It wasn't until 1960 that most American homes had a TV set, and television, with its demands for images and sound bites, started to become the arbiter of presidential politics. His loss was felt in an intensely personal way by people with little or no interest in politics, and by people whose politics were opposed to his.

With JFK, the concept of "charisma" entered the American political lexicon. The men and women who worked in Kennedy's campaign considered themselves crusaders fighting for the spirit of youth and vigor (pronounced in broadest Bostonian as "vigah") and enlightenment that JFK embodied following the long, dull decade of the 1950s. The two Roosevelt presidents—Teddy and Franklin—had generated a fair amount of personal interest, but nothing like the devotion, bordering on worship, that JFK inspired. Of course, never before had this kind of media been available to provide movie-star coverage for a politician.

The Washington of JFK's New Frontier became a magnet for talented, ambitious, and idealistic young people. "The best and the brightest" (as David Halberstam famously called them) developed a uniquely personal commitment to the president himself. In many respects this attachment was also motivated by self-interest: Support for the Kennedys could lead to power, prestige, and considerable career advancement. In the three years of his presidency Kennedy salted the federal government with fervent (Ivy-educated) supporters who sincerely believed that they knew what was best for America and for Americans. The same was true for a generation of journalists who were excited by the idea that JFK, someone like themselves— young, educated, liberal, modern—was in power. The fact that the young president and his colorful family provided excellent copy was the icing on the cake.

Paradoxically, John Kennedy also attracted some distinctly more rough-and-tumble types, men for whom his deep roots in the decidedly unidealistic world of Boston Democratic ward politics were his principal appeal. For these people JFK was a cigar-chomping party boss who understood that eggs had to be broken to serve omelets to the voters. These two equal and opposite constituencies—the Arthur Schlesingers and the Kenny O'Donnells—lived in uncomfortable coexistence, but they were both vital to the survival of Kennedy Clan Democrats, and to the perpetuation of the Kennedy mystique.

When JFK was killed the Kennedy Clan Democrats felt both devastated and wronged. In addition to the loss of their hero and leader, many of them also suffered—or feared—the loss of the power and influence they had so briefly and tantalizingly tasted. They also were deeply offended by Lyndon Johnson—the crude and vulgar Texan whom JFK had only taken on the ticket as a matter of expediency, and who was now occupying the Oval Office surrounded by his yokel cronies.

The only answer was a restoration of the Kennedy dynasty—and of themselves along with it. Even before the mourning had ended, loyalties and energies were shifting to the next Kennedy, to John's younger brother Robert.

It is this mystical symbiosis between the Kennedys and their very talented supporters that explains the extraordinary intensity and longevity of their association, and its ability to survive the deaths of John and Robert and the disappointments of Edward.

Less than five years after President Kennedy's assassination, it looked like the Camelot restoration was on track. Robert Kennedy seemed likely to win his party's nomination, and then the general election. Then he, too, was shot. And once again, underneath the shock and grief, there was a transfer of loyalty to the next—and now the last—Kennedy, Edward.

With RFK removed from the '68 race, Richard Nixon managed to squeak out a narrow victory over Hubert Humphrey; he won by only half a million votes out of seventy-three million cast. Even before he got to spend his first night in the White House, the pollsters and the pundits were predicting he would be a one-term president. Nixon would be easy pickings in '72, and Teddy Kennedy would be the one to take him out. By now, for the large numbers of Kennedy Clan Democrats, returning a Kennedy to the White House had become almost a religious quest.

Politics as practiced by the Kennedys was truly something new under the sun. Before the Kennedys, politics—without many pretensions to nobility—had been rough and tumble, cut and thrust; with the Kennedys—beneath the veneer of youthful idealism—it would become slash and burn, search and destroy.

Almost two decades later, Richard Nixon would still remember:

> *I had been through some pretty rough campaigns in the past, but compared to the others, going into the 1960 campaign was like moving from the minor to the major leagues. I had an efficient, totally dedicated, well-financed, and highly motivated organization. But we were faced by an organization that had equal dedication and unlimited money that was led by the most ruthless group of political operators ever mobilized for a presidential campaign.*

Being on the receiving end of Kennedy politics wasn't an experience reserved for Nixon or Republicans. Hubert Humphrey, the liberal icon who had served as senator and vice president, long remembered how

Kennedy politics sabotaged his chance to run for president in 1960. In his memoir *The Education of a Public Man,* Humphrey wrote that "underneath the beautiful exterior there was an element of ruthlessness and toughness that I had trouble either accepting or forgetting."

But instead of being called out and criticized by the media for such questionably moral or legal conduct, it was either ignored or accepted as just part of an irrepressibly macho component of the Kennedy character. Reporters who were strong-armed for not writing to the Kennedys' liking somehow found the experience exhilarating; professors who were pushed into swimming pools at parties (as was Harvard's Arthur Schlesinger, Jr.) considered it a badge of honor rather than an insult to their position or intelligence.

To Republicans—and to any Democrats who made the mistake of opposing Kennedy candidacies or interests—it seemed that if you were a Kennedy, you could get away with murder.

I realize that all these events happened a long time ago. At the rate news and events move today, the Nixon administration now borders on being ancient history. But this story is still vitally important because the disturbing—and deeply undemocratic—trends that began with the Camelot Conspiracy during Watergate are still shaping—and subverting—our politics over three decades later.

Teddy Kennedy and his supporters still command attention and headlines, thanks to vast staffs accumulated over years of seniority, and continuing uncritical acceptance by the media; it doesn't go too far to say that he influences virtually every aspect of activity on Capitol Hill. Many people—including those who oppose him—have come to respect his consistency and commitment to the liberal values he so ardently espouses. Now in his seventies, and settled into an apparently solid and supportive second marriage, he is firmly ensconced in the Senate, without any apparent regrets at never having occupied 1600 Pennsylvania Avenue.

Time and events have moved on, and there is now no possibility of a Camelot restoration. If Teddy was the weak link in the first generation's chain, subsequent generations have diluted the line almost to obscurity. The Kennedy dynasty has imploded with a resounding whimper.

But although no Kennedys have played a part in any recent presidential contests, many of the current contenders have adopted some of Camelot's least attractive characteristics. Besides, many Kennedy operatives involved in Watergate are still active, and still injecting lessons learned from the dark side of Camelot into our political process: The folks who did in Robert Bork's Supreme Court nomination, and who almost succeeded in doing the same with Clarence Thomas (by finding, nurturing, and representing Anita Hill, his chief accuser); the folks who defended Al Gore in the Buddhist Temple fund-raising scandal and three times successfully prevented a compliant attorney general from appointing an independent prosecutor to investigate those scandals; the folks who founded and run the private investigatory agency that hounds political opponents of the Kennedys and the Clintons; the folks who sealed Vincent Foster's White House office following his mysterious death; the folks who defended Bill Clinton, both in the House during the impeachment inquiry and in the Senate during the actual trial—all got their start and cut their political teeth working under the tutelage of the original Kennedy Clan Democrats during the glory days of the Camelot Conspiracy and its all-out efforts to exploit Watergate.

The politics of personal destruction perfected by the Kennedys for their campaigns, radically expanded with Watergate, and cynically weaponized by the Clintons, is now the rule rather than the exception in our nation's capital.

The self-righteous willingness to criminalize policy differences and abandon notions of equal protection where ideological opponents are concerned now permeates congressional committees and far too many American courtrooms (when even one would be far too many). The appointment of run amok special and independent prosecutors has become the first refuge of partisans with scores to settle and a taste for easy solutions and cheap headlines. The fact that the independent prosecutor law turned out to be a double-edged sword, and not nearly as much fun when used against Democrats as when used against Republicans, resulted in the statute being allowed to expire without protest in 1998. But distance has begun to lend enchantment, and the new Democratic majority appears to be rediscovering as if anew the myriad charms of special prosecutors.

And the shameless symbiosis between the press corps and the permanent leakocracy in the executive and legislative branches of government that first flexed its muscles during the Watergate era now sets the pace for politics at every level in America.

1

Two Summer Nights:
The Bridge at Chappaquiddick and the Watergate Break-in

Two summer nights. Three years apart.

Both were disasters.

But one was skillfully handled and successfully contained; its details were largely covered up. Indeed, even today simple factual information, like time sequences and specific locations, remains in some dispute. Eventually the intensity of the feelings surrounding it was diminished by the passage of time and the rush of events.

The other was badly handled and then successfully exploited into a major scandal that resulted in the first resignation by a president in American history.

FRIDAY JULY 18, 1969

It was supposed to be one of those typical Kennedy Cape Cod weekends that required tremendous preparation so that everything would look easy. It would involve tickets, reservations, rentals, victuals, and coping with the inevitable glitches. Twelve people would be arriving from several destinations; their flights would have to be arranged and met; rooms would be required at two different inns; some would need cars; some would need a boat charter; all would need food and drinks; and a cottage would have to be rented for a party and cookout. But somehow with the Kennedys everything always got done, and everyone always had fun.

The focus of the weekend was the annual Edgartown Regatta. Ted Kennedy would be competing at the helm of *Victura,* the classic wood Wianno Senior twenty-five-foot racing sloop that had been a fifteenth birthday present to his elder brother Jack. His crew would be his cousin, Joe Gargan, who had been raised with the Kennedy children and was now a lawyer, and Paul Markham, a lawyer and former U.S. attorney for Massachusetts.

Because of Bobby's death, no Kennedys had sailed in the '68 regatta, so it was decided that this year's event could both resume the tradition and provide the occasion for a reunion of the "boiler room girls"—a half dozen young women who had worked at the heart of RFK's short and intense presidential campaign.

Joe Gargan made all the arrangements. The girls would be at the Katama Shores Inn; Teddy and the other men would be at the Shiretown Inn; and they could all relax at the Lawrence cottage, a private house that was near the beach on Chappaquiddick—a mile-long island that was separated from Edgartown by a five-hundred-foot channel and connected by a ferry.

The girls arrived on Thursday and spent the day shopping and swimming. The senator arrived at one o'clock on Friday afternoon and was met by his chauffeur, Jack Crimmins. It was a hot day, and he asked if there would be time for a swim, so they took the ferry over to Chappaquiddick, and Crimmins drove him to the beach—which was reached by a dirt road leading to a narrow wooden bridge over Poucha Pond that led to the wide Atlantic beach.

The next day, while the girls watched and cheered aboard a chartered boat, *Victura* finished ninth in a field of thirty-six. Paul Markham hurt his leg and returned to the inn instead of attending any of the parties after the race. By 8:30 P.M., however, everyone was at the Lawrence cottage. After false starts getting the charcoal lit—without which no cookout is complete—the steaks were finally ready around 9:45 P.M.

The Lawrence cottage's nearest neighbor—the island's fire captain, who was expert at lifesaving—was kept awake by the loud music and noise coming from the party next door. He didn't know it was Senator Kennedy's rental, and he considered going over to complain.

Ted Kennedy and Mary Jo Kopechne left the cottage together. He asked Crimmins for the car keys, saying that she wasn't feeling well and wanted to catch the last ferry back to Edgartown. He refused the chauffeur's offer to drive. They left without saying good-bye to anyone, and Mary Jo didn't take her purse.

Around 1:20 A.M., one of the partygoers, Ray LaRosa, a former firefighter and Kennedy campaigner, had gone outside to have a quiet smoke. He was startled when Ted Kennedy suddenly walked up the path and asked him to go inside and get Gargan and Markham. He told them that he had driven off the wooden bridge into the water, and his attempts to free Mary Jo had been unsuccessful; she was still in the car.

So the three men drove to the bridge. It was an almost eight-foot drop into six feet of water, and they could see part of a wheel and a rear fender just breaking the surface. Gargan and Markham stripped and started diving, but there were strong currents and almost no visibility. Their rescue efforts were unsuccessful.

Exhausted, his friends considered the enormity of what had happened, and what they could possibly do about it.

The senator was silent about his intentions, but it appeared he did not want to report the accident at this time. Kennedy was having alternative ideas about the situation. Why couldn't Mary Jo have been driving the car? Why couldn't she have left him off, and driven to the ferry herself and made a wrong turn?

Kennedy asked to be brought back to the cottage to establish the story. After a while he could leave. Kennedy suggested that when he was back at the Shiretown Inn, Gargan could "discover" the accident and report to police that Mary Jo had been alone in the car. How this was going to be worked out insofar as "details" were concerned, the senator didn't say.

Gargan rejected the idea out of hand. Mary Jo was the only other person who could possibly have been driving the accident car, but neither the senator nor Paul Markham knew her very well, Gargan said later. "Nobody had any idea if she could drive a car, or even had a license."

By 1:45 A.M. they were at the ferry landing, urging Teddy to report the accident as soon as he got back to the inn. Instead of calling the ferry and waiting for it to arrive, Kennedy dove into the water and swam across the channel. At 2:25 A.M., dressed in slacks and a blazer, he told a room clerk at the inn that he was being disturbed by the noise from a party next door.

At 7:00 A.M., the senator asked a desk clerk to reserve a copy of the *Boston Globe* and *The New York Times* for him as soon as they arrived. Then he said he had forgotten his wallet and asked if he could borrow a dime to make a collect phone call. He called Helga Wagner, the wife of a campaign contributor with whom he was having an affair, and told her that something serious had happened and that he needed to reach his brother-in-law, Steve Smith, in Spain. When the call was completed he returned the dime to the desk clerk.

He met some other guests in the lobby and idly talked with them for about twenty minutes before returning to his room. By 8:45 A.M. Gargan and Markham were back from Chappaquiddick and were disturbed to learn that the accident hadn't been reported. Once again, Kennedy said, "I'm going to say that Mary Jo was driving." Once again his friends said he couldn't do that; he could be placed at the scene of the accident.

He said that before he reported it he wanted to talk to his chief of staff in Washington, as well as to his lawyer. There was sure to be a line waiting to use the inn's only public phone, so they decided to take the ferry back across to Chappaquiddick, where there was a pay phone at the dock.

The car had been discovered by two fishermen around eight in the morning; they ran to the house about four hundred feet from the bridge and used the phone to call police. Divers found a young woman's body but no identification. When they ran the license plate it showed up belonging to one of seven cars registered to the Kennedy family.

The police chief reached Teddy at the boat dock pay phone and arranged a meeting. By noon the story had spread around the world—and by the next day it was challenging man's first walk on the moon for headline space.

On its face the story was tragic enough. A young woman had died. But as the details began to emerge, for those who wanted to see it, they added insult to injury. Why were six young married men spending a weekend partying with six young unmarried women? What was on Teddy Kennedy's mind when he made a sharp turn and left a clearly marked paved road for a dirt road that only led to the bridge and the beach?

The amount of alcohol consumed by the senator and nine others also came under close scrutiny. (Markham had been sidelined by an upset stomach and was drinking only Cokes; LaRosa was a teetotaler.) Aside from the rum and Cokes and beers consumed at the race, Crimmins had stocked Lawrence cottage with three half gallons of vodka, four one-fifth bottles of Scotch, two bottles of rum, and two cases of beer. When the owner, having heard about what had happened in his house, arrived on Saturday afternoon, he found all the beds neatly made and everything meticulously cleaned. The garbage contained only eight empty Coke bottles.

Although nothing would ever be the same for Teddy Kennedy after Chappaquiddick, the way in which he was able to deal with it was a paradigm of Kennedy macho and privilege.

The first phone calls he made weren't to the police or for medical help (although that, sadly, was clearly no longer appropriate for the situation), but to one of his current girlfriends (his pregnant wife would be called later), the chief of staff of his Senate office in Washington, and Kennedy family legal adviser Burke Marshall.

The fact that he had been driving with an expired license was quickly fixed behind the scenes and not revealed to the police or the court. The local police and prosecutors were like deer caught in headlights: surprised by the sudden tsunami of media attention and naturally deferential to their U.S. senator, who was also a member of Massachusetts's most prominent family. Their questioning was tentative and restrained. The many anomalies of Kennedy's story and conduct weren't probed at all.

And then, suddenly, he was gone, and unavailable for questioning, holed up behind the high white fences of the Kennedy compound in Hyannis Port and hunkered down with growing numbers of high-powered attorneys and advisers and speechwriters. Among those who flew in to help were: former Defense secretary Robert McNamara; Yale Law School professor and former RFK Justice Department official Burke Marshall; Harvard professor and writer Arthur Schlesinger, Jr.; Washington lawyer and long-time Kennedy friend Milton Gwirtzman; and superspeechwriters Richard Goodwin and Ted Sorensen. Writer and Harvard economist John Kenneth Galbraith was consulted on the phone.

They crafted a speech and, four nights after the accident, Ted Kennedy was on television, from his father's house in the Kennedy compound, sitting in a pale blue easy chair with bookshelves and an American flag in the background, and maintaining eye contact by reading from a teleprompter. Kennedy superspeechwriter Richard Goodwin expressed one of the main hurdles the speech had to jump. "They were trying to say something and still avoid the connotation of immorality," he said, "the old Irish Catholic fear of ever suggesting that you were screwing anybody outside of marriage."

Teddy evoked the tragedies that had befallen his family, and, at several points, said that he just couldn't remember what he did or logically explain what he remembered. Some observers had thought that he might conclude the speech by announcing his resignation from the Senate. Instead, he said that he would leave his fate in the hands of the voters of the Commonwealth of Massachusetts in the upcoming election.

Even *The New York Times* had a hard time swallowing Teddy's confused and confusing version of events. The title of the next day's editorial was "Still a Tragedy and a Mystery." The paper of record stated, "His emotionally-charged address leaves us less than satisfied with his partial explanations for a gross failure of responsibility, and more than ever convinced that the concerned town, county and state officials of Massachusetts have also failed in their duty thoroughly to investigate this case because of the political personality involved."

If the *Times* remained unconvinced, apparently the voters of Massachusetts were still buying whatever the Kennedys were selling. Sixteen months after his car went off the bridge on Chappaquiddick, and despite the myriad unanswered questions and suspicions that had only grown in the months following Mary Jo Kopechne's death, Teddy Kennedy was re-elected with 61 percent of the vote.

The law courts were as understanding as the court of public opinion for the errant Kennedy. While not permitted by statute, he was given a suspended sentence.

I have often wondered what would have happened if the Chappaquiddick cover-up had been investigated in a manner similar to Watergate's.

- What would have happened if the nonpartisan career prosecutor who had been handling the case and was ready to issue indictments was suddenly replaced by a Chappaquiddick special prosecutor, a longtime Republican partisan, who postponed the indictments for almost a year in order to continue exploring other potentially embarrassing or illegal activities of Ted Kennedy and his family and friends?
- What if the Chappaquiddick special prosecutor had built a staff of close to one hundred people, including some sixty lawyers, to carry on investigations into every aspect of Teddy Kennedy's personal conduct and finances?
- What would have happened if interviews had been conducted under oath with everyone who attended the party that fateful night, and with the recipients of Teddy's first phone calls before he reported the accident to the police? (And where was the media or public shock that such interviews weren't conducted?)
- What would have happened if the Chappaquiddick special prosecutor made himself easily available to the press ("off-the-record," of course—for the little he would have known was worth) and willing to respond to an endless series of "what-if" hypothetical questions?
- What if investigatory materials revealing that the Kennedys had made payments in undisclosed amounts to the Kopechne family and others had been leaked to the press or revealed during televised hearings?

- What if, instead of being largely ignored by the media, Chappaquiddick judge James Boyle, who said that Kennedy had clearly lied at the trial, was lionized in the same way as Watergate judge John Sirica, who said the burglars were covering up for others?

Could even a Kennedy have survived such treatment? Would even the voters of Massachusetts have been unaffected by such revelations?

I often wonder because there is no way that we will ever know. Because the Kennedys successfully swept Chappaquiddick under the rug.

Friday June 16, 1972

The broad streets of Washington were unusually quiet for an early summer Friday night. Hurricane Agnes, an unexpected preseason storm, had touched ground in Florida a few days earlier, and was now wreaking havoc, with floods and storms up the Eastern Seaboard.

The seven men in the private dining room at the posh Watergate Hotel weren't worried about the rain outside. They were dining on lobster and revisiting old times. With an otherwise unlikely mix of backgrounds—a former FBI agent and congressional candidate; an ex-Yalie thriller writer; a lieutenant colonel in the Air Force Reserves; and four Cuban-born Miamians who had fought against Castro—they shared two things. All, but one, had worked or were working for the CIA. And all, with no exceptions, were burglars.

As the silverware reflected the candelabra at the center of the table, they toasted their upcoming caper. The two leaders, clearly, were G. Gordon Liddy and E. Howard Hunt. The four Cuban Americans went by more than five names; all had aliases, some more than a few. According to their birth certificates, the others were: James McCord, Frank Sturgis, Eugenio R. Martinez, Virgilio R. Gonzalez, and Bernard L. Barker.

The night's target was, literally, next door. The Watergate complex was an architecturally adventurous combination of residential condos, upscale retail shops, the most fashionable hotel in Washington, the capital's most expensive restaurant, and a luxury office building. It was centrally located on the banks of the Potomac River—hence its name—midway between Georgetown and the White House.

Around ten o'clock they went back to their rooms. They were already wearing suits—everyone (and certainly everyone dining at the Watergate) did in 1972—so they only had to freshen up and collect their briefcases. They met in the lobby and walked across the small interior courtyard to the entrance to the office building's underground parking lot. From the basement they methodically advanced to the sixth-floor offices of the Democratic National Committee. At each floor one of them put a piece of masking tape over the lock on the door leading from the corridor to the stairwell.

For Gonzalez, a CIA lock expert who worked in Miami at the Missing Link Key Shop, the DNC's door was a piece of cake. Safely inside the target, they fanned out and went to work.

Across the street, on the balcony of room 727 of the decidedly more downscale Howard Johnson's Motor Inn, Alfred Baldwin was watching with binoculars. He had been there for the previous two weeks, monitoring the results from the first bugs these same burglars had placed. A lot of it was garbled; a lot of it was gobbledygook; some of it was about setting men up with available and willing young women.

A hundred feet across Virginia Avenue and one floor down, first Baldwin saw shadows moving through some of the rooms, darker against lighter. Then some lights came on, and he could clearly see the men in dark suits and dark ties. At that distance the surgical gloves they all were wearing were not so visible.

Baldwin also noticed when the police car pulled up in front of the building and three men emerged. He activated his walkie-talkie—he had been assigned to the balcony as a lookout—and tried to inform the men across the street about what he was watching. All he got was static.

About half an hour earlier, Frank Wills, a twenty-four-year-old security guard who had recently arrived in Washington from South Carolina, noticed a piece of masking tape over the lock into the basement parking garage when he was making his regular rounds. This was a major breach of security, but it was hardly the first time it had happened. The overnight cleaning crews frequently taped over the locks in order to facilitate floor-to-floor access. He removed it and moved on. Ten minutes later, when he passed by the same door, another piece of tape had been placed over the lock. *That* wasn't right. So he called the cops.

As it happened, the cops were already right outside the building. They entered the stairwell from the basement. They found the taped locks on each floor, but everything else seemed to be in order. When they saw that the entrance to the DNC on the sixth floor had been jimmied, they drew their weapons and entered the premises.

The DNC offices occupied the entire floor; twenty-six offices held seventy employees. At first nothing seemed awry, but then the officers entered an office with drawers open and papers strewn everywhere. Advancing into the next office, they flipped on the lights. As the harsh fluorescent light suddenly flooded the room, from behind the desks in front of them, three men emerged with their hands in the air. "Don't shoot," they said. The police found two more men crouching on the balcony outside.

Lined up against the wall, these five middle-aged men in their suits and ties and surgical gloves made a highly unlikely picture. As briefcases were opened and pockets were emptied, the situation became no less bizarre.

They had highly sophisticated, state-of-the-art equipment, including walkie-talkies, burglary tools, more than five thousand dollars in cash (in sequential one-hundred-dollar bills), forty rolls of unexposed film, two 35-millimeter cameras, and three pen-sized tear-gas guns. One of them had a small yellow breast-pocket notebook with a key taped to its cover. Another had a small address book. Within a couple of days one of the addresses in it ("HH," whose phone number began with the letters "WH") would tie the burglars to Howard Hunt and the White House. But it would be more than two decades before it was discovered that the key was to the desk of the secretary of the DNC official who was in charge of arranging the liaisons between visiting Democrats and the local good-time girls.

The five men were handcuffed and taken in for processing and booking. They were all charged with felonious burglary and possession of the implements of the crime.

The police report, number 316–823, filed at 4:45 A.M., described the crime of the century in typical just-the-facts-ma'am style:

Complainant's Name: Democratic National Convention [sic] . . .
Describe Location or Type of Premise: office building . . . Crime: Burglary
II . . . Weapon, Tool, Force Or Means Used: lockpicking tools, screwdriv-
ers, tape . . . Method Used: taped door locks open . . . Type of Property
Taken: none . . . Loss Value: unk. . . . Point of Entry: stairway.

2

Watergate:
What Really Happened—And Why

It would take several months for most of the story of the Watergate break-in to emerge. Behind it was a long and complicated backstory—one involving a few villains, many extras, and, ultimately, no heroes.

At the beginning of 1971, in anticipation of a tough reelection battle the following year, the White House decided to set up an independent campaign committee. To emphasize the strengths of Nixon's incumbency, an intentionally impressive name was chosen: the Committee to Re-elect the President. (This impressive name unfortunately yielded a less impressive acronym. It was referred to as "the C-R-P" by a few insiders, but snarkily called CREEP by everyone else.) The site chosen for the CRP headquarters was an office building at 1701 Pennsylvania Avenue, kitty-corner from the White House one block south at 1600.

Jeb Stuart Magruder, a handsome, clean-cut young White House staffer, was sent to get the CRP up and running. From the beginning, things were chaotic. There was too much money coming in and too many macho campaign types itching to show how much more money they could raise and how much bigger a majority they could pile up for their president in 1972. There was also too little adult supervision. There was a lot of bitterness among many Nixon veterans, who felt that they had been on the receiving end of political dirty tricks for so long that it was finally time to even the score.

Much of the intensity was driven by the fear that despite the setback of Chappaquiddick, Teddy Kennedy would end up being the Democratic nominee. No one could believe that the Democrats would nominate a candidate as weak as Senator George McGovern. As Magruder remembered it:

> McGovern was obviously running a strong campaign but he was the weakest of the Democratic contenders, because of his far-left record. He was our most-favored opponent, but for a long time we just couldn't believe we'd be that lucky. Our biggest fear was a deadlocked Democratic Convention and a draft of Senator Kennedy, because we felt that despite Chappaquiddick he was the strongest Democratic candidate.

Around the time that Magruder moved over to the CRP, Haldeman tasked John Dean with setting up what Dean later described as a "perfectly legitimate campaign intelligence operation" for the campaign.

Knowledge is power, and gathering intelligence in political campaigns is an activity as old as campaigning itself. Over time the concept of "campaign intelligence" has come to cover a wide range of activities, from simple opposition research (acquiring and analyzing an opponent's speeches, statements, and votes), to basic infiltration (sending workers to report on public events or joining an opponent's staff to gain inside information), to classic prankish dirty tricks (ordering large numbers of flowers or pizzas, printing phony posters), to outright illegalities (bugging, forgery, libel).

Nixon had been the target of some extremely dirty tricks during every stage of his long career. He felt, with considerable bitterness and not without justification, that when Democrats were the perpetrators and he was the target, they were excused or indulged or—in the case of Dick Tuck, the Democratic activist who had made a minicareer out of embarrassing Nixon—even celebrated as cult-hero pranksters.

One of the first widespread uses of bugging was by Robert Kennedy, when he was attorney general. Most of it was directed against the targets of Justice Department prosecutions. But some of it was directed at people who could cause political trouble for the Kennedys (such as Martin Luther King, Jr.), or people who could actually threaten their power (such as a troublesome former mistress). Indeed, Carmine Bellino, a longtime Kennedy family operative, was accused of having arranged wiretaps on an Engelhard Industries executive thought to have been gathering evidence concerning a JFK affair with a Radcliffe student.

Lyndon Johnson, who was already a consummate practitioner and connoisseur of the art of gossip, in the days when it still depended on word of mouth, couldn't resist using the new technology to bug his friends as well as his enemies.

Although a lot of pious public rhetoric is expended denying or decrying bugging, and milking the public's surprise and revulsion when examples are revealed, the fact is that since the 1960s bugging had been a fairly common practice in the political campaigns of both parties. Campaign security had become a flourishing industry, and only the most naive candidate those days would speak openly in a room or on a phone that hadn't been recently swept for bugs.

That is why Nixon's first reaction to the story about the bugging of the Democratic National Committee (DNC) registered dismay rather than disapproval. If he was shocked, it wasn't because he thought it was wrong but because he thought it was dumb. Anyone with any political savvy knew that the party headquarters was usually the last place where anybody knew what was actually going on. The action was all in the camps of the individual candidates.

When John Dean was assigned by Haldeman to set up a campaign intelligence operation, there is every reason to believe that his superiors had in mind a tough, inventive, and aggressive operation that might cut some corners but, if worst came to worst, could be publicly defendable. This presumption was indicated by the choice of John Dean, the White House's chief legal officer, to set it up.

Dean in turn discussed Haldeman's assignment with Jack Caulfield, a member of his staff. Caulfield was a retired New York City police detective who had been in charge of security for Nixon's 1968 campaign, and then been brought into the White House counsel's office as the White House's liaison to the Secret Service, to add an element of street smarts, and to deal with local police departments for presidential visits.

In a plan he code-named "Sandwedge," Caulfield proposed setting up a separate private investigative agency that could be contracted to supply intelligence services to the CRP. This would, at the very least, put a layer of separation between the two entities. It was decided, however, that Caulfield wasn't up to the assignment.

Just about this time, Jeb Magruder asked Dean to help find a lawyer for the CRP. In fact, Magruder had someone in mind: He helpfully suggested Dean's own deputy White House counsel, Fred Fielding. Fielding declined the honor. Then Dean asked Bud Krogh, an associate director of the Domestic Council, if his colleague David Young could be made available. Krogh instead suggested that Dean take a look at G. Gordon Liddy.

Liddy, a lawyer and former FBI agent, was already known to be a colorful character. He had joined the White House staff in June to work for Krogh—and soon found himself part of a small group assembled on the president's orders to track down and prevent the leaks of classified information that had plagued the new administration from its first weeks in office. Because their job was to plug leaks, they referred to themselves as the "Plumbers."

In August and September 1971, Liddy had been involved in the highly sensitive—and badly botched—break-in of the Beverly Hills office of Dr. Lewis Fielding. Daniel Ellsberg, a former Defense Department aide and current RAND Corporation consultant, had just been identified as the man who had stolen the Pentagon Papers, and Dr. Fielding was his psychiatrist.

After interviewing Liddy, Dean was sufficiently impressed to offer him both jobs: setting up the campaign intel operation and serving as the CRP's general counsel for Magruder.

In early November, Dean introduced Liddy as his choice for both assignments to John Mitchell, who was still attorney general but would soon leave to run the CRP. With Mitchell's blessing, Liddy officially joined the CRP in December 1971.

Gordon Liddy, newly ensconced in his CRP office, boasted to Magruder that Dean had promised him a million-dollar budget for the intel operation he had been hired to set up. Magruder insisted that only John Mitchell could approve such a substantial expenditure. Accordingly, he arranged a meeting for January 27, 1972, in Mitchell's office at the Department of Justice.

Mitchell, Magruder, and Dean were all there that chilly Thursday morning for Liddy's presentation: Dean, because the campaign intelligence plan was his responsibility; Magruder, because the meeting was being held at his insistence; and Mitchell, because his express approval was deemed necessary for the intel op's megabudget.

Liddy produced several professionally prepared charts. He proposed a number of activities, each with a colorful code name, that amounted to a comprehensive program of mugging, bugging, kidnapping, and prostitution.

The Republican convention was planned for San Diego, and large crowds of angry protesters were expected. Protesters would obviously attempt to wreak the kind of convention havoc on the Republicans in '72 that had derailed the Democrats in Chicago in '68. But Liddy had the answer. While the mugging squads roughed up the hostile demonstrators, the kidnapping squads would seize the radical leaders and hold them just across the border in Mexico until all the delegates had gone home.

For the Democratic convention in Miami, he proposed compromising prominent Democrats by installing professional prostitutes (and not any old skanks, he insisted, but "high class and the best in the business") on yachts near the delegates' hotels. The bugging initiatives he proposed included electronic surveillance and wiretapping, as well as break-ins to collect information and photograph documents.

Liddy's plan was rejected, but not on the grounds that it was somewhere between completely over-the-top and utterly barmy. Although Dean later remembered that Mitchell had winked at him from time to time, Liddy was only told that what he was proposing was too expensive and not quite what they had in mind. In the car afterward, Liddy complained that he had been assured of a million dollars, and Dean and Magruder urged him to submit a revised plan.

Liddy's revision, now priced at $500,000, was presented to the same group the following week. The proposals for mugging, kidnapping, and prostitution were gone; but three specific targets were now identified for bugging: the DNC offices in the Watergate office building in Washington; the DNC's Miami convention headquarters at the Fontainebleau Hotel; and the offices of the front-runners for the party's presidential nomination.

Dean, although he had arranged the meeting, arrived slightly late. He soon said that such proposals shouldn't be discussed in the presence of the attorney general, and instructed Liddy to limit future discussions to Magruder and himself; they would be responsible for dealing with Mitchell. The meeting ended without any specific action taken, but the message was delivered that the plan was still too expensive, and still in need of further revision.

As long anticipated, Mitchell resigned as attorney general on March 1 to take full-time charge at the CRP. At a meeting in Key Biscayne at the end of that month, Magruder presented Liddy's latest revised plan. Version three, now priced at $250,000, was the last of dozens of pending matters reviewed during a long meeting with Mitchell and one of his CRP lieutenants, Fred LaRue.

Stories differ about what actually happened at this March 30 meeting. Magruder claimed that he obtained Mitchell's express approval for this third version of Liddy's intel plan. Both Mitchell and LaRue agreed that the plan was discussed, but insisted that Mitchell had once again put off any decision. (LaRue maintained this position even after he had reached a plea bargain and had no reason not to tell the truth.)

Whatever happened, Magruder acted as though Mitchell had approved it. He immediately telephoned the CRP and authorized disbursal of eighty-three thousand dollars in cash to Liddy.

Several weeks later, on May 28, Liddy's plan for eavesdropping on the DNC at the Watergate offices was implemented, when the first break-in occurred. Files were photographed, and wiretaps were placed on the phones of Chairman Larry O'Brien and Spencer Oliver, who was the director of the Association of State Democratic Chairmen.

Back at the CRP offices at 1701 Pennsylvania Avenue, the voluble and dramatic Liddy hadn't been getting along very well with the preppy and somewhat wimpy Magruder. Suffice it to say that, at one point, Liddy threatened to kill him. Magruder, naturally unsettled, wanted Liddy fired. To alleviate a very strained situation, at Dean's suggestion Liddy was transferred to a new position—legal counsel to the CRP's finance committee—that would call for minimal interface with Magruder. He would, however, retain his responsibilities for campaign intelligence.

Photos and wiretap transcripts from the initial Watergate break-in started going to Magruder on May 31. He kept them in his office in a file marked "Gemstone." He shared information gleaned from these taps with select CRP officials, and with Gordon Strachan, Haldeman's White House staff member who had been assigned as liaison to the CRP. It isn't clear whether Magruder informed Strachan of the source of the Gemstone information—indeed, the answer to this question would become central to the government's case against Haldeman and Nixon.

Sometime in early June, Liddy was told by Mitchell and Magruder that the wiretap material wasn't satisfactory. He explained that the bug on O'Brien's phone had stopped working, and said he would take care of it.

He took care of it on the night of June 16, when roughly the same cast of characters broke into the Watergate for the second time—but with very different results.

There are no records of any contact between John Dean and Gordon Liddy during the four months between the February 4 meeting, when break-ins and bugging were discussed, and June 17, when the Watergate burglars were arrested. Liddy has never talked, and Dean would have no interest in any such admission. Gordon Strachan later testified that he was never involved in intelligence matters, and that Dean continued to shoulder this responsibility.

On June 17, when the burglars were caught, Dean was flying home from Manila. When he landed in San Francisco, he called his office, and was told to get back to Washington ASAP. Arriving on the morning of the nineteenth, he wanted to find out what had happened at the Watergate. Not surprisingly, the first person he met with was Gordon Liddy.

That must have been quite a meeting. Learning that the Watergate break-in was part of the Liddy program that he had initiated and helped to develop, Dean would immediately have realized that he was at serious risk of prosecution. In a heartbeat, he heard that his dreams of power and prestige were threatened by certain disbarment and possible incarceration.

So he became, by his own description, the "chief desk officer" of the attempt to cover up the true story of who was responsible for what had happened at the Watergate. Despite his later claims, he was far from reluctant to assume this role. In fact, after the initial shock wore off, he may even have thought it might turn out to be a blessing in disguise. At least at the beginning, when it seemed that keeping things under control could be managed fairly easily, this new role offered him extraordinary opportunities, not only to cover his own tail, but to garner credit from the most important men in the White House—including the president himself, who began recognizing him on sight and calling him "John." Dean had never even met with Nixon during his first two years as the White House counsel; their first meeting was on September 15, 1972, the day that the Watergate burglars were indicted.

Besides, the alternative was unthinkable. Unless he wanted to turn himself in and accept the consequences, he had no choice but to cast his lot with those at the CRP, whose only chance of evading prosecution was for the cover-up to succeed. He must have breathed a sigh of relief when neither Haldeman nor Ehrlichman apparently remembered his earlier involvement with the intel op assignment, and his patronage of Gordon Liddy. His assurance that no one from the White House staff had been involved in Liddy's operation was taken at face value. While what he said may have been literally true, it was totally misleading, because *he* was involved by virtue of his earlier connection with Liddy. Dean's failure to disclose his own conflict of interest, while still functioning as the president's lawyer, lies at the very core of his unethical conduct—and of what became his treachery.

Nixon's immediate concern had been that Chuck Colson, his White House special counsel who dealt with labor unions and political interest groups, might have had his fingerprints on the Watergate break-in. But once Dean assured Nixon that Colson hadn't been involved, there was no reason for anyone to question his further assurances. Their concern then shifted to CRP boss John Mitchell, who was the president's good friend and had been the country's attorney general. As embarrassing and painful and sad as the outcome might be if Mitchell were involved, at least he wouldn't involve the White House directly.

I believe that the White House—which, for Watergate purposes, means Haldeman, Ehrlichman, and the president—thought that John Dean was doing exactly what the White House counsel would be expected to do in a case like this, indeed what any lawyer would be expected to do for his client: He was investigating what had happened, finding out who was responsible, and making sure that his client's interests were protected. There would have been a natural presumption that Dean would, where possible, try to minimize any political damage.

The first order of business would be to find out if anyone from the White House was involved, and, if so, who and to what extent. Assuming the White House was cleared, the next thing would be to assess the consequences for the president if his reelection committee was involved.

From the very first day he started handling Watergate for the White House, however, Counsel Dean was leading a double life—principally to protect his own interests. And his own interests were antithetical to those of his client, the president of the United States. Even aside from any personal loyalty or professional ethics involved, what he did—and what he did not do—during the cover-up can be summarized under the heading "obstruction of justice."

Despite the widespread acceptance of the image he has worked so hard and so successfully to cultivate, the facts remain that entirely on his own and without direct proof of any direction from above, and in order to hide his own criminal involvement from anyone who could compel him to accept responsibility for it, John Dean may well have committed crimes in addition to those to which he pled guilty. Based on my reading of WSPF investigatory files, these would include:

SUBORNATION OF PERJURY. Subornation of perjury is the active encouragement of others to commit perjury—which is, itself, a felony. Dean advised, counseled, and rehearsed Jeb Magruder for his appearances before the Watergate grand jury while knowing full well of Magruder's intent to testify falsely. Dean has admitted that he played the role of prosecution, cross-examining Magruder, to help with his expected testimony. He also helped to coordinate the testimony given by other original Watergate burglars.

MISUSE OF GOVERNMENT INFORMATION. At his own initiative and insistence, Dean arranged to receive progress reports from the Department of Justice's Criminal Division about their investigation. Ostensibly he was doing this to further his own investigation on behalf of the president and the White House. In fact, he was also doing it to keep himself, literally, one step ahead of the sheriff.

He even requested access to raw FBI files and witness interviews; Attorney General Richard Kleindienst and Associate Attorney General Henry Petersen rightly denied this request. Unbeknownst to them, however, Dean later arranged for access to this material through acting FBI director Pat Gray. He also obtained internal memoranda from the U.S. attorney's office that would indicate their theories of the case. Dean illegally and improperly shared this information with CRP officials and their defense counsel, revealing to them what he had learned about the status of the government's investigation and its direction.

DESTRUCTION OF EVIDENCE. Much has been written about the circumstances surrounding John Dean's opening of Howard Hunt's White House safe and the subsequent transfer of its contents, some to the FBI agents and some handed directly to acting FBI director Pat Gray.

It is now known that Dean did not, in fact, turn over all of the safe's contents. He held back, and personally later destroyed, Hunt's two cloth-bound notebooks and an address book. He didn't disclose this fact to the prosecutors for over six months following his agreement to work with them in exchange for leniency for his own wrongdoing. It was only when he was forced to (by Hunt himself, who, after he had been convicted and then given immunity from further prosecution, insisted that the safe had also contained his personal notebooks) that Dean finally fessed up. His belated admission is described in a WSPF memo dated November 2, 1973. (Reproduced in Appendix A.)

WITNESS TAMPERING. Dean was an active participant in arranging and supervising the efforts to buy continued silence from the seven Watergate burglars. Since he knew they possessed information that put him at risk of prosecution, he could not claim the kind of innocent motive (such as providing legal fees for their defense and support for their families) that would later be claimed by other members of the White House staff who had been involved in raising funds for these payments.

Indeed, some defendants later claimed that because their lawyers knew their legal fees were being paid by money from the CRP, they had been improperly influenced to plead guilty rather than to stand trial.

Dean also tried to convince Magruder to omit his name from the list of attendees at the two meetings in Mitchell's office at the Department of Justice during which Liddy first presented his intelligence plans.

EMBEZZLEMENT. During the course of the payoffs, Dean came into possession of $22,000, which he kept in his office safe. When he found himself short of cash for his planned honeymoon, he helped himself to $4,000. While he claimed that he left a note in the safe recording this "loan," and his intent to repay it, this was an empty gesture, because he was the only one with the safe's combination. The honeymoon was postponed, but he failed to return the money. Many months later his lawyer placed $4,000 in a safe deposit box and gave the key to Judge Sirica as a sign of good faith. Even today, one searches in vain for any record of the ultimate disposition of that money—or, indeed, of the remainder of the $22,000.

One indication of at least one prosecutor's view of Dean's conduct is an undated, unsigned handwritten page found in the WSPF file on Dean at National Archives. It is labeled "Dean Violations" and lists two of the above items. (Reproduced in Appendix B.)

In addition to Dean's potentially criminal activities during the cover-up, he was the central figure in preventing any effective White House disclosures about Watergate as the scandal grew. The White House tapes contain dozens of discussions of "getting this behind us," "getting the facts out," and "getting the truth out." Even the much mocked "limited, modified hang-out" was an attempt to divulge some information. The goal, admittedly, wasn't full disclosure in the service of truth: The motivation was necessity, based on having no other options. But whatever the reason, the upshot was that, however reluctantly, Nixon was clearly willing to cut his losses by going public with additional facts.

But while the president and his aides importuned Dean to produce a statement they could release, he hemmed and hawed, and said that because the investigation was ongoing and there were conflicting versions of the events, the White House couldn't say anything without prejudicing the rights of the defendants. He also adamantly maintained that any policy of disclosure would inevitably lead to exposure of other White House problems, especially the break-in at Daniel Ellsberg's psychiatrist's office.

Because John Dean continued to lie about his own involvement, Richard Nixon continued to assess the costs only in terms of problems for his reelection campaign, with the likely criminal prosecution of several CRP honchos. There would be enough embarrassment to go around, but the only real carnage would be confined to the CRP offices one block up Pennsylvania Avenue.

The White House wasn't alone in wanting to take the offensive. Maury Stans, the CRP's finance chairman, was under pressure because of the adverse publicity surrounding some of the campaign contributions he had received. He repeatedly urged Dean to allow him to issue a public statement clarifying the situation. But Dean remained adamant: The policy was silence.

It wasn't only the president and his aides who Dean fooled; there were also senior officials at the Department of Justice. During the summer of 1972, before the indictments of the burglars were handed down on September 15, Associate Attorney General Henry Petersen urged Dean to advise the president to instruct Attorney General Kleindienst to press forward with a thorough investigation. Dean said he would, but he didn't, and Nixon remained unaware of Petersen's advice until he met with him personally in April 1972, after the cover-up was blown.

Dean's every comment and action throughout the cover-up worked in opposition to any White House disclosure—right up until the day he jumped ship.

3

The Hidden Hand of Edward Kennedy

PRESIDENT NIXON AND JOHN DEAN, FEBRUARY 28, 1973

Dean: *I am convinced that he [Ervin] has shown that he is merely a puppet for Kennedy in this whole thing. The fine hand of the Kennedys is behind this whole hearing. There is no doubt about it. When they considered the resolution on the Floor of the Senate I got the record out to read it. Who asked special permission to have their staff man on the floor? Kennedy brings this man [his Subcommittee Counsel, James] Flug out on the floor when they are debating a resolution. He is the only one who did this. It has been Kennedy's push quietly, his constant investigation. His committee did the [unintelligible] subpoenas to get at [Nixon's personal lawyer Herbert] Kalmbach and all these people.*

President: *Uh, huh.*

Dean: *He has kept this quiet and constant pressure on this thing. I think this fellow Sam Dash, who has been selected counsel, is a Kennedy choice. I think this is also something we will be able to quietly and slowly document. Leak this to the press, and the parts and cast become much more apparent.*

President: *Yes, I guess the Kennedy crowd is just lying in the bushes waiting to make their move.*

Although to this day his name is not closely associated with any of the Watergate investigations, Teddy Kennedy was in fact their real progenitor. This ongoing modesty—not usually characteristic of the Kennedys—was both consciously sought by Kennedy himself and wisely imposed by Democratic Party leaders, who worried that a Kennedy in full-bore pursuit of Nixon could smack of partisan politics and leave a bad taste with many voters.

Conventional wisdom is that John Dean was motivated by the combination of a guilty conscience (he finally had enough of the wrongdoing in which he had been caught up) and the letter Watergate burglar James McCord wrote to the judge alleging that there was an ongoing cover-up (which made Dean realize that the cover-up was doomed to failure).

But conventional wisdom is at best half right.

I submit that John Dean had two earlier and more significant Watergate wake-up calls—and both of them came courtesy of Senator Edward M. Kennedy. It was Teddy and his well-honed collection of henchmen and hatchet men—James Flug, Carmine Bellino, Terry Lenzner—who put the fear of God in John W. Dean, and really started the Watergate cover-up unraveling.

Richard Nixon, the thirty-seventh president of the United States, had the singular misfortune to be the first president in 120 years (since Zachary Taylor, the twelfth president, in 1849) to enter office with both houses of Congress controlled by the opposition party. The agency of Kennedy's Watergate activity was the Senate Judiciary Committee, and principally its Administrative Practices and Procedures Subcommittee, which he chaired. Both seniority and rank hath their privileges; the committee's staff of six professionals included four Democratic lawyers (including the chief counsel, James F. Flug) and chief investigator, Carmine Bellino; there was only one Republican counsel.

In October, an attempt in the House of Representatives' Banking Committee to hold public hearings and obtain subpoena powers covering campaign dirty tricks had been thwarted by Republican opposition. It was expected that Teddy Kennedy's attempt to do the same would be quietly squelched by Judiciary chairman James Eastland. Indeed, Republican committee member Ed Gurney announced as early as October 14 that he would insist on a full committee meeting if Kennedy proceeded with his subcommittee plans. Undeterred, Kennedy characteristically did exactly what he wanted.

In mid-October—weeks before the 1972 presidential election, and while Watergate was still a relatively minor campaign issue—Kennedy's subcommittee had issued—solely on its chairman's authority—five subpoenas to four banks and business firms and the telephone company, for records and documents relating to "authorization, financing, direction, control, operation, products, beneficiaries, participants, methods, and results of the alleged wiretapping and related political espionage and sabotage activities" that had constituted the small dirty tricks operation run by CRP agent Donald Segretti.

On October 28, a front page story in the *Washington Post* by Bob Woodward and Carl Bernstein was headlined "Sen. Kennedy Prepares for Probe—Watergate Data Subpoenaed." Four days later they were back with a story about Segretti headlined "Kennedy Panel Summons Watergate Figure": "The subpoena is the most persuasive indication to date that Kennedy intends to pursue an investigation by his subcommittee into the Watergate break-in case and related alleged acts of political sabotage and espionage."

For anyone with eyes to read—much less with John Dean's highly sensitive political antennae and knowledge of his personal vulnerability—the fact that Teddy Kennedy had the Watergate bit between his teeth was well and widely known for three months before James McCord even thought about writing his letter.

Among those who understood this perfectly well was Senate Democratic majority leader Mike Mansfield. Aware that Kennedy was not to be deterred, Mansfield was at least able to convince him that taking the public lead in such a determined way on Watergate (which was then considered to be a relatively minor and tangential matter) would risk having the whole thing seen as a purely partisan—and even personal—attack by a Kennedy against Nixon.

The fact that Teddy was willing to take the highly uncharacteristic step of surrendering the limelight (and his chief staff members) to such an unserious and unprepossessing figure as Sam Ervin (this was before the media turned the undistinguished North Carolina senator with the long-standing anti–civil rights voting record into a national folk hero) seems to me to indicate two things.

First, Kennedy had an assurance that Watergate would continue to be pursued under his direction, if not his direct leadership. And second, that he already had another agenda in mind.

The upshot was that on February 7, 1973, the Senate voted to create the Select Committee on Presidential Campaign Activities under Senator Ervin's leadership, and Kennedy handed over his files and his staffers.

The second wake-up call was even more attention getting and disturbing for John Dean, because, literally, it had his name written all over it.

The Senate Judiciary Committee's confirmation hearings of L. Patrick Gray to succeed J. Edgar Hoover as director of the FBI began on February 28, 1973. Gray seemed to be the ideal nominee—the pick of the litter—and little if any resistance was expected. His only announced opposition was from a small group of Kennedy-led senators (including the usual liberal suspects: John Tunney, Phil Hart, Birch Bayh, and Quentin Burdick) and the few newspapers that followed their lead.

Gray had seemed to be a sure thing for a quick and easy confirmation, but he turned out to be a spectacularly incompetent witness; he also turned out to have made some serious errors of judgment, which he compounded by making the fatal mistake of trusting his White House contact John Dean.

It emerged that he had kept Dean regularly informed about the FBI's Watergate investigation, and that he had, at Dean's behest, burned in his own home fireplace material from Howard Hunt's White House safe that Dean had given him. (Dean had assured him that the documents had nothing to do with Watergate, but said that "they should never see the light of day.") Gray admitted to the senators that Dean had "probably" lied to the FBI.

Just as with the establishment of the Ervin Committee three weeks earlier, both Senator Kennedy and the Senate Democratic leadership decided Kennedy should take a backseat in the Gray hearings, lest his involvement allow them to be painted as another Kennedy anti-Nixon canard. Robert Byrd of West Virginia and John Tunney of California, who had been Ted Kennedy's law school roommate, became point men, but it is hard not to conclude that Kennedy was really supplying the ammunition and pulling the strings.

The opposition ramped up considerably, and it became clear that Gray's nomination would be dead in the water unless Dean himself also testified. On March 13, John Tunney led the committee in a unanimous vote to "invite" Dean to testify about his dealings with Gray; without Dean's appearance, Gray's nomination was doomed.

Thus, at least a fortnight before he even knew about the McCord letter, Dean found himself directly in Teddy Kennedy's very precise and unforgiving crosshairs. Byrd and Tunney were lightweights, but Kennedy, Flug, and Bellino were hell on wheels.

On April 5, the president put Pat Gray out of his misery—and took John Dean off the hot seat—with a statement issued from the Western White House in San Clemente:

> *Pat Gray is an able, honest, and dedicated American.*
>
> *Because I asked my Counsel, John Dean, to conduct a thorough investigation of alleged involvement in the Watergate episode, Director Gray was asked to make FBI reports available to Mr. Dean. His compliance with this completely proper and necessary request exposed Mr. Gray to totally unfair innuendo and suspicion, and thereby seriously tarnished his fine record as Acting Director and promising future at the Bureau.*
>
> *In view of the action of the Senate Judiciary Committee today, it is obvious that Mr. Gray's nomination will not be confirmed by the Senate. Mr. Gray has asked that I withdraw his nomination. In fairness to Mr. Gray, and out of my overriding concern for the effective conduct of the vitally important business of the FBI, I have regretfully agreed to withdraw Mr. Gray's nomination.*

With this background in mind, it is not surprising that when he decided to hire his own criminal defense lawyer, Dean retained Charles Shaffer, an attorney who was in the innermost circle of—who was, indeed, a hero of—the Kennedy Clan Democrats.

4

Kennedy Politics: Long Memories and Sharp Knives

Led by patriarch Joseph P. Kennedy, Sr., the Kennedy family pioneered a new kind of presidential politics in America. They introduced, in ways and to degrees that had not been known before, what might be called the three Ms: money, macho, and media.

MONEY

A friend of JFK's once observed, "Politics is like war. It takes three things to win. The first is money and the second is money and the third is money." In that war, JFK had all three fronts covered.

Of course, money had always played a role. The politician who called money the "mother's milk of politics" wasn't kidding. Wealthy men have spent fortunes on their campaigns since the beginning of the republic. But no one had done so on the scale, and with the unalloyed dynastic ambitions, of Joseph P. Kennedy. There was no question he could afford it; in 1957 *Fortune* magazine listed him as one of America's sixteen wealthiest men.

Joe, Sr., never got to spend his money on himself. His disastrous tenure as FDR's ambassador to the Court of St. James's (where he went a tad too native and espoused Prime Minister Neville Chamberlain's policy of appeasing Hitler) nipped his own presidential ambitions in the bud. Without losing a beat, he transferred his expectations and attention to his eldest son, Joseph P. Kennedy, Jr. When Joe, Jr., died a hero's death flying a dangerous mission over the English Channel, the mantle passed to the next son, John Fitzgerald Kennedy.

The Kennedy campaign MO was established with JFK's first race for Congress in 1946. His father spent more than a quarter of a million dollars (almost two million dollars in 2008) to get the nomination. This was a phenomenal amount, as Joe, Sr., himself acknowledged. "With that sort of money," he quipped, "I could elect my chauffeur."

Six years later, when JFK ran for the Senate, his father lent more than a hand. The race was uncomfortably close, and when he learned that a major Boston newspaper planned to endorse his son's opponent, Joe Kennedy solved the problem by extending a half-million-dollar "loan" to the paper's owner, who was skating on the edge of bankruptcy. As John Kennedy later put it, "You know, we had to buy that paper or I'd have been licked."

By Election Day, Joe Kennedy had poured several million dollars into the race. As President Eisenhower saw it, JFK's Republican opponent—the popular incumbent Henry Cabot Lodge—was "simply overwhelmed by money."

The investigative writer and journalist Peter Maas, who specialized in police and Mafia stories, uncovered one of the ways Joe Kennedy used his money. The leader of Boston's Roman Catholics, Richard Cardinal Cushing, was a friend of the family, and where his son's political career was involved, Joe Kennedy saw no reason to separate church and state. If, for example, one Sunday's collections in the Boston archdiocese netted $950,000, Joe Kennedy would write the church a check for $1 million in return for the cash. That way the church earned an extra $50,000; Kennedy could take a $50,000 tax deduction for the donation; and he had almost a million untraceable dollars for use in his son's campaign. It was a win/win/win situation. It is even conceivable Joe took the full $1 million deduction, since you never knew for sure just what he was up to.

In an interview in 1958 Eleanor Roosevelt, who didn't know the half of it, said, "Senator Kennedy's father has been spending oodles of money all over the country, and probably has a paid representative in every state by now." She said she had been told that Joe Kennedy would spend "any money" to make his son president. She warned, "Building an organization is permissible, but giving too lavishly may seem to indicate a desire to influence through money."

The test case for what Kennedy money could do in presidential politics turned out to be the West Virginia primary. Held on May 10, 1960, the primary pitted JFK against Hubert Humphrey, a liberal senator from Minnesota, in a do-or-die shoot-out for the Democratic nomination.

West Virginia was a big labor state, and Humphrey had a long history of supporting union interests. A month before the vote, he was leading in all the polls. Legendary Boston political and former House Speaker Tip O'Neill remembered how Joe Kennedy turned the tide. He sent Eddie Ford, a Boston real estate man, to West Virginia with "a pocket full of money." Ford, O'Neill said, would "see the sheriff, and he'd say to the sheriff, 'Sheriff, I'm from Chicago. I'm on my way south. I love this young Kennedy boy. He can help this nation, by God. He'll do things for West Virginians. I'll tell you what. Here's $5,000. You carry your village for him or your county for him, and I'll give you a little reward when I'm on my way back.'"

As Tip O'Neill somewhat wistfully remembered, "They passed money around like it was never seen."

If there were any doubts that money talks, the West Virginia results put them to rest. In four weeks JFK's campaign turned a 20 percent deficit into a 60 percent lead. The next day Humphrey withdrew from the presidential race, and JFK waltzed to the nomination two months later.

Plainspoken former president Harry Truman, who lost no love where the Kennedys were concerned, put it bluntly: "He [Joe Kennedy] bought West Virginia. I don't know how much it cost him; he's a tightfisted old son of a bitch; so he didn't [spend] any more than he had to, but he bought West Virginia, and that's how his boy won the primary over Humphrey."

The stories about Kennedy money swamping West Virginia were so widespread that JFK finally had to address them. Characteristically, he adopted humor as a way to defuse the controversy, while finessing the facts. "I have just received the following telegram from my generous father," he joked. "'Dear Jack: Don't buy a single vote more than is necessary. I'll help you win this election, but I'll be damned if I'm going to pay for a land-slide!'"

Adlai Stevenson, the party's standard-bearer in 1952 and 1956, said that "the amount of money being spent" by the Kennedys in 1960 was "phenom-enal, probably the highest amount spent on a campaign in history."

Once JFK was his party's presidential nominee, large amounts of offi-cial campaign funds were automatically available, and success no longer depended so much on the family's private fortune. But old habits die hard. In Illinois, where the downstate Republicans had to be outnumbered by the Chicago Democratic machine in order to carry the state, Joe Kennedy became the conduit for mob money. G. Robert Blakey, a former federal prosecutor, confirmed that FBI wiretaps had recorded details of a plot to run contributions to the Kennedy campaign from the corrupt Teamsters union pension fund through the candidate's father.

Kennedy intimate Ben Bradlee recorded a late-night phone call the anxious candidate made to Chicago's mayor Daley: "Mr. President," the mayor reassured him with a greeting that in itself must have allayed a lot of worries, "with a little bit of luck and the help of a few close friends, you're going to carry Illinois." A few hours later, Chicago came through with enough votes to win the state.

MACHO

As Chris Matthews, an unabashed Kennedy clan worshipper puts it:

> *They play hard. They ski hard. Every sport they get into seems to be an ultimate endurance question. They don't just go out and swim in a swimming pool. It has got to be in the ocean. They have got to go out and they have got to go out and sail in the ocean. They have got to ski 100 miles an hour. They've got to climb mountains.*

Kennedy macho, reflecting the nature and mores of the times, was a combination of physical bravado and personal assurance. British author Ian Fleming started publishing his James Bond spy novels in the early

1950s. JFK was one of their biggest fans, and he clearly identified with the personality—and morals—of the supersmooth Agent 007. James Bond accepted every challenge, laughed at danger, sniggered at pretension, trusted no one but himself, and considered the admiration of men and the availability of women as his rightful due.

In the political arena Kennedy macho manifested itself in risky associations and a roughshod approach to desired goals; in the personal area it took the form of male chauvinism and sexual voracity.

The Kennedys' deep and dangerous connection with the Mafia was a case of macho run amok. A lot of Joseph P. Kennedy's first fortune had been made by bootlegging booze during Prohibition. In the course of that career he rubbed shoulders with some unsavory types. In *Brothers,* his recent book about the Kennedys, David Talbot, founder and former editor of the online magazine *Salon,* candidly observed:

> *Running liquor during Prohibition brought the kind of windfall profits the drug trade does today. But it also meant doing business with the Mafia if you valued your life, and Kennedy went right to the top to ensure the security of his business. He forged a partnership with Frank Costello, the dapper, politically wired "prime minister of the underworld."*

But by the late 1950s, the postwar Mafia was reaching for new levels of phony respectability at the same time that it was pioneering new levels of violence. When the Kennedys cultivated organized crime connections with labor unions to turn out the vote in the West Virginia primary, when they made use of mob-laundered funds for walking-around money in Chicago, and when they encouraged the Mafia to take out Castro in Cuba they were truly dancing with the devil. How high a price they paid for their failure to keep dancing is still being debated today.

Once JFK was in the White House and RFK was heading the Department of Justice, the Mafia bosses, not unreasonably, expected the new administration at the very least to lighten up where some of their activities were concerned. Instead, the president insulted them by snubbing their idol Frank Sinatra, and the attorney general unleashed an unprecedented attack on organized crime—especially that connected with unions. At first the bosses were confused; then they were annoyed; then they were angry. FBI wiretaps started to pick up talk about revenge.

Robert Kennedy was convinced that the Mafia had had a hand in his brother's assassination. As we will see, he had a trusted confidant infiltrate the staff of the Warren Commission for the specific purpose of reporting any evidence of such a connection directly back to him.

Unlike his three brothers, Robert was small and wiry. He had a wrestler's body topped by a large handsome head. What he may have lacked in charm and affability he made up in intensity and toughness. The word he brought to mind for many people was "ruthless."

Novelist, essayist, and dabbler in Democratic politics Gore Vidal wrote in 1963: "There are flaws in his persona hard to disguise. For one thing, it will take a public relations genius to make him appear lovable. He is not. His obvious characteristics are energy, vindictiveness and simplemindedness about human motives, which may yet bring him down. To Bobby the world is black and white. Them and Us. He has none of his brother's human ease; or charity."

Robert Kennedy's determined crusade against organized crime and labor boss James Hoffa was a prime example of Kennedy macho. His focus and intensity even caused problems within the family. Both Joe, Sr., and JFK were less than enthusiastic about anything that could rock the boat where labor and union support for Democrats was concerned. But despite bitter quarrels with his father, and only lukewarm encouragement from his brother, Bobby would not be deterred.

His obsession started in the mid-1950s, when he was chief counsel of the Senate Select Committee on Improper Activities in the Labor or Management Field, better known as the McClellan Rackets Committee. Senators John Kennedy and Sam Ervin also were members. He wrote a bestselling account of his racket-busting activities called *The Enemy Within*.

By the early 1960s, James Hoffa, president of the largest and richest union, the 1.3-million-member Teamsters, was the enemy. Almost nothing was more important to Bobby Kennedy than putting Jimmy Hoffa behind bars. Their conflict had an intensely up close and personal element: Hoffa had succeeded in thwarting and outmaneuvering Kennedy many times. "I used to love to bug that little bastard," Hoffa said, once calling him a spoiled rich kid during a public hearing.

As soon as Bobby became attorney general, he set up an organized crime section in the Criminal Division of the Justice Department, and brought aboard dozens of special prosecutors. Because of the way organized crime works, any serious attempt to shut it down involves a totally different kind of attitude and approach from that appropriate to prosecuting other crimes. Mafia bosses are neither stupid nor willing to get their hands dirty in the actual commission of violent crimes. To bring them down, you must begin with the assumption that their very existence is irrefutable evidence of evil—and that they need to be destroyed by any means possible. Bobby Kennedy, indeed, said he believed in Hoffa's "absolute evilness"; he said that aside from the government itself, the Teamsters were the most powerful institution in the country. He told Americans: "Quite literally, your life—the life of every person in the United States—is in the hands of Hoffa and his Teamsters."

To bring down such an evil adversary—immensely powerful and insidiously wily—it would be necessary to push the federal government's power and authority to the absolute limit, and be willing, even eager, to find any charge—no matter how tangential or contrived—to secure a conviction and imprisonment.

Indeed, to bring down the big Mafia bosses required reliance on thought crimes—ephemeral concepts like conspiracy charges and perjury—where the real crime is membership in an already presumed criminal group, and where very little real evidence of other criminality is required for conviction. That was how Eliot Ness and his untouchables finally managed to get Al Capone: on income tax charges. Civil libertarians might object—and many did, worrying that Kennedy was turning the Fifth Amendment into an admission of guilt. The press, however, was dependably Kennedy-friendly, happy to be on the side of the angels in the good-versus-evil drama the attorney general was presenting, and grateful to him for providing dependably colorful copy.

While officially a part of the Organized Crime Section of the DOJ's Criminal Division, the Labor and Racketeering unit was headed by a nonlawyer, former FBI agent Walter Sheridan, who reported directly to Robert Kennedy. Carmine Bellino, the Kennedy family retainer who had been Bobby's go-to investigator on the McClellan Committee, was also part of what became widely known as the Get Hoffa Squad, which before long comprised some twenty specially recruited attorneys.

Victor Navasky, in his generally admiring book, *Kennedy Justice*, explains the extrajudicial tactics that Bobby was prepared to use where Hoffa was concerned:

> *Personally he felt Hoffa was involved in a conspiracy of evil, and where evil men were concerned, Kennedy's image of justice, of the role of law, had elements of a morality play. Although he had no systematic jurisprudence, his public and private observations showed him sympathetic to St. Thomas Aquinas' idea of a natural law, which meted out justice in accordance with Aristotelian principles of retribution and reciprocity—a jurisprudence ideally suited to accommodate a Get-Hoffa Squad. That Robert Kennedy simultaneously entertained other conceptions of justice, which emphasized protection of the personality, freedom and equity, proved no barrier at the time, since in a rather naïve way he felt that these were the prerogative of the pure, the young, the poor, the disadvantaged. Robert Kennedy in the early sixties had little difficulty accommodating the notion that there were two kinds of justice; one for society's enemies, another for its victims.*

RFK's pursuit of Jimmy Hoffa, likened by some to Captain Ahab's obsession with Moby Dick, extended over seven years and involved massive eavesdropping and wiretaps—and five separate trials. Ultimately it required the insertion of a mole as a spy within Hoffa's inner circle. The idea wasn't to catch him for having committed an already known crime, but in the hope the mole would be a witness to some future crime committed by the Teamster boss.

After several acquittals, Bobby finally prevailed: Jimmy Hoffa was convicted in separate trials for jury tampering and for pension fraud.

Although no one doubted the ultimate justice represented in these verdicts, there were serious doubts inside and outside the Justice Department about the corners that had to be cut and the principles that had to be over-looked in order to secure them. Some viewed Kennedy's Hoffa obsession as a vendetta plain and simple, based on a considerable amount of macho-laced bad blood. The troubling specter of selective prosecution was unavoidable. Few could claim that had the target not been Hoffa, the amount of time and effort and resources would have been allocated to the cases based solely on their legal merit or worthiness.

Victor Navasky expressed these concerns concisely:

> *Does the Justice Department have the right to go fishing into every area of a person's activities, looking for possible crime? Or should the Department investigate only specific charges where it has reasonable assurance that a crime has been committed? The government has a right to subpoena a particular businessman if it has reasonable grounds to believe that he made a payoff to Hoffa to get a loan from the Teamster Pension Fund. But it has no right to subpoena a hundred business-men or even to send FBI agents to interrogate them, just on the chance that one of them did make such a payoff. Yet, the Justice Department is following the latter course, hitting in all directions in the hope that something will be uncovered which can be used to "get Hoffa."*

In March 1960, two months after he had announced his candidacy for president with the declaration that the White House should be "the center of moral leadership," JFK began an affair with Judith Exner, who also hap-pened to be sleeping with Chicago mob boss Sam Giancana. This was a perfect paradigm of the kind of bold—bordering on foolhardy—risk tak-ing that characterized the Kennedy family's approach to life. A presidential candidate; an extramarital affair with a mistress who is connected with the Mafia—what's to worry?

And, for various reasons, including the deep cushion of family money, the complicity of the media, and a reservoir of charm, Kennedy transgres-sions resulted more in knowing winks and nudging elbows than in negative headlines.

And Kennedys trusted only Kennedys. John appointed his brother Bobby keeper of many family secrets—including the political debt they owed to organized crime, the real state of the president's health, the role of money and intimidation in their election campaigns, and their plots to murder foreign leaders, among many others. The brothers also shared that trait inherited from their father—a voracious appetite for women—and indulged it with a sometimes daily abandon that was deeply disturbing to the Secret Service agents who witnessed it. Kennedys could do exactly what they wanted and still evade any charges that might actually be brought against them. Kennedys wrote their own moral code.

Where sex was concerned, the Kennedy family—father and sons—not only shared the same attitudes; in many cases they shared the same women. JFK flapped the usually unflappable British prime minister Harold Macmillan by revealing that unless he could have a new woman every three days he would get headaches. Macmillan, observing the wide sexual and political swath the Kennedys were cutting through Washington, was reminded of the notorious family that raped and pillaged its way to power during the Renaissance. Watching the Kennedys in the nation's capital, he said, was "like watching the Borgia brothers take over a respectable North Italian City." Years later, after the press had finally reported many of these kinds of stories, *Time* magazine described JFK as "a one-man Roman orgy." By the 1980s that description was seen as a bad thing; in the macho atmosphere of the Kennedy White House of the early sixties it would have been taken as a pat on the back of downright Bondian dimensions.

When thorny issues or difficult questions could no longer be avoided, the Kennedy way was to deflect them with humorous self-deprecation. During the presidential campaign Bobby Kennedy was asked by a TV interviewer about the persistent rumors that he would be appointed attorney general if his brother became president. Looking levelly into the camera, he replied, "There is absolutely no truth to that at all. That would be nepotism of the worst sort." When the newly elected president was called on the appointment of his thirty-two-year-old brother, who had no prior legal experience, as attorney general of the United States, he quipped, "I can't see that it's wrong to give him a little legal experience before he goes out to practice law."

When Teddy, at age thirty and with no prior experience holding any office, ran for the U.S. Senate, he expressed concern about how to answer a question he was sure to be asked in an upcoming debate: Why are you running? Bobby Kennedy said, "Tell them you don't want to be sitting on your ass in some office in New York."

MEDIA

John Kennedy enjoyed excellent press—partly because he was a natural as far as the media was concerned, and partly because he knew how to manipulate reporters (and when that didn't work, how to punish them) into writing what he wanted. He understood how important reporters were to presenting and projecting an image of him and his administration, and he always made sure that their needs were met, and, where possible, even anticipated.

In addition to looking good, he also knew how to look good for the camera—which can be a very different thing. He always seemed at ease, but he always knew exactly what he was doing, and was prepared to do it differently if that would look better. Joe, Sr., who had learned a great deal about visual presentation during his years in Hollywood, appreciated the role that television would come to play in American politics. He arranged for a media coach to work with JFK as early as the 1952 Senate race, when only a handful of homes had a TV set.

The Kennedy White House had a voracious appetite for journalism. Merriman Smith, UPI's senior White House correspondent, wondered, "How they can spot an obscure paragraph in a paper of 3,000 circulation 2,000 miles away is beyond me. They must have a thousand little gnomes reading the papers for them."

No more immune to flattery than anyone else, reporters were disarmed when JFK could quote their columns and praise their work. Before the Los Angeles nominating convention, a prominent journalist boasted that Jack Kennedy had called to ask him who he thought should be his floor manager. He surprised the influential muckraking (and not particularly Kennedy-friendly) columnist Drew Pearson by showing up at his home for a chat. His late-night visits to columnist Joseph Alsop became the stuff of immediate legend in the capital's tightly knit and highly competitive journalistic community.

JFK also knew how to provide reporters with the kinds of interesting angles, strong visuals, and colorful quotes that make for the best stories. In at least one recorded instance, a reporter returned the favor. At a White House briefing held for Texas reporters, Ted Dealey, the crusty and outspoken publisher of the *Dallas Morning News*, launched into a detailed account of what he considered to be the administration's abject weakness in the face of Soviet aggression. JFK maintained a fixed smile as Dealey told him, "The general opinion of the grass-roots thinking in this country is that you and your administration are weak sisters."

This unexpected tirade produced an uneasy reaction in the room, but the president maintained his silence and, at least apparently, his equanimity. Charles Bartlett, the Washington correspondent of the *Chattanooga Times*, was an old Kennedy friend; it was at one of his dinner parties that JFK first met his future wife, Jacqueline Bouvier. Bartlett helped the White House invent, and then falsely reported on, an account of the Dealey incident, in which the president emerged as a bold and eloquent leader. "The difference between you and me, Mr. Dealey," according to the words Bartlett crafted for his friend the president, "is that I was elected President of this country and you were not, and I have the responsibility for the lives of one hundred eighty million Americans, which you have not. Wars are easier to talk about than they are to fight. I'm just as tough as you are, Mr. Dealey. And I didn't get elected by arriving at soft judgments."

Dealey and the eighteen other Texans present were surprised by their inability to remember such a dramatic and articulate exchange having taken place, but the story was widely reported.

If charm failed, or when manipulation wouldn't work, the president was perfectly prepared to play hardball. When a newspaper's coverage angered him, he publicly canceled the White House subscription—in those days a serious blow to a paper's public image that any reporter or editorial writer would think twice before risking. If a reporter wasn't friendly enough his access would suddenly dry up. Even Ben Bradlee knew what it felt like to be consigned to Siberia. In the early 1960s, controlling access to the president gave the White House far more leverage than it does today. An inside track to the president and the White House was a feather in a newsman's cap, and might even make the career of a television reporter.

There was hardball—and then there was hardball. Instead of experiencing the more subtle forms of presidential displeasure, some reporters received calls—or, worse, a summons—from the attorney general. Bobby wasted no time with pleasantries, much less with being pleasant. His shouting tantrums became well-known and widely feared. One reporter described an RFK "lecture" when his paper's coverage of a scandal displeased the new president. He "expected at any moment he would throw himself to the floor, screaming and bawling for his way. Instead, he paced back and forth, storming and complaining. It was something to see."

The administration's conduct during the 1962 conflict over steel prices was condemned by *The New York Times* as smacking of a "personal vendetta." FBI agents—acting on orders from the attorney general and without authorizing warrants—were sent to conduct dawn interviews with reporters in an attempt to uncover sources and influence coverage. The liberal pundit Max Lerner wrote, "This may make sense if you want to catch a spy before he vanishes, but these were reporters, not spies, and this invasion of their privacy suggested a police operation." The *Richmond Times-Dispatch* stated, "The indefensible abuse of personal power by a hired public servant highlights the intemperate reaction of the Brothers Kennedy toward any and all who presume to cross their ambition."

Teddy Kennedy and the Three Ms

Edward Moore Kennedy was the fourth of the four Kennedy brothers. Joe, Jr., died before Teddy was even a teenager; John and Robert had been born seven years apart; but John and Teddy were separated by fifteen years. As a result, Teddy grew up largely on his own and—much more important—somewhat below his father's unforgiving radar. Not being driven like Joe, John, and Robert, he lacked their drive. He was gregarious and outgoing; he was rich and popular. But he wasn't necessarily a gentleman, and he certainly wasn't a scholar.

JFK jokingly referred to his hard-partying youngest brother as "the gay illiterate." The word "gay" was used in its older sense—because there was absolutely no question about Teddy's overweening interest in women.

Admitted to Harvard as a legacy student (because his father and three older brothers were alumni), Teddy was expelled in his second year when he paid someone to take a test for him. After two years in the Army (where he never rose above the rank of private) he was allowed to return and graduate.

While in law school at the University of Virginia, he was known as "Cadillac Eddie." His big, flashy, new car stood out from the usual college-town jalopies, and he was cited by police four times for reckless driving.

His reputation was so widespread that when Robert Kennedy came to the law school to speak, he joked that their mother had asked him to find out "what side of the court my brother is going to appear on when he gets out of law school, attorney or defendant." Once again humor was enlisted to put a kinder, gentler face on consistently questionable conduct.

Three years later, in 1962, at the age of thirty, thanks to his family's celebrity and a large infusion of his father's cash, Teddy Kennedy was sitting in the U.S. Senate.

His brothers' assassinations and the massive debilitating stroke his father suffered in 1968 left Teddy on his own and adrift. Within the short span of five years he had gone from being the most peripheral member of a vital political dynasty to being its sole survivor and last standard-bearer. When both brothers died so publicly and tragically, Teddy was automatically anointed and moved up next in line, whether he wanted it or not.

Even the most devoted Kennedy supporters were hard-pressed to place EMK on equal footing with JFK or RFK. He had settled comfortably into a Senate seat that amounted to a sinecure; as long as he wanted to be the senator from Massachusetts, the job was his.

Personally wealthy, with his Senate seat secure and a ready-made cadre of able and devoted supporters eager to work for him, at least one of the three Ms—money—wouldn't be a major concern for Teddy Kennedy.

As far as macho was concerned, Teddy embodied it every bit as much as his brothers but without their arguably redeeming, or at least modulating, qualities. While they were able to maintain the reality or the facade of happy and stable marriages despite their serial philandering, Teddy engaged in flagrant and risky conduct, even as his marriage dissolved and his wife's physical and mental problems compounded in public. His sexual conduct lacked the sophistication and cynicism of that of his siblings; and totally unlike them, his drinking was often excessive and indiscreet. Even as admiring an observer as Adam Clymer, the *New York Times* reporter who became his unofficial biographer, had to report instances of Teddy's drinking and sometimes public intoxication (noting, "In the convention of the time, no one wrote about it for publication").

Despite the fact that his conduct didn't make it easy for them, reporters still gave him the benefits of many doubts, and his media coverage—the third M—was extremely positive. While he was a senator in the shadow of his more prominent brothers, he was able to avoid detailed coverage and too close scrutiny. And after his brothers were dead, reporters had personal and professional reasons for treating him gingerly.

He may not have been up to his brothers' level of intelligence, charm, or ambition—but he was the only Kennedy left. He was the heir apparent, albeit by default, and that was enough to cover a multitude of sins.

It was hard to imagine that anything could prevent Teddy from taking up the stricken standard his brothers had left on the field and rejoining the battle in 1972. From the first days after Nixon moved into the White House the polls indicated that he would have an uphill battle to win reelection against Teddy Kennedy.

As if to leave no doubt in this regard, Teddy decided to challenge the incumbent Russell Long, his Louisiana colleague, for the role of Senate Democratic whip. On January 3, 1969—three weeks before Nixon was inaugurated—Teddy won the whip position with a comfortable thirty-one to twenty-six vote. *The New York Times* story called this whip win a "stepping stone to the presidency." Both *Newsweek* and *Time* put Teddy on their covers and said his presidential candidacy was all but inevitable.

Senator Long provided a telling commentary to his defeat.

> *Having had the experience that Lyndon Johnson experienced in 1960, Richard Nixon experienced in that same year, and a number of other people have had in taking on a Kennedy, I can say it is a very interesting experience. I would suggest that Mr. Nixon himself should be very careful and watch himself for the future, because in all probability he has a very able opponent ready for him.*

Of course, all that was before July 19. But by the beginning of 1972, Chappaquiddick was going on three years past. His refusal to allow it to end his career, coupled with a containment plan and truly exceptional staff work, had apparently paid off. It would always be a problem and vulnerability for him with some voters, but it wouldn't be a deal breaker with a majority of them. While his apparent diffidence about running for president in 1972 (and again in 1976) was troubling to Kennedy Clan Democrats impatient for the restoration of Camelot, and to the reporters who wanted the excitement his candidacy would generate, it was attributed to strategy rather than indecision—much less indifference.

Such was the power of the Kennedy mystique that the loyalists and supporters were self-motivating and self-supporting. Confident that EMK was only biding his time before taking his place in the pantheon alongside JFK and RFK, Kennedy Clan Democrats were content to wait on the sidelines until he decided the time was right to lead them in their noble quest.

5

John Dean's Cover-up Collapses

The 1972 Watergate break-in took place on June 16; the burglars were indicted on September 15; the trial began on January 8.

Shortly thereafter, in Judge Sirica's courtroom, E. Howard Hunt and the four Cubans pled guilty. McCord and Liddy refused to cooperate and were found guilty by the jury. Sirica set March 23 as the sentencing date for all defendants.

The prosecutors, well aware that some kind of cover-up was in effect, adopted the standard approach of counting on the prospect of spending time in prison to start changing minds and loosening tongues. The fact that Judge Sirica was nicknamed "Maximum John" because of the severity of his sentences could only help in this regard.

From the time the burglars were arrested, the CRP had honored Liddy's commitment to pay their attorneys' fees and to provide support for their families. The lawyers were paid directly and the amount of family assistance was relatively modest. In the two months following the guilty verdicts, however, Howard Hunt's demands for money reached the point that they could no longer be thought of as anything but blackmail.

Watergate burglar James McCord, having been convicted on all counts, was facing a substantial prison sentence. With his CIA and law enforcement background, he was worried about how he would fare on the wrong side of the bars in prison. So on March 19, he submitted a letter to Judge Sirica. This was exactly the kind of break that the prosecutors had been counting on. McCord wrote:

> *There was political pressure applied to the defendants to plead guilty and remain silent.*
>
> *Perjury occurred during the trial in matters highly material to the very structure, orientation, and impact of the government's case and to the motivation and intent of the defendants.*
>
> *Others involved in the Watergate operation were not identified during the trial, when they could have been by those testifying.*
>
> *The Watergate operation was not a CIA operation. Others may have misled the Cubans into believing it was a CIA operation. I know for a fact that it was not.*

On that Monday morning, the letter was delivered to Judge Sirica. That same night, unaware that McCord's time bomb was now ticking, Richard Nixon and John Ehrlichman sat down for a discussion about where the Watergate matter currently stood. Their conversation lasted over an hour, and several things are clear from listening to it today. They were both aware of the impending sentencing at the end of the week, and of John Dean's concerns, expressed earlier to Ehrlichman, that something might "blow" because of it. They speculate on whether McCord will be the one to blow, because Dean has characterized him as out of touch with the defense team and absolutely terrified of going to jail. Nixon and Ehrlichman are more curious than concerned about this question, because they are confident that whatever McCord does, it can only impact officials at the CRP.

The president says that he can't be seen as supporting any "stone-walling"—his role must be one of wanting full disclosure.

They are clearly unaware of Dean's own vulnerability. They know he is concerned, but they have no idea that his concern stems from a fear of being prosecuted for his own criminal conduct.

Dean's increasingly desperate attempts to keep Watergate under control behind the scenes had not been successful, and his ability to remain behind the scenes was about to come to an end. He had to do something. What he did was ask for a private meeting with President Nixon.

MARCH 21, 1973, OVAL OFFICE MEETING

BETWEEN PRESIDENT NIXON AND JOHN DEAN (EXCERPT)

Dean: *Uh, the reason I thought we ought to talk this morning is because in, in our conversations, uh, uh, I have, I have the impression that you don't know everything I know*

President: *That's right.*

Dean: *. . . and it makes it very difficult for you to make judgments that, uh, that only you can make . . .*

President: *That's right.*

Dean: *. . . on some of these things and I thought that—*

President: *You've got, in other words, I've got to know why you feel that, uh, that something . . .*

Dean: *Well, let me . . .*

President: *. . . that, that we shouldn't unravel something.*

Dean: *. . . let me give you my overall first.*

President: *In other words, you, your judgment as to where it stands, and where we go now—*

Dean: *I think, I think that, uh, there's no doubt about the seriousness of the problem we're, we've got. We have a cancer—within, close to the Presidency, that's growing. It's growing daily. It's compounding, it grows geometrically now because it compounds itself. Uh, that'll be clear as I explain you know, some of the details, uh, of why it is, and it basically is because (1) we're being black-mailed; (2) uh, people are going to start perjuring themself* [sic] *very quickly that have not had to perjure themselves to protect other people and the like.*

And that is just—and there is no assurance—

President: *That it won't bust.*

Dean: *That, that won't bust.*

President: *True.*

Just after ten o'clock the next morning—March 21, 1973, a fateful day in any Watergate chronology—Nixon met alone with John Dean. Dean opened the above meeting, which had been arranged at his request, by saying that he thinks it's important for Nixon to learn about some things that he clearly doesn't know. He outlines some aspects of the cover-up and tells the president that Howard Hunt's recent demands for money were seen by Dean as blackmail.

This is John Dean's pivotal "cancer on the presidency" speech, in which he later claimed to have made a full disclosure of all wrongdoing. It was hardly the comprehensive review he would claim. In fact, it was a highly selective account. And, as we have seen, far from being motivated by a guilty conscience and the desire to make a clean breast of things, the meeting was triggered by Teddy Kennedy's subcommittee's investigations and Pat Gray's disastrous confirmation hearings—two events that had suddenly threatened to put John Dean directly in the firing line for criminal prosecution.

Dean's purpose, now that he could no longer keep all the balls in the air on his own, was to bring the president at least partially into the loop. He had no intention whatever of fessing up and informing Nixon that he had been running the cover-up out of the White House counsel's office. He only went as far as describing how the break-in came about. It was too little and too late, but for the very first time he revealed that *he* had been present with Mitchell when Liddy's plan was first presented. It was almost as if he were rehearsing his story for the lawyers he would retain exactly one week later.

What he chose to tell Nixon, he soon realized, hadn't been enough for the president to grasp the immensity and complexity Watergate had by now assumed. When Dean described the March 21 conversation to the federal prosecutors, he told them that "Nixon just didn't get it."

One thing Nixon got very clearly was the concept of blackmail. He is riveted by that news, and toys with the idea of meeting Hunt's latest demands. The discussion concludes with the understanding that Dean will get together with Haldeman and Ehrlichman to decide, along with John Mitchell, what they are going to do. The principal question is how to influence the manner in which unpleasant disclosures that can't be avoided will now have to be made.

A couple of hours later, at five o'clock on the afternoon of the twenty-first, the president met with Dean, Haldeman, and Ehrlichman. The three advisers had hashed the situation out and now make recommendations about what to do. The idea of meeting Hunt's blackmail demands is off the table; the issue now is how the White House can trigger a renewed investigation of CRP wrongdoing. Thus, even before they are aware of McCord's letter, they have decided that Nixon will have to call for another grand jury to investigate Watergate.

The real question is how to handle John Mitchell, whom they have asked to come down from New York the next day. They realize that calling for a new Watergate grand jury while waiving any claim of executive privilege will amount to forcing Nixon's friend, the former attorney general, to walk the plank.

The meeting ends with the idea that Dean will prepare a report on everything he has found out about what went on at the CRP. The president can then cite this report as the reason for requesting a renewed investigation—even calling for a new Watergate grand jury. It is apparent that Nixon, Haldeman, and Ehrlichman still persist in their belief that any fallout will only affect people from the CRP.

John Mitchell flew down on the shuttle the next morning. At two o'clock that afternoon, Wednesday, March 22, he met with the president, Dean, Haldeman, and Ehrlichman. Dean says very little at this meeting other than to confirm that he can and will write a report about what his investigations have uncovered. Strangely, he also urges the president to grant immunity to everyone concerned—he even offers to go with Attorney General Kleindienst to Congress to explain why presidential grants of immunity have been deemed necessary.

The reaction to Dean's suggestion was immediately and unanimously negative. Granting immunity to White House staff would send exactly the wrong signal; if no one in the White House had been involved, why should everyone in the White House be granted immunity? Because none of the other participants understand Dean's personal stake in gaining immunity, the notion seems to come from left field and isn't pursued. History might have been very different if they had just agreed to this odd and ostensibly unnecessary proposal.

Dean's report was now central to any further action, and the president suggests that the author retire to the calm and seclusion of Camp David as a way to hasten its completion.

The next day, Friday March 23, was sentencing day for the Watergate break-in defendants in Judge Sirica's courtroom. Only the judge knew about the bombshell he would drop by reading McCord's letter. Only the judge knew—but at least one other interested party had been given a heads-up.

A month before, when Sam Dash was named chief counsel of the Senate Watergate Committee, Judge Sirica had written his friend and Georgetown Law colleague a congratulatory note. Thus encouraged, Dash soon found time to call on the judge for what was somewhat more than a social visit. His pretext was to withdraw a request the Ervin Committee had previously submitted to inspect some of the Watergate grand jury's notes. As Dash later wrote, this could have been handled in a letter, but he saw an opportunity to talk privately with Sirica in his chambers.

Dash, well aware of the delicacy of the situation, emphasized that he wasn't recommending anything regarding the sentencing of the Watergate defendants. He then proceeded to plant what turned out to be a very fruitful seed, by referring the judge to the recent *Sweig* case.*

In *Sweig*, the Supreme Court declined to overturn a judge who had handed down harsh preliminary sentences while holding out the possibility of remission in exchange for cooperation with the authorities. Dash had been a counsel on the losing side (and thought the decision was very bad law), but he saw that *Sweig* could at least have a silver lining where Watergate was concerned. He was a man with a plan as he sat chatting in Maximum John's chambers.

Sirica noted that neither Dash nor the committee was making any requests of him, which was a good thing, because they had no right to do so. But he said he would study all the law and impose such sentences as he felt would serve the interests of justice.

Dash didn't have to wait long for results:

---

*One of the many coincidences (for those who believe in coincidences) with which Watergate abounds is that three of the principal attorneys we will soon discuss—Samuel Dash, Richard Ben-Veniste, and Charles Shaffer—had all worked on the *Sweig* case: Ben-Veniste as prosecutor, Dash and Shaffer representing defendants or potential defendants.

A few days later, on Wednesday, March 21st, my secretary buzzed
me and told me Judge Sirica was on the line. "Sam, you know I'm
sentencing the Watergate defendants this Friday, the twenty-third,"
Sirica's heavy deliberate voice announced as I picked up the phone. "I
think you should be present in the courtroom when I sentence them.
What I plan to do should be of special interest to you and the committee.
That's all I can say, you understand." I told Sirica I would be in his
courtroom early enough to get a seat on Friday morning.

After flamboyantly unsealing the official envelope into which he had
placed McCord's letter after reading it, Judge Sirica proceeded to read it
aloud. His dramatic flair was not without effect. There was pandemonium
in the courtroom as reporters ran to find the nearest phones.

With order restored, the judge announced that he would take Mc-
Cord's letter under advisement and postpone his sentencing for another
week. He then proceeded to throw the book at the other defendants: Everyone would serve the maximum prison time allowed by law. He sentenced Hunt to up to thirty-five years and Liddy to a term of six to twenty
years; the hapless Cubans received only somewhat lesser sentences.

Then, in what surely was an unprecedented example of judicial
activism—even for Maximum John Sirica—he specifically conditioned possible future reductions in these final sentences not only on cooperation with
federal prosecutors, but on cooperation with the Senate's Ervin Committee
and its chief counsel, Sam Dash. He spoke directly to the defendants.

I recommend your full cooperation with the grand jury and the
Senate Select Committee. You must understand that I hold out no
promises or hopes of any kind to you in this matter, but I do say that
should you decide to speak freely, I would have to weigh that factor in
appraising what sentences will be finally imposed in each case. Other
facts will, of course, be considered but I mention this because it is one
over which you have control.

This was *Sweig* with a vengeance. As Dash himself put it, Sirica "really turned the screw on the defendants." Those inclined may see irony in

the fact that a decision intended—unsuccessfully as things turned out—to expose Democratic political corruption ended up providing the first link in a chain of events that led to the resignation of a Republican president.

Now you may think that judges do this kind of thing all the time—impose maximum final sentences with the possibility of later reduction conditioned on favorable Senate testimony. In fact, it had never been done before, or since—and even the idea of such provisional sentencing would be disallowed under subsequent Supreme Court rulings.

Was it improper for Dash to call on Sirica for the express purpose of seeking this assistance? It was certainly unethical. That may be why there is no mention of the whole exchange in Judge Sirica's otherwise very detailed book published in 1979 *To Set the Record Straight: The Break-in, the Tapes, the Conspirators, the Pardon.* From Sirica's perspective, such a secret ex parte meeting in advance of sentencing would appear to be a clear violation of the canons of judicial ethics. Had it been disclosed—as it should have been—defense counsel could have insisted on his removal from the case for the sentencing phase as well as from any further involvement in Watergate, including the evidentiary hearing, and from presiding at the cover-up trial itself.

At least one of the defendants in Sirica's courtroom that Friday morning received the judge's message loud and clear. By the time Dash got back to his office there was already a note on his desk that James McCord had called. An hour later, they had their first face-to-face meeting.

In those days, before the twenty-four-hour news cycle, weekends were generally accepted as media downtime that should only be disturbed by acts of God or outbreaks of war. It's hard to guess which category Sam Dash felt McCord's revelations fit, but he called an unusual Saturday morning press conference to announce that McCord had provided proof of a Watergate cover-up. Apparently lost in the heat of the moment was any thought of including the minority staff in the McCord interview, or even of informing any of the committee Republicans about the pending press conference.

As Sirica had hoped it would, his disclosure of McCord's letter and Sam Dash's ensuing press conference publicly blew the lid off the Watergate cover-up, reinvigorated the investigation, and soon led to almost daily disclosures in the *Washington Post,* as potential targets started scrambling to make their own deals with the prosecutors and to spin the story to their benefit.

Yet, even after the release of the McCord letter, the White House still didn't know any specific details of the cover-up, or anything at all of Dean's own criminal involvement. They were still waiting for the report he had promised to write, which they expected to use as the basis for Nixon's own cleansing initiatives.

When the McCord letter suddenly burst on the public, those most intimately involved in illegal acts (especially Dean, Magruder, and Mitchell) realized their vulnerability to prosecution far sooner than those not nearly as familiar with what had really been going on (Nixon, Haldeman, and Ehrlichman).

Several overall observations are in order at this point:

First, there is nothing illegal per se about a policy of containment—limiting the political damage from an adverse event, as Haldeman described it—or of paying defense costs or family support for defendants in trials. The question, of course, is if and when such actions cross the line into criminal acts, and paying for support becomes paying for silence.

Second, there's no question that Nixon, Haldeman, and Ehrlichman—and everyone else on the White House staff, for that matter—did not want to know the details of what Dean was doing to contain the Watergate problem. They clearly knew that money for legal fees and family expenses was being given to the original Watergate defendants. But it is reasonable to assume that they thought that Dean—who was a lawyer and would be conscious of the kind of conduct expected from the White House counsel—wouldn't do anything that was actually illegal, or even publicly undefendable. Lawyers frequently cut corners; sometimes they look the other way; but they know when a cut corner or an overlooked action crosses the line from omission to commission. Every day, all across America, lawyers defend the guilty without themselves committing any crimes, and this is what I believe his White House colleagues would have expected Dean's role to be in sorting out the CRP's responsibility for Watergate.

Third, at the same time, it is quite possible that John Dean felt that he was doing precisely what his White House superiors wanted him to do—including the commission of illegal acts in furtherance of the goal of containing the Watergate problem. He certainly appears confident that he was doing the right thing to save John Mitchell, his mentor and father figure, and the others at the CRP with whom he shared the risk of prosecution for the original Liddy intelligence plan. It also seems reasonable to assume that he deliberately chose not to inform his White House superiors of any specifics so that they would not become tainted with guilty knowledge. This is precisely the approach he had articulated in Mitchell's office during Liddy's second plan presentation: This needs to be done, but without specific involvement of those higher up. It is likely that Dean orchestrated the cover-up under the same premise, and felt he knew what "they" wanted, and that he was carrying out "their" plan, without having ever discussed it with "them."

This lack of a meeting of the minds among the alleged coconspirators explains some subsequent reactions by all the parties. Haldeman, Ehrlichman, and Nixon, for example, were clearly appalled to learn of Dean's conflict of interest, and what Dean had been doing with his White House authority. And Dean was equally appalled—with a fury not unlike that of a jilted lover—to learn that they now claimed he had been doing everything of his own volition.

Perhaps worse from the White House perspective is that after Dean's departure in late April, no one remaining, or arriving later, had any idea of the full extent of the cover-up or the extent of Dean's participation in it. As selective as the information he gave them was, I believe it was, essentially, the only information they had gotten. It wasn't until some three months later, in late June, that the president and his new team of senior advisers (Al Haig, Fred Buzhardt, Mel Laird, Bryce Harlow, Dean Burch, etc.), along with the rest of the nation (but not the Kennedy clan, who were already very well informed), began to learn from the newspapers, the TV, and the Ervin hearings all the details of John Dean's handiwork.

John Dean took the president's suggestion and—accompanied by his wife, Maureen—went to Camp David over the weekend. Nixon's idea in offering the bucolic retreat was to get Dean's report as quickly as possible. That report, after all, was to be the action-forcing event that would provide the basis for presidential action.

But after a few days, when it was clear that no Dean report was going to be forthcoming, Haldeman called him back to Washington on Tuesday; on Thursday he was relieved of the responsibility of overseeing the White House response to the Watergate situation, and he was replaced by John Ehrlichman.

Now, after all the months of scrambling and dissembling—and just plain hoping that somehow things would work out—John Dean saw his cover-up crashing down around him. Nothing if not a survivor, his actions give every indication that he now fixed his eye firmly on one single overriding goal: to avoid prosecution for his criminal misdeeds by obtaining personal immunity.

As we have seen, he had already raised the possibility of immunity—for everyone—on March 22, before agreeing—or pretending to agree—to go to Camp David to write his long awaited, much promised report. Not realizing what Dean's reason had been for raising the notion of immunity, it was quickly passed over as irrelevant and inappropriate. Dean also raised it in several subsequent phone calls to Haldeman, who, still steeped in Dean's reassurances and apparently ignorant of the real situation, continued to be puzzled why the counsel wanted immunity. How different history might have unfolded had Dean only been more straightforward—or his superiors had only been more suspicious.

We don't know precisely when, or the process by which, Dean decided to switch sides. But his options were clearly narrowing. He realized that his own criminality would soon be discovered, and Magruder had told him that he had already decided to retain his own lawyer. On March 28, the day after he was recalled—reportless—from Camp David, John Dean formally retained Charles Shaffer as his criminal defense attorney.

John Dean wasn't particularly smart, but he was plenty bright. And whether or not he knew it (and after his too close for comfort brush with Teddy Kennedy, with the subcommittee subpoenas and the Gray hearings, it's hard to believe he didn't know it full well), in Charles Shaffer he had retained one of the Kennedy clan's most tried and trusted insiders. In a conversation with Nixon just before he retained Shaffer, Dean described Howard Hunt's lawyer as "an excellent criminal lawyer from the Democratic era of Bobby Kennedy." It would only make sense that he would look for just such qualities in his own.

A brilliant and feisty New Yorker, a graduate of Fordham University's law school, Charles Shaffer had been personally recruited for the Get Hoffa Squad by Robert Kennedy. In due course, working with fellow squad member James Neal, Shaffer had captured the Holy Grail that had evaded so many for so long when he obtained a conviction against Jimmy Hoffa in a Tennessee trial for jury tampering.

The degree of Robert Kennedy's trust in Shaffer was indicated by his subsequent choice of the young New Yorker for a truly unique and sensitive assignment. Almost from the minute he learned about his brother's assassination, Robert Kennedy was convinced that organized crime in general, and Jimmy Hoffa in particular, had played some part in it. This concern was not very far-fetched. The Kennedy Justice Department had been leaning hard on the mob; Jack Ruby, Oswald's assassin, had organized crime connections; there were phone calls to known Hoffa associates during the critical period before Oswald's assassination of JFK; and among the many wiretaps on Hoffa, there were at least two serious discussions of the methods and benefits of a mob hit on Bobby or Jack. The technique for the hit discussed for Bobby—a single assassin shooting into an open car proceeding along a known parade route—bore an eerie similarity to Oswald's actual MO.

For all its distinguished members and large staff, Robert Kennedy didn't trust the Warren Commission—the official investigative group appointed by President Johnson—to operate aggressively enough. He needed to know for himself whether there was any evidence, no matter how remote, connecting the Mafia or Hoffa to that moment in Dealey Plaza. Receiving such information secretly and from a trusted source was particularly important, because J. Edgar Hoover had specifically directed the FBI to cut off the attorney general from any reports it supplied to the Warren Commission.

So Bobby decided to have one of his most trusted people infiltrate the Warren Commission staff, with the specific assignment of ferreting out any mob or Hoffa connections. The man Robert Kennedy chose for this most delicate and vital mission was Charles Shaffer. Shaffer's loyalty was unquestioned, and his toughness on the Get Hoffa Squad demonstrated that he could be counted on to get the job done. The commission never learned that it had been infiltrated, but fifteen years later, when the House of Representatives reviewed the commission's findings, it considered the incident sufficiently important to be mentioned in its final report.

> The committee learned that Attorney General Kennedy and his aides arranged for the appointment of Charles Shaffer, a Justice Department attorney, to the Warren Commission staff in order that the possibility of Teamster involvement be watched. Shaffer confirmed to the committee that looking into Hoffa was one purpose of his appointment.

Here's how Richard Ben-Veniste, Neal's second in command of the Watergate Task Force, subsequently described the Shaffer-Dean relationship.

> For his attorney Dean chose a brilliant, aggressive criminal lawyer named Charles N. Shaffer. Shaffer was a liberal Democrat and former Kennedy Justice Department prosecutor who had previously worked with Jim Neal on a prosecution of James Hoffa. Ben-Veniste had also dealt with Shaffer in connection with Shaffer's representation of an important witness in the Volshen-Sweig case. When Shaffer debriefed Dean, he was stunned to learn the extent of the information Dean stood to provide the prosecutors.

A few pages later, Ben-Veniste describes Shaffer's influence on Dean's own testimony.

> Shaffer played a critical role in assisting Dean's preparation of a written opening statement for the Ervin Committee. Shaffer debriefed Dean, drove him, harangued him, subjected him to hours of mock cross-examination. . . . Shaffer reached in to the corners of Dean's recollection and pulled chunks out. . . . The result, a 245-page

*typewritten statement, was a testimonial to the touch of a fine crimi-
nal lawyer.*

There is no question that Charles Shaffer, the ultimate Kennedy insider, helped shape all of John Dean's recollections and testimony.

From the moment John Dean retained Shaffer, everything changed,
and the circumstances were ripe for hatching the Camelot Conspiracy. The
Kennedy Clan Democrats now had the president's own lawyer in their
thrall, very much panicked and willing to tell them what he knew in exchange for immunity. When immunity proved hard to obtain, it appears
that it didn't take them long to learn that he was willing to alter his recollections of events in ways that could help him get what he wanted.

A fter a brief initial period of lying low, Teddy Kennedy had slowly begun to reassert himself after Chappaquiddick—first, as a major player
on the national scene, and then as a potential presidential candidate for
1972 or 1976. By the beginning of 1970 he was leading the opposition to
President Nixon's first Supreme Court nominations.

Judge Clement Haynsworth, a South Carolinian, was nominated on
August 21, 1969; after he was defeated, Floridian judge G. Harrold Carswell was nominated on January 19, 1970.

In retrospect, the rejection of Haynsworth has been seen as a purely
politically motivated exercise—payback on the part of the Democratic-
controlled Senate for Nixon's success in implementing the so-called Southern strategy that had paved his way into the White House. Whether or not
that is true, Haynsworth's nomination was certainly subjected to a double
standard when contrasted with judges nominated under the earlier Kennedy and Johnson administrations.

Haynsworth had served for over a dozen years on the Fourth Circuit
Court of Appeals. He had a solid record of upheld decisions, and was considered to be a legal thinker and writer of some distinction—but his actual record became almost irrelevant. In practical political terms, he had committed
the unforgivable sin of JWS—Judging While Southern. The fact that he had
been nominated to fill the superliberal Abe Fortas's seat added an extra fillip
of sweet revenge to the opponents of Haynsworth's nomination.

Kennedy and Flug spearheaded a fierce campaign of opposition that resulted in Haynsworth's becoming the first Supreme Court nominee defeated by the Senate since 1930. The vote was 55 to 45. Nixon was bloodied but unbowed; more to the point, he was bloody-minded, and he pledged to keep nominating Southerners until the Senate forswore politics and recognized the right of an entire region to be represented on the High Court.

Unfortunately, his next nominee, Carswell, a federal district court judge, was not so wisely chosen—nor, apparently, very well vetted. His record was undistinguished, and his résumé turned out to present some problems. But even Justinian, if he had hailed from below the Mason-Dixon Line, would have fallen before the Kennedy-Flug onslaught. Carswell was defeated on April 8 by a vote of 51 to 45.

It was apparent that the Kennedy-led liberal Democrats had the influence and votes to continue defeating Southerners. Nixon, after making the reasons for his capitulation clear, and thus further cementing his relationship with the South, nominated a Minnesotan—Warren E. Burger—who was quickly confirmed.

Emboldened by his successes defeating the new administration's Supreme Court nominees, Kennedy began to feel more comfortable as the leading liberal challenger to the Nixon presidency. Each issue, each debate, each vote put Chappaquiddick a little bit more behind him. The Watergate break-in occurred one month short of Chappaquiddick's third anniversary, and Ted Kennedy was ready to reemerge with a vengeance—literally and figuratively. Recognizing the scent of political blood in the water, as we have seen, he used one of the Senate subcommittees he chaired to undertake his own investigation. No actual hearings were held, but the information he was able to gather turned out to be the starter dough for the Ervin Committee's national extravaganza.

On Teddy Kennedy's subcommittee, staffers Jim Flug, Carmine Bellino, and LaVern Duffy started delving into Donald Segretti's contacts with the White House. Segretti had been given a small budget to play political dirty tricks on Democratic presidential contenders. Only a few years out of the University of Southern California, his term for what he did was "ratfucking," and it ran the gamut from conventional political pranks to outright slander (forging a letter accusing a candidate of fathering an illegitimate child with a seventeen-year-old).

Any actual records of the Kennedy-Flug investigations other than a contemporary news account have, apparently, vanished. The only two tantalizing survivors are an exchange of letters from Watergate special prosecutor Leon Jaworski (the Houston attorney who succeeded Archibald Cox as special prosecutor on November 1, 1973) to Senator Kennedy, dated July 15, 1974, seeking records of any "verbatim or contemporaneous statement" in the subcommittee's files from a specified list of defendants and other key Watergate players. The senator's undated response (stamped as received on July 30) stated that "on no occasion did the Subcommittee formally meet to receive testimony, in open or executive session, from any of the identified persons, and on no occasion were stenographic or taped records made when Subcommittee staff did interview or talk with them." Since Donald Segretti and other early Watergate figures didn't appear on the list of identified persons, we can only wonder what might have been disclosed if the WSPF request had not been so carefully phrased.

If you Google James Flug you will learn very little except that in 2005, at the age of sixty-five, he rejoined Teddy Kennedy's Senate staff with the avowed purpose of repeating their earlier successes by defeating President George W. Bush's Supreme Court nominees. But Jim Flug was not just a two-trick pony. His skills extended far beyond sinking Supreme Court nominations.

Although he was one of the most influential and well-known men in Washington during the 1970s, Jim Flug left a very light footprint on the public record. Like the consummate staffer he was, he operated behind the scenes.

Sam Dash acknowledged that he got advice from Flug when he was deciding what approach the Ervin Committee would take to Watergate. Flug recommended that "our investigation and hearings should begin with Segretti and political dirty tricks, and urged me to have my staff meet with him for a background briefing before we conducted our own interrogation of Segretti." Dash observes:

> *This advice to start out with Segretti rather than the Watergate break-in surprised me. The major reason for the creation of the*

committee was the widespread belief that the Justice Department had done a poor job in the Watergate prosecution in not uncovering the real higher-ups behind the burglary. But Duffy and Flug had experience in Senate investigations and had been working with the material they had collected. I was starting from scratch. Until I knew more, I thought it would be wise for me to be guided by their judgment.

Carmine Bellino, as we have seen, had been a high-level Kennedy operative for decades. He had been J. Edgar Hoover's personal assistant in the decade prior to World War II, and then personal secretary to Joseph P. Kennedy and the Kennedy family's accountant. In the run-up to the 1960 presidential campaign, his services to the Kennedys were alleged to have included wiretapping an official of Engelhard Industries to learn whether the company's chairman was planning to disclose a liaison JFK had with a nineteen-year-old college student.

During JFK's administration, Bellino had maintained offices both in the White House and in Bobby Kennedy's Department of Justice. An accountant by training, the partisan application of forensic accounting was a particular Bellino forte. For the Watergate investigations and hearings, Carmine Bellino moved from Kennedy's Subcommittee on Administrative Practices to the Ervin Watergate Committee as its chief investigator.

6

The Camelot Conspiracy Commences

The seeds of the Camelot Conspiracy appear to have taken root when several of Nixon's opponents realized that John W. Dean III was willing—indeed, was eager—to change his story if it would save his own skin. Because Dean could supply a direct link between Watergate and the president, the possibilities were as intriguing as they were endless.

There was, however, a major problem: Dean himself was the guilty man at the very center of the planning that had led to the Watergate break-in, and of the subsequent attempts to cover up the involvement of himself and others. Many would consider him a despicable, weaselley figure, who had misled and entrapped the president and his White House colleagues. Anything he was now willing to say could inevitably be compromised by these inescapable facts.

But . . . maybe the facts weren't all that inescapable. If Dean's role could be downplayed, if details of his own actions could be withheld, and if any prosecution could be delayed at least until after he had testified before the various congressional committees that were investigating Watergate, then changes from the initial account he gave the career prosecutors wouldn't be as easily undermined by the inconvenient truth of his own actions and self-interest.

The critical months of April and May 1973 were ground zero for hatching the conspiracy. To carry it off required intense concentration and careful coordination by Kennedy Clan Democrats.

Throughout the month of April, Dean was cast into the role of double agent. Officially he was still working on the White House staff as the president's lawyer. But at the same time, below the radar and behind the scenes, Dean's actions suggest he had sold the president out and was actively working on behalf of the Kennedys.

One of the most remarkable aspects of the whole Watergate story is how the Dean-Shaffer-Kennedy connection went essentially unnoticed—or, at least, unreported and unexplored. It isn't even mentioned in any of the literature (including the few "pro-Nixon" books where, had it been known, it would have been given great prominence). Although research was more onerous in those pre-Google days, there were scores and more people who knew about Shaffer's background. Yet the fact that John Dean—the soon-to-be darling of the Nixon haters—had retained an ultimate Kennedy insider as his counsel remained hidden in plain sight.

The federal prosecutors—Earl Silbert, Seymour Glanzer, and Donald Campbell—had been working full time on the Watergate case ever since the day after the break-in on June 17, 1972, and so had their grand jury. A new grand jury had been impaneled two weeks before the break-in, so it was already sitting when the burglars were arrested and arraigned. Before long, Watergate would become its sole focus, even leading to legislation extending its term well beyond the original eighteen months.

Frustrated by what seemed an orchestrated cover-up, the prosecutors were counting on stiff prison sentences to loosen at least some of the burglars' tongues. Following their convictions, they had moved quickly to immunize the defendants from further prosecution and to bring them back before the grand jury. They got a real boost after Sirica's sentencing when other potential defendants also started to come forward. There were dozens of grand jury appearances during this critical time—involving at least thirty individuals—but we can only confirm the names of those that were disclosed in one of the trials or during the impeachment hearings—a list of which can be seen from a memo to Cox dated June 4, 1973 and entitled "Post Watergate" Grand Jury Testimony Trial (Reproduced in Appendix C.)

Charles Shaffer, representing Dean, and James Bierbower, representing Magruder, both approached the U.S. attorney's office in an attempt to negotiate pleas on their clients' behalf. Dean "won" the race by getting there first. Typically, he did so because of insider knowledge; Magruder had made the mistake of telling Dean not only the name of his expected lawyer but that he was currently unreachable at a legal conference in Bermuda.

Shaffer debriefed Dean for six days—from the time Dean retained him on March 28 until Shaffer first approached prosecutor Seymour Glanzer on April 2. Given what others have said about Shaffer's forte of defending white collar criminals, there is no doubt that Dean's story was already well hammered out even before the meetings began with the prosecutors to see what kind of deal they would be willing to cut. As other facts emerged, his story continued to evolve to accommodate them. The hapless Magruder, typically late to the party, didn't begin his negotiations with the prosecutors for another two weeks.

In these negotiations Dean and Magruder took characteristically different approaches. Magruder confessed everything he knew up front and reached an immediate agreement to plead to a single conspiracy count. But Dean wanted immunity from prosecution, which the prosecutors were reluctant to give, so his path took many twists and turns.

While still the president's lawyer by day, John Dean not only began to confide the circumstances of his own wrongdoing to Shaffer, he also threw in non-Watergate-related damaging information that he had learned in his official capacity as counsel to the president. His disloyalties, his breaches of the lawyer-client relationship, and his revelations of government secrets increased exponentially during that month.

When Dean decided to jump ship in late April, he arranged for a van to take boxes of confidential files from his office.

He and Shaffer selectively began to share these with the U.S. attorney's office as bargaining chips for personal immunity. Some of these files involved matters that later came to be known as the "White House horrors." These included the break-in of Daniel Ellsberg's psychiatrist's office; White

House involvement in the ITT antitrust scandal; and materials relating to several other sensitive situations (including the Robert Vesco embezzlement case, the milk producers case, and the Townhouse Project—all discussed in Chapter 19).

Dean also later traded on information about President Nixon's personal tax returns—information that only came into his possession in the course of his legal work as counsel. Senator Lowell Weicker recounts in his 1995 book (*Maverick: A Life in Politics*) about how he learned of confidential tax information directly from Dean, and prides himself on using it to great effect to further ruin the president.

Information being gathered by the U.S. attorney's office, including summary reports from dozens of daily FBI interviews and secret grand jury testimony, was shared on a daily basis in only two directions—upward with Henry Petersen, the head of the Criminal Division at the Justice Department, and laterally with Mark Felt, the acting director of the FBI. We now know that Felt—recently the self-proclaimed Deep Throat—was leaking information from this fast-breaking investigation to Bob Woodward of the *Washington Post*.

The resulting articles fanned the flames of public discontent. The information in these leaks was not attributed to government investigators, but—by implication—to someone inside the administration who was frustrated by the wrongdoing that was being successfully covered up. Indeed, the name "Deep Throat" appears to have been invented only in response to an observation made during the editing process that early drafts of Woodward's book, *All the President's Men* (coauthored with Carl Bernstein), lacked an organizing principle. Because Felt's position was deliberately kept secret, the public was given the false impression that the government itself was not moving quickly and professionally to resolve the case. In fact, exactly the opposite was true. Deep Throat wasn't leaking hints or clues that needed to be followed in order to uncover the story. He was leaking what the prosecutors had already uncovered and were about to use for their indictments.

One might even suspect that Woodward's articles—indeed, the entire coverage by the *Washington Post*—were purposely designed to fool the public—but that is a topic to be explored in a future chapter.

Under circumstances such as these, where leaks were occurring daily and the press was in hot pursuit, the government is placed in a difficult position, because federal prosecutorial guidelines clearly forbid making any public comment regarding ongoing investigations. The awkwardness of the situation is usually only temporary, because it is resolved as soon as indictments are announced. As we shall see, however, it was the purposeful intent of the Kennedy conspirators to postpone any actual indictments. And thus no indictments—even of those defendants who had already agreed to plead guilty—were handed down for many months following the March release of the McCord letter: Magruder's on August 16, Dean's on October 19, and the comprehensive Watergate cover-up indictment wasn't handed down until March 1, 1974. Let us be clear about this: It is my belief that deliberately delaying indictments, especially for purely partisan political purposes, can be construed to be an obstruction of justice—and those involved in such activities as criminal conspirators.

John Dean's story changed dramatically—and "dramatically" is a very good word for how it changed—between March 28, 1973, when he first retained Charles Shaffer, and April 2, 1973 (when his lawyer first met with the federal prosecutors), and May 4 (when he reneged on his grand jury appearance, scheduled for the next day, and cast his lot with the Ervin Committee) and June 25, when he began his public testimony. In fact, his story continued to change right up to and including his testimony at the cover-up trial in the late fall of 1974. We can now follow a lot of this process thanks to several sources, including some I was able to uncover while researching for this book: the handwritten notes from the meetings Shaffer and Dean held with prosecutors Silbert, Glanzer, and Campbell in April 1973; a memo that Silbert prepared for Archibald Cox in early June; Dean's Ervin Committee testimony; and a memorandum of conversations with WSPF prosecutors later that November.

When Dean and Shaffer first began discussions with the prosecutors in the first week of April, they claimed that if Dean were granted immunity, he could "deliver" both John Mitchell and Jeb Magruder as having been at the heart of the Watergate break-in and nothing more.

When the U.S. attorney—who was the prosecutors' boss and called the shots—declined to grant such immunity, Dean offered to approach Attorney

General Kleindienst personally in order to get around any authority problem with regard to his own immunity. The prosecutors also rejected this idea.

Sometime around April 15, realizing that he wasn't getting any closer to immunity, Dean started to volunteer information on matters unconnected with Watergate that he knew only as a result of his position as counsel to the president.

On April 17, the president announced that there would be no immunity for anyone in his administration involved in the cover-up. Dean's accusations then suddenly shifted from the CRP to the White House itself. He began suggesting—for the first time—that Haldeman and Ehrlichman might have been involved, and might have been keeping things from the president. This allegation was undoubtedly intriguing, but as the prosecutors pointed out, Dean was short on any corroborating evidence. Yet even at this stage of his shifting story in search of immunity, his revelations were confined to Haldeman and Ehrlichman. Dean never mentioned a cover-up or conspiracy—or any Nixon involvement—until after he was fired on April 30.

With immunity negotiations with the federal prosecutors stalled, Dean began talking with the Ervin Committee. There is more than one way to skin a cat, and his strategy was clear: play one branch of the government off against the other to see which would reward him with the most immunity.

Silbert names April 20 as the date on which the competition between the prosecutors and the Senate committee became apparent. Dash's version is a little different, but he does confirm that he was competing with the prosecutors, and suggests that Dean had a rose-colored view of himself and his role in the cover-up (with which Dash disagreed—at least at first).

> At the time of our meeting, he saw himself as a young lawyer who had pulled himself out of a powerful conspiracy and was expiating the wrongs he had committed by his willingness to expose them to the public and to testify to facts that only he was able and willing to reveal. He thought his informer role displayed courage, which merited the friendship and good will of those who were investigating the conduct in which he was so enmeshed. Indeed, as he talked to me that evening, he

spoke in a cold, matter-of-fact way, as though he was describing some-one else's conduct, and not his own.

I viewed Dean differently. He was much the same as his colleagues in the Watergate conspiracy—Magruder, Mitchell, Haldeman, and Ehrlichman. Although Dean had turned informer, I thought he had done so in an effort to save his own skin. By now he knew he was cornered.

Dash says he was willing to grant Dean immunity at this very first meeting, which he places on May 9. That date appears highly suspect as the commencement of their communications, coming as it does almost three weeks after the time frame consistently identified by federal prosecutors as the beginning of their competition with the Ervin Committee.

Finally, it is important to note that according to the prosecutors' own notes, Dean did not begin even to accuse the president of any complicity in the cover-up until May 3, several days after his forced termination as President Nixon's lawyer.

Dean had agreed with the prosecutors to testify—without any promise of immunity, but with the expectation that his cooperation would be taken into account in determining his punishment—before the grand jury on May 5. His indictment would surely have followed almost immediately.

At the eleventh hour, however, he had a change of heart. Now confident that he had a deal with the Ervin Committee for at least limited immunity in exchange for his testimony at their hearings, scheduled to begin on May 17, Shaffer telephoned the prosecutors late in the evening of May 4 to say that his client wouldn't be keeping his date with the grand jury the next morning.

It is no wonder that Silbert noted, in his May 31, 1974, memo to Cox:

> *At the outset of Dean's relationship with the prosecutors his disclosures were focused on John Mitchell and Jeb Magruder. He discussed the pre–June 17 meeting at the Department of Justice for example. Then he shifted to the post–June 17 obstruction, but the participants were limited to the re-election Committee. Subsequently, he escalated his revelations to implicate Ehrlichman and Haldeman. When Dean*

began to get pressure from the President and was ultimately eased out
he began focusing on the President as being culpable. In other words,
there has been a gradual escalation by Dean as to who is culpable.

In Silbert's own words, "there has been a gradual escalation by Dean
as to who is culpable." The WSPF couldn't ignore this uncomfortable
fact—but they could downplay it, shifting blame to a lack of thorough interrogation by the career prosecutors. Richard Ben-Veniste acknowledged
simply that "Dean's testimony before the Ervin Committee that electrified
the country went far beyond what Dean had told the Silbert team in his
meetings with them, in both scope and detail."

It is reasonable to assume that Shaffer, as part of his zealous representa-
tion of his client, was also reaching out to his Kennedy clan connections
and relaying all of Dean's escalating accusations to Ted Kennedy and his
veteran staffer Jim Flug. The essential equation was crystal clear: Dean
could sink Nixon, but his credibility would depend on his not being indicted for his own crimes. And immediate action was required, because the
federal prosecutors were well along toward completing their case.

On April 30, 1973, the president spoke to the American people for the
first time about Watergate. He announced that he had asked for Haldeman's and Ehrlichman's resignations, and that he had fired John Dean. He
also announced that Attorney General Kleindienst had resigned, and that
he would nominate Elliot Richardson to replace him.

In words that seemed of small significance in terms of the overall content of the speech, the president essentially sealed his own doom by saying
that the new AG would have the discretion to name a special supervising
prosecutor for Watergate.

> *As the new Attorney General, I have today named Elliot Richard-*
> *son, a man of unimpeachable integrity and rigorously high principle. I*
> *have directed him to do everything necessary to ensure that the De-*
> *partment of Justice has the confidence and the trust of every law-abiding*
> *person in this country.*
> *I have given him absolute authority to make all decisions bearing*
> *upon the prosecution of the Watergate case and related matters. I have*

instructed him that if he should consider it appropriate, he has the authority to name a special supervising prosecutor for matters arising out of the case.

As it developed, Nixon soon discovered that he had been persuaded to strip himself of his closest and most loyal aides just as the Kennedy clan began to mount their all-out assault.

7

Obstructing Justice:
Postponing Dean's Indictment

It seems clear that without Cox's intervention, the federal prosecutors would have issued indictments at least by August 1973, and the public's desire to know that the government was seriously pursuing the Watergate case would have been fully satisfied. Indeed, on May 24, 1973, the U.S. attorney publicly stated that comprehensive indictments were imminent; and the prosecutorial memo submitted to Cox on his arrival stated that the case was all but closed.

Sam Dash's book seems to confirm this speculation: In spite of many meetings and requests seeking assurances from the Silbert team and Henry Petersen, Dash admits that he couldn't get these career prosecutors to guarantee indictments were not forthcoming.

Yet Magruder's plea agreement, made in early April, was not formalized in a court appearance until August—five months later. Dean's agreement wasn't formalized for almost half a year. And the comprehensive cover-up indictments of Ehrlichman, Haldeman, and Mitchell were not brought until March 1974. This inordinate and highly unusual delay, which cries out for scrutiny, is a topic no one has seen fit to explore until now.

James Neal arrived from Nashville on May 29, the first day the WSPF opened its doors for business. Knowingly or not, the headline writer at *The New York Times* perfectly captured the portent of Neal's arrival in Washington. The front page story was headed: "Hoffa Prosecutor Named to Aid Cox on Watergate."

Neal was the assigned Kennedy point man for co-opting federal prosecutors Silbert, Glanzer, and Campbell. The concern was that Silbert and his team—and the grand jury with which they had been working for the twelve months since the break-in arrests—might actually take the next step in the process and hand down indictments. Jeb Magruder and Fred LaRue had already worked out pleas, and could be indicted at any time (they may, in fact, already have been under sealed indictments). Because everyone pleading so far had implicated John Mitchell, the former AG was an indicted man walking. And because John Dean double-crossed the prosecutors by failing to testify at the grand jury on May 5, he too was a prime candidate for indictment. Indictments of Haldeman and Ehrlichman also seemed imminent; indeed, Henry Petersen had demanded Nixon remove them precisely because they might well be indicted.

That's what was already in the works. Timely indictments would have been handed down—if the Kennedy conspirators hadn't intervened in the course of Richardson's confirmation hearings to demand a special prosecutor, one who could be depended on to derail the investigation, and then redirect it away from Watergate itself and toward Nixon and the Republican Party. Such an orderly unfolding of the judicial process would prevent any possibility of prolonging the investigations in order to assist a Kennedy candidacy. Immediate action was clearly called for.

WSPF press secretary Jim Doyle confirms this interpretation with his description of that Tuesday, May 29, in the special prosecutor's office.

> *Neal arrived at Room 1111 the first day and received simple instructions: Inform yourself completely about the Watergate case; ride herd on Silbert's team; make sure they don't do anything without the special prosecutor's knowledge.*

The focus of their discussions must have been almost exclusively on Dean, because on May 31, only two days later, Silbert and Glanzer submitted a thirteen-page memo that clearly had been produced in great haste, and under such stress that it contains a number of handwritten additions and interpolations, and is carelessly entitled "Contacts Between Prosecution of John W. Dean III From April 1, Up to Date."

Neal's purpose in demanding this memo was to find out, and fast, just how much Silbert, Glanzer, and Campbell already knew about how much Dean's story had changed in order to get what he wanted. When the memo indicated that they knew a great deal, Neal realized that he had to take immediate and forceful action. So, on June 1, the day after receiving Silbert's status memo on Dean, Neal wrote a memo to Silbert instructing him not to make any more judgments regarding potential defendants without having received clearance in advance from Cox.

On June 14, Cox himself went so far as to formalize these instructions to Neal in a memo requesting a daily briefing from him on any planned actions on the Watergate cover-up case. The next day Cox wrote a memo informing Silbert that he had instructed Neal to sit in on all important interviews. (Reproduced, respectively, in Appendices D and E.)

What had happened to prompt such a vigorous statement of interest on Cox's part? Could it have been because on June 11 John Dean had been formally subpoenaed by career prosecutors to appear before the grand jury? Shaffer first filed a motion to quash the subpoena. Failing that he instructed him to take the Fifth Amendment. It is hard to believe that this instruction to take the Fifth before the grand jury hadn't been cleared with Neal in advance.

A rather candid recap of these events is found in an internal memo recounting Shaffer's efforts to put off Dean's scheduled appearance, reproduced in Appendix F. Note the memo also indicates the less than high regard the career prosecutors had come to hold Dean's public claim of just wanting to tell the full truth about his past actions.

By the next day, June 15, the WSPF takeover of the federal prosecutors was virtually complete. Possession truly was nine points of the law, and Silbert, Glanzer, and Campbell, along with all of their investigatory files, were forcefully relocated from the U.S. attorney's offices to the WSPF's new offices at 1425 K Street. Although they had hoped and expected to be invited to stay on to complete the case they had brought so far, by the end of the month their formal letters of resignation were announced as having been submitted and accepted.

Having been forced out, the Silbert team was deluged with requests for interviews. They accepted an invitation to appear on CBS's Sunday morning talk show *Face the Nation*. The possibility that Silbert and his colleagues might go public and accurately indicate that the case was, for all intents and purposes, already solved was too great a risk for Cox's army to take. One of the very few memos actually written by Cox himself summarizes a conversation he had on July 2 with Attorney General Richardson. It notes that Richardson had agreed with him that it would be inappropriate for Silbert, Glanzer, or Campbell to have any contact whatsoever with the media.

On July 4, CBS news reported that Richardson had ordered the federal prosecutors not appear on *Face the Nation*. It also revealed several of the details from Silbert's eighty-seven-page transition memo, and claimed that the grand jury's investigation was 85 percent complete. This was exactly what the Kennedy conspirators had feared.

The public controversy couldn't be ignored, and a WSPF press release was issued dismissing the CBS story, saying that it was grossly premature to be thinking in terms of indictments. Of course, CBS had gotten the story exactly right, and the press release was at the same time inaccurate and misleading, and purposely intended to throw the media off the scent. Silbert's exhaustive transition memo set out the all but completed Watergate case in great and precise detail. But it would not, however, become available for public scrutiny until my research uncovered it several decades later.

Leaking wasn't much fun when it was aimed in your own direction, and Cox publicly condemned the "gross breach of professional ethics" on the part of the CBS leaker. Internally, his reaction was decisive—and, in view of the amount of leaking he and his office practiced and countenanced, ironic. He demanded sworn depositions from everyone who had access to the Silbert memorandum—including Silbert himself, his boss, U.S. Attorney Harold Titus, and his colleagues Glanzer and Campbell—stating that they had not been the source of the leak to CBS.

Given the unlimited power vested in the special prosecutor as a result of the Kennedy-inspired Guidelines (detailed in Chapter 11), removing and silencing Silbert and his team wasn't much of a challenge. These men were, after all, only career federal prosecutors and assistant U.S. attorneys.

But this was only the beginning. What the Kennedy clan needed in order to have full and free rein for the Get Nixon Squad was the neutralization of the entire Department of Justice and, principally, the two men in it who had both the professional reputations and access to public attention that could put a serious crimp in the Kennedy agenda: Henry Petersen, the highly respected career head of the Criminal Division, and the new attorney general himself, Elliot Richardson.

Richardson, despite his excellent reputation and spectacular résumé, was not, fundamentally, a strong man. He was a politician who knew how to calculate the odds and advantages of taking stands on any given issue, and who understood the advantages of living to fight another day. Besides, by actually defending President Nixon he would risk losing the positive and flattering media coverage he was receiving by allowing Cox a free rein.

Unaware of the Kennedy plans for John Dean when he had agreed to be bound by the Guidelines, Richardson had been, for all intents and purposes, effectively sidelined from the outset. He was apparently slightly disturbed when he realized what was actually happening, because he did make one attempt, albeit a feeble one, to stem the tide of direct referrals to Cox. At a meeting he called on July 12, he presented a proposal for a prescreening of referrals to Cox. When Cox and his principal assistants, James Vorenberg and Henry Ruth, raised objections, however, he quickly withdrew it. This skirmish then led to a minor dustup when he met with Cox on the twenty-third. On the agenda was the question of who would be assigned the responsibility of investigating the allegations that members of Nixon's National Security Council staff had been wiretapped. You can feel the hauteur of Cox's rebuke in the memo he wrote about the meeting.

The Attorney General went on to say—there is no potential criminal liability in such cases, and he would be disposed to determine that they were outside my jurisdiction and instruct me not to deal with them. . . . I expressed the view that he was personally heading for trouble and should very carefully review his testimony before the Judiciary Committee when he was appointed before he attempted to give me instruction based upon his views concerning the scope of my jurisdiction.

The chilling effect of these icy words was immediately felt, and there is no further record of any Richardson involvement in WSPF jurisdictional issues—criminal, noncriminal, investigatory, or otherwise.

Henry Petersen would prove to be a tougher challenge. He was not only head of the Criminal Division but had been at the Justice Department for his entire career, serving under twelve attorneys general. He was respected—even revered—by the hundreds of other attorneys who had worked alongside him. But he had spoken to Nixon about Watergate—had even met with him—and he was therefore suspect. It didn't matter that all of Petersen's conversations with Nixon had taken place the month before Dean even began to hint at his belief that the president was personally involved in the cover-up. Nor did it matter that the purpose of Petersen's meetings had been to demand the resignations of Haldeman and Ehrlichman. In light of the special prosecutor's new goal, these facts became trivialities. If the game plan was to get Nixon, a career prosecutor of Petersen's integrity and reputation could actually be an obstacle.

The first step in removing Henry Petersen was a confrontational interrogation on the evening of May 29, the same Tuesday that James Neal arrived. Cox and Vorenberg met with Petersen for two hours. They took the extraordinary—and extraordinarily offensive—step of having the session transcribed by a court stenographer.

They also were troubled because Petersen, concerned with issues of lawyer-client privilege, did not feel free to disclose his conversations with the president without the president's approval. This was clearly not a man who would sign on to the Kennedy game plan and cut the necessary corners in order to achieve the greater good of a Camelot restoration; this was obviously a man whose independence could spell trouble.

There were three almost immediate results of this confrontation with Henry Petersen.

First, a memo was issued by Attorney General Richardson himself—at Cox's "request"—instructing that all pending investigations of the Nixon administration within the Justice Department—no matter how remote from Watergate—be immediately turned over to the office of the special prosecutor.

Second, an article appeared in *The New York Times* saying that Petersen himself was under investigation. Silbert immediately sent Cox a memo complaining about the article and urging a public statement to clear Petersen's name. Of course, no such statement was forthcoming. Instead, Cox sent Petersen a brief handwritten note with the bleak reassurance that "we did not leak this." Not surprisingly, there is no record of any effort to discover the leaker. This exchange, including Cox's handwritten response, is reproduced in Appendix G.

Third, Cox sent a memo to the Criminal Division assuming direction and control of all Election Unit investigations, as well as directing the FBI and the GAO (what was then called the General Accounting Office, now the Government Accountability Office, which was responsible for enforcing the 1972 campaign finance law) to report all allegations concerning the CRP's finance committee to his office.

Later, there is a "memo to file" from Neal detailing the information that Petersen had given to and received from John Dean over the preceding year, and concluding that it wouldn't be necessary to bring Petersen before the grand jury to testify prior to Dean's scheduled Ervin Committee appearance. This conclusion was irrelevant; the memo's sting wasn't in its tail. The sting was in the notion that the special prosecutor had felt it necessary to even explore the notion of putting the assistant attorney general of the United States in charge of the Criminal Division under oath before the grand jury.

Cox soon took care of Petersen's concerns about lawyer-client privilege. On June 11, he wrote to Fred Buzhardt, the president's new counsel, asking for the waiver of any such privilege (while being careful to deny that it actually existed). When Buzhardt confirmed, on June 16, Nixon's agreement to waive any privilege as to his April conversations with Petersen, Vorenberg and Neal immediately summoned Petersen and interviewed him again about those meetings and conversations.

The result of these maneuverings by Cox and his Kennedy cohorts to position themselves above the law and apart from any review within the executive branch was that Earl Silbert and Henry Petersen, two of the finest career prosecutors in the long and distinguished annals of the Department of Justice, and the men really responsible for uncovering the Watergate cover-up and demanding that cleansing actions be taken by the Nixon White House, were removed entirely from the Watergate case; their reputations trashed; and any concerns or reservations about WSPF's use of overly aggressive tactics in the future effectively precluded.

The Kennedy Clan Democrats had achieved a one-two punch with the arrival of Special Prosecutor Cox. Silbert and Petersen had been corralled long enough for Dean to appear before the Ervin Committee "unencumbered" by any government response to his criminal acts. Any oversight by the Department of Justice had been effectively neutralized. Now the real goal of the conspiracy could be achieved: the refocus of their unrestrained investigatory powers away from the Watergate cover-up and toward a full-scale inquiry into every aspect of the Nixon presidency.

One critical ingredient was James Vorenberg's aggressive staffing initiative that enabled the fledgling operation virtually to hire at will. Press secretary James Doyle describes Vorenberg's interview technique. He would ask prospective hires which task force they were interested in joining. The normal hesitation in answering led him to suggest a temporary assignment to the "boiler room"—which Doyle described as "a converted conference room at the far reaches of the offices . . . jammed with young lawyers who had been handed transcripts of Senate Watergate Committee or Grand Jury hearings and told to summarize the testimony on index cards so it could be cross-referenced." This was in line with Neal's belief that the first order of business was to master all the facts. This operation would later be computerized, but for the first two months, as Doyle notes, "the work was a strictly manual operation that made necks sore and minds numb."

Two observations seem in order: first, the recruitment of young lawyers followed the same course as dissembling with the public. The WSPF used the legitimate outrage over Watergate as a cover to pursue its own purposes by recruiting the number of lawyers necessary not to work on Watergate but to launch full-scale investigations into every aspect of the Nixon presidency.

Second, while Doyle naively appears not to have grasped the concept, the fastest way for these eager young lawyers to escape the boiler room would be to find new theories of prosecution amid all those file cards. The more determination—and creativity—you showed, the faster you could get out of that windowless room and onto a Get Nixon Squad. The boiler room represented a casebook example of Supreme Court Justice Robert Jackson's nightmare, in which a young prosecutor was tempted to "pick people he thinks he should get rather than pick cases that need to be prosecuted."

This Kennedy cohorts' operation refocus also required gently disabusing the media and the public of the idea that Watergate indictments could be expected any time soon. This would require some fancy footwork because, as we have seen, the U.S. attorney's office had only recently promised them, and they had been the topic of some interest at the WSPF's first press conferences.

Vorenberg was asked about it on June 15.

Question: *Mr. Titus [the U.S. attorney for the District of Columbia] said a few weeks ago in a statement that the grand jury was maybe two months away from returning indictments, if I recall correctly. Where do you stand right now on your first indictment?*
Mr. Vorenberg: *I don't want to talk about the timing of indictments. I can't talk about them.*
Question: *Is it beyond two months?*
Mr. Vorenberg: *I am not going to discuss the timing of indictments.*
Question: *Would Mr. Titus's public statement still stand, in your opinion?*
Mr. Vorenberg: *I am not going to discuss that. It is still there.*

So much for a gentle backing away. The same topic was raised again at a press conference three days later, this time with Special Prosecutor Cox himself.

Question: *Mr. Cox, Mr. Titus said sixty and ninety days was the period he expected before indictment. Do you still expect that period?*

Mr. Cox: *I really can't speculate when indictments, if any, would be returned. I think that really would be improper.*

Both Vorenberg and Cox leave the clear—and entirely erroneous—impression that the question of indictments is too sensitive to discuss, perhaps because they are actively in process.

Of course, it would have been impossible to tell the truth. Imagine the reaction if either had said, "We've decided it is in Senator Kennedy's political interest to string this out as long as humanly possible. So, far from being imminent, the central indictment in this case won't be handed down for another eight months—well after our colleagues on the Ervin Committee finish their ostensible inquiry into what the career prosecutors and the FBI already know occurred and are already prepared to prosecute."

The third and final aspect of their refocus was to divert the public's outrage over the existence of a Watergate cover-up into the other areas of their expanded scope of inquiry. Vorenberg first articulated this kind of fishing expedition free-for-all at his June 15 press conference. After mentioning the Watergate, Segretti, ITT, and campaign finance cases, he added:

> We have initiated several lines of investigations on our own in addition to those that were under way. We have a number of requests outstanding to the FBI for information and new lines of inquiry. We have begun what is in some ways the most important job we have of building up a central information system that will try to pull together and let us analyze all data relating to this case, cross-indexed by people and by incidents, events, chronology, so that we can begin to see this whole situation as a whole and be able to follow down each piece of it separately.
>
> Many leads and suggestions have come to us from outside of our offices, some from governmental agencies, some from people around the country. We have begun to investigate some of these. As our staff builds up, we will pursue them all. We are, at the outset, taking a broad view of the Special Prosecutor's jurisdiction. Undoubtedly, some of the

suggestions or leads will turn out to be unrelated to the area that we are supposed to be converging, but we are going to start with the assumption that we will at least look into everything. We are not going to assume that some piece that at the outset seems not to be directly related is not worthy of investigation.

We strongly urge people in this country with information that they think may bear on the Watergate case, campaign contributions, or any other aspect of the Special Prosecutor's jurisdiction to come forward and provide Mr. Cox and his staff with information. We will continue, as we have in the last several days, to run down those leads as fast as our staff needs and staff resources make that possible.

This statement gives the real feel of what the Kennedy Clan Democrats had in mind. They had achieved the almost unimaginable position of being able to couple their intense partisanship with the awesome and unsupervised investigatory power of a special prosecutor—assured that much of what they did would forever remain hidden behind the secrecy of grand jury proceedings.

The real key to appreciating the Kennedy conspiracy lies not in trying to figure out why the indictments were so long in coming. The reasoning for that seems obvious: to let the Ervin Committee take the lead with its public hearings in order to fan the flames of public discontent with the Nixon administration. Because the cover-up case was already broken, and there was no danger that the guilty would escape, many benefits would flow to a Kennedy candidacy from delivering a one-two punch: the Senate hearings followed by the WSPF indictments.

From a political perspective it was clearly better for Ervin's committee to go first, because there would be no rules of evidence or rudiments of due process required for Senate hearings. The senators, not known for being reluctant to grandstand, could set their own agendas and ask any questions they wanted. There would be no right of cross-examination or opportunity to put on rebuttal witnesses. Equally advantageous, selective leaks to a predictably voracious media would further whet the appetite for the testimony itself. The media-savvy Kennedy Clan Democrats saw the way to get double and triple shots at coverage out of individual areas of interest.

From an investigatory perspective, there was almost unlimited potential for symbiosis. The Ervin Committee staff could interview prospective witnesses with the benefit of having already reviewed grand jury testimony summaries and FBI interviews; they could confer with WSPF staff, and perhaps get suggestions for questions that would close any gaps in prior testimony or provide occasion for misstatements that could be turned into perjury traps—since WSPF lawyers could then pore over transcripts of committee testimony for discrepancies and possible perjury charges.

Put another way, the question isn't *why* the special prosecutor decided to let the Senate proceed. The benefits of that to the Kennedy cause were obvious. The question is *how,* under any concept of due process, an office within the executive branch (and therefore subject to the constitutional requirement that the president "take care that the laws be faithfully executed") could allow known crimes to remain unprosecuted for so long.

One looks in vain both in the public record and within WSPF files for any record of discussion or consideration of how this situation was allowed to persist. There is no memo in the WSPF files that says, for example, "There are fantastic benefits that will accrue if we just sit on our hands for several months—but there are serious legal concerns involved in such a course of action, because our system of justice normally requires that criminal cases be pursued with great vigor." There is no decision by Judge Sirica, for example, stating, "I think it would be best if you allowed the Senate to go first."

While we can detect a vast and coordinated effort to prevent Dean's indictment, the idea of taking a backseat to the Ervin Committee hearings seems to occur without any record of its ever having been discussed or debated. The real issue—the lack of legal justification for deliberately holding back any indictments while the Ervin hearings were under way—is nowhere addressed in any WSPF memos; at least, not in any that survive.

The whole rationale for giving Congress investigatory and oversight authority is to allow it to examine issues or situations that it doesn't think the executive branch is taking seriously enough, or with which it doesn't agree. It was, for example, the executive branch's failure to react to the corruption in organized labor that was the genesis of the McClellan Rackets Committee on which Robert Kennedy cut his investigative teeth.

But that was hardly the case with the Ervin Committee. The executive branch already knew about the wrongdoing and had vigorously pursued the wrongdoers. Indeed, most of the committee's investigatory information originated from within the executive branch itself. The answer was that such a single-minded focus had worked with the Get Hoffa Squad. Get Hoffa—Get Nixon: It amounted to the same difference as far as the Kennedy cohorts were concerned. What worked then would work now. And, as it turned out, they were right in both cases.

But allowing the Ervin Committee to proceed first, as well as the degree of cooperation between the committee and the WSPF, raises very serious constitutional questions about the separation of powers and due process.

You may not fully agree with me that this prosecutorial inversion was the result of a deliberate conspiracy. If I have succeeded in establishing the existence of the Camelot Conspiracy, you are convinced. If I haven't, you aren't. But even if you are still unconvinced, you can't really believe that all the things I have described could have occurred simply by chance.

8

The Pious Fraud of the Ervin Committee

I n January 1973, at the conclusion of the original Watergate break-in trial,
Judge Sirica had vented his frustration that the whole truth had not come
out. He expressed the hope that the Senate might do a better job. On February 7, 1973, the Senate approved a resolution to impanel the Senate Select
Committee on Presidential Campaign Activities to investigate Watergate.
Popularly known as the Senate Watergate Committee, or the Ervin Committee, for its chairman, North Carolina senator Sam Ervin, who had served
with both JFK and RFK on the McClellan Rackets Committee.

The vote establishing the Ervin Committee was 77 to 0, so it may be
assumed that almost two dozen Republicans chose to abstain. They had,
presumably, already read the writing on the wall when two Republican-
offered amendments were each defeated on party-line votes by the Democratic majority.

The first amendment would have provided for equal committee repre-
sentation from each party—half Democrats and half Republicans. But the
amendment lost; the seven-member Ervin Committee would comprise
four Democrats and three Republicans. This ratio meant the Democrats
would get two thirds of the staffing budget, and of the important perks
(space, equipment, etc.), that that entailed.

The second amendment the Republicans offered was to provide some frame of reference for the kinds of subjects being investigated (campaign finance and fund-raising abuses, dirty tricks, etc.) by including reviews of prior presidential campaigns. Only if both parties were scrutinized could there be some objective basis for judging campaign excesses and establishing acceptable campaign practices.

Senator Ervin, in his book *The Whole Truth: The Watergate Conspiracy*, camouflaged a real whopper in homespun language when he described why he opposed the two Republican amendments.

> *I opposed the first of these amendments because it created the possibility that the committee might suffer from paralysis. I objected to the second on the ground that there were no charges of improprieties in the presidential elections of 1964 and 1968, and that if the Senate directed the committee to investigate them, it "would be about as foolish as the man who went bear hunting and stopped to chase rabbits."*

Coming from North Carolina, a state that was not a stranger to some almost gothic political practices, it is hard to take his statement that "there were no charges of improprieties in the presidential elections of 1964 and 1968" at anything near face value. The charges were both credible and legion, but they primarily involved Lyndon Johnson, whose colorful and expansive conception of the powers of his office would not have made comfortable hearing material for any Democrats. Senator Ted Kennedy, who certainly didn't want any of the 1960 campaign's dirty linen to be aired, was influential in arranging the party-line vote that put a quick stop to this notion.

Maurice Stans, Nixon's secretary of commerce and head of the CRP's finance committee, has described why preventing a bipartisan review of campaign finance abuses was also of critical importance.

> *What the public did not know was the blatant hypocrisy of the four Democratic members of the Committee, all of whom sanctimoniously interrogated witnesses, they said, to "get the facts on the record."*

In 1964, when Bobby Baker, a protégé of Senators Lyndon Johnson and Robert Kerr, was charged with running an influence-peddling operation in Washington for high stakes, the Democrats controlling the Senate had blocked an investigation; Ervin, Talmadge and Inouye voted time after time to prevent the facts from coming out.

Three of them had campaign finance problems, too. In 1970 . . . Montoya and his campaigners had used nonreporting committees in the District of Columbia to launder the sources of more than $100,000 of funds for his Senate race, and then destroyed the records, to circumvent disclosure laws; and Inouye's organization was found guilty of accepting an illegal corporate contribution in 1974, which was after the Committee's work had been substantially completed. In 1978, Talmadge was in the headlines for a variety of unorthodox and possibly illegal financial transactions over a period of years, including being reimbursed for campaign expenditures in 1973 and 1974 that he never reported making, and receiving many thousands of dollars in gifts from constituents. The discrepancies were explained by his staff as due to "clear oversight" and "careless recordkeeping."

Sam Ervin, then seventy-seven years old, was nearing the end of twenty years in the Senate. The self-styled old country lawyer had an Ivy League pedigree: He graduated from Harvard Law School in 1923. Fifty years later he was understandably fading, and not expected to seek reelection, although his partisan instincts and powers of personal presentation remained formidable.

Two of the committee's other Democratic members—Daniel Inouye of Hawaii and Joseph Montoya of New Mexico—were amiable but undistinguished men who would, like Ervin, be willing to let the committee staff do the work and guide the hearings. On the majority side, then, three of four senators could be counted on to follow the Kennedy activists' lead. Only Georgian Herman Talmadge might be expected to exhibit some independent thinking.

On the Republican side—at least from Nixon's perspective—things were scarcely more encouraging. Senator Howard Baker of Tennessee, the committee's vice chairman and ranking minority member, had presidential aspirations of his own. While fighting hard (and consistently losing) for a more balanced approach in private, his own political calculations did not leave much room (or provide much incentive) for defending Nixon in public.

Edward Gurney of Florida and Lowell Weicker of Connecticut were both in their first terms as senators. Gurney was inclined to defend Nixon but lacked experience; besides, he was not a very forceful personality. Weicker had already begun his own Watergate investigation, and made no secret about his intense dislike of Nixon.

The Ervin Committee's seven senators were served by seventy-five lawyers, investigators, administrative aides, and staff, one third of whom were allocated to the minority.

To say that the Harvard Law School was the primary source for the majority staff would be an understatement. Indeed, Senator Ervin had turned to law professor Arthur S. Miller, who he made chief consultant, for help in selecting the staff. Miller, in turn, had recommended Georgetown law professor Samuel Dash (Harvard Law, '50) as chief counsel. Dash, who had been a trial attorney in the Justice Department's Criminal Division during the Truman administration, immediately hired David Dorsen (Harvard, '56; Harvard Law, '59), James Hamilton (Yale Law, '63), and Terry Lenzner (Harvard, '61; Harvard Law, '64) as his senior associates.

Dorsen had been an assistant U.S. attorney in the Southern District of New York from 1963 to 1968, an office that had been one of the primary sources for both RFK's Get Hoffa Squad and WSPF attorneys. Hamilton had worked for Covington & Burling, a prominent D.C. law firm. Lenzner was a paradigm of Kennedy closeness and Nixon hatred. He had worked for Robert Kennedy's Civil Rights Division under Burke Marshall and John Doar. In 1969 he was heading the Office of Economic Opportunity's legal services program, where he had defended the Berrigan brothers' antiwar actions. Not surprisingly, he was fired by Donald Rumsfeld, the Nixon administration's newly appointed director of OEO.

Three assistant counsels also came from Harvard Law: Marc Lackritz (Princeton, '68; Harvard Law, '73), Ron Rotunda (Harvard, '67; Harvard Law, '70), and Alan Weitz (University of Pennsylvania, '67; Harvard Law,

'70). A fourth, Scott Armstrong, dropped out after his first year at Harvard Law School to join Lenzner's group.

At Kennedy's insistence, Dash hired Carmine Bellino as the committee's chief investigator. Bellino, as we have seen, had long-standing and intimate Kennedy family connections; he had already begun to investigate Watergate for Kennedy's subcommittee.

On the Republican side, Howard Baker inexplicably appointed Fred Thompson as the committee's minority counsel. Thompson later became a distinguished senator and actor and, in 2008, a presidential candidate. At the time of his appointment as minority counsel, however, he was a newly minted small-town attorney whose only practical political experience came from having managed Baker's 1970 reelection campaign in the middle district of Tennessee. Up against the massive majority staff of Washington-savvy Harvards and hard-bitten Kennedys, and a cynical and anti-Nixon national press corps, Fred Thompson experienced a baptism by fire that kept him effectively pinned down throughout the hearings.

At Sam Ervin's behest, Sam Dash was also in touch with LaVern Duffy, who had worked for Bobby Kennedy when he was chief counsel of the McClellan Rackets Committee, and had assisted in Kennedy's earlier investigation. Duffy advised Dash not to focus on the Watergate break-in, because the trial had just ended and the newspapers had covered the prosecutors' activities in considerable detail. Instead, he suggested pursuing campaign dirty tricks in general, and Donald Segretti in particular, as the key witness. Duffy said that he had already collected information about Segretti that was hearing-ready.

Dash, apparently naively, observed:

> *Coincidentally, I received the same advice from James Flug, chief counsel of Senator Kennedy's Administrative Practices Committee. Flug had conducted a preliminary investigation of Watergate when Kennedy thought his committee would be assigned the Major Senate Watergate probe and had interviewed Segretti sometime in November 1972. He endorsed Duffy's view that our investigation and hearings should begin with Segretti and political dirty tricks, and urged me to*

have my staff meet with him for a background briefing before we con-
ducted our own interrogation of Segretti.

Who would have imagined that the advice of two Kennedy clan members would be the same where Watergate was involved? The cynic might suspect that a more active collaboration was under way: that during the crucial months of April and May, attorney Charles Shaffer had been privately spreading the word about what Dean was capable of saying—even while negotiating for immunity on his behalf in a sort of quid pro quo.

In their respective books, both Dash and Weicker confirm late night meetings with Dean in Shaffer's law office in Rockville, Maryland. Similar meetings were held with the three career prosecutors (Silbert, Glanzer, and Campbell). Who is to say such meet-the-witness sessions were not also held with many others, as Shaffer sought support for his client?

Of course, there was nothing illegal per se with the Democrats deciding to use their substantial Senate majority to establish a committee whose sole goal was to trash a Republican president. It's just that when such a massively partisan witch hunt is undertaken, the American public should have a reasonable expectation of being informed of what's really happening.

But the media uncritically reported the committee's composition and lionized its majority members and staff. Nobody seemed to notice—or perhaps nobody cared—that the PR spin wasn't necessarily connected to the reality of what was actually going on. An early *Congressional Quarterly* interview with Sam Dash was typical.

> *"The success of the investigation will depend on the staff," Dash said. He expects the initial public hearings to last about a month, followed by continued investigation by the staff through the summer and more extensive hearings in the fall, he said. The investigation is expected to be broad in scope, exploring not only the details of the Watergate, but other charges of wrongdoing by both the Republican and Democratic Parties.*
>
> *"The ultimate goal of the committee," said Dash, was to discover "what impact [all this] has on the election process in a Democratic*

country. The final report," he said, "might contain recommendations to reform existing election laws."

The Ervin Committee was run by its large and able staff, led by chief counsel Sam Dash. The public hearings, which often gave the appearance of being spontaneous, and sometimes even bordering on chaotic, were, in fact, carefully stage-managed from the outset. In a May 30, 2004, article in *The New York Times,* Warren E. Leary wrote:

> *Professor Dash said he was nervous before the hearings but over-came any jitters with preparation. He made sure all senators on the committee were supplied with questions that probed key issues without slowing the proceedings with repetition or going off the point.*
>
> *Realizing he was involved in a historic constitutional and presidential event, Professor Dash said he wanted people to understand what they saw in the unprecedented televised hearings. "I scripted it like a story, like a detective story," he said in an interview last May [2003] with the* Philadelphia Inquirer *on the 30th anniversary of the hearings. "The most important thing I had to do was convey the information to the public in a way they could understand."*

Senator Lowell Weicker played such a unique role in the deliberations of the Ervin Committee that he deserves special consideration. Over time he assigned five members of his own staff to be full-time investigators. One indication of Weicker's enthusiasm may be seen in a Vorenberg memo, re-capping his conversation with a Weicker aide, regarding their intent to as-sist FBI agents in reviewing some 300,000 items that had been identified in response to earlier Weicker request letters to Cox and to the deputy attor-ney general. The memo, reproduced in Appendix H, is rather entertaining and well worth reading.

Coincidentally, Weicker and John and Maureen Dean were neighbors. They lived on Quay Street, on the Potomac River, in Old Town, the his-toric section of Alexandria, Virginia, and continued to socialize as the Watergate scandal unfolded. In fact, the senator helped the Deans leave town by purchasing their town house in April 1974—not to live in, but to facilitate their planned relocation to Los Angeles.

The third of the committee's three Republicans, Weicker nonetheless consistently voted with the Democrats on procedural issues. Most importantly, he provided the critical single Republican vote that was required to grant Dean immunity prior to his committee testimony.

At first, Sam Dash took to heart the advice he had received from Jim Flug and LaVern Duffy: Avoid focusing on Watergate itself, because that had just been the subject of a full trial. Dash's game plan had been refocused to pursue the topic of political dirty tricks. As he described it later:

> It was my plan to start out with little-known witnesses, who would provide the details necessary for the public to understand the background roles and activities of the major witnesses. Such a plan would call for a long witness list and a rejection of a "bombshell" opening. The use of innumerable witnesses would be opposed by some of the senators; the lack of instant drama would bring me the displeasure of the press. Nevertheless, I was committed to this plan. The witness list my staff and I developed was formidable. I estimated it would take the committee all summer to complete public hearings on the Watergate break-in and cover-up phase. But as I and my staff contemplated this prospect we saw no acceptable shortcut.

"Particularly after talking to Flug, Duffy, and Shaffer" is the phrase perhaps missing from the end of this paragraph—especially in light of Dash's earlier comment about the identical advice he received from at least two of them.

So when Sam Ervin gaveled his Senate Watergate Committee hearings to order on May 17, there was little impact outside of the nation's capital and the Beltway that cushions it. At least, until John Dean appeared in mid-June, the Ervin hearings were well on their way to becoming a nonevent. But this was just as Dash's plan envisioned. The hearings would move slowly enough to take all summer on the Watergate phase alone. What he had in mind was a steady drip, drip, drip of leaks, innuendos, disclosures, and public posturing that would gradually wear away respect for the Nixon presidency.

That was the game plan before news of Dean's evolving—and, apparently, pliable—accusations seem to have been shared among the Kennedy cohorts, and new possibilities involving Watergate itself began to appear. The offer of immunity led to Dean's casting his lot with the committee and stiffing the prosecutors and the grand jury. Now the dirty trick focus faded fast, and the new priority was to build up anticipation for Dean's testimony.

It is also quite telling that Dash soon became confident that his hearings would precede any criminal trials; he wasn't the least concerned about the possibility of any pending indictments—at least, after Cox was appointed.

9

First Blood: John Dean Testifies

While nutcases and damn fools surface with some regularity in politics, there has simply never been anyone quite like John Wesley Dean III.

He is unique in our political history, and possibly even in the all-time annals of lawyers gone bad. There have been many amoral, self-serving young men on the make in Washington before—the type isn't exclusive to Hollywood or to Wall Street. But only one has been able to apply his unique lack of talents and integrity in such a way as to change the course of history and bring down a president.

As we have seen, John Dean was first the midwife of the campaign intelligence plan that led to the Watergate break-in, and then the architect and project manager of the attempt to cover it up. As the scandal worsened, he almost single-handedly prevented any meaningful White House moves to cut its losses by making timely disclosures. He breached lawyer-client confidences by the boatload. And, when he found that the true story of what happened wouldn't be enough to get him immunity from prosecution for his crimes, he dramatically changed his story to implicate higher-ups and to save his own skin.

While others—including a president of the United States—went down in flames during Watergate, John Dean managed to jump ship and crawl to safety with an agility that reflected his prep school swimming prowess. As the star government witness against his former bosses and colleagues, he testified before the Ervin Committee in June 1973 and during the Watergate cover-up trial in the fall of 1974. It may be true that no bad deed goes unrewarded, because all the scrambling and hustling and betrayal came pretty close to achieving their purpose when John Dean ended up serving the shortest sentence of any of the major Watergate figures.

To many today Dean is thought of as the young aide who finally couldn't live with what was going on around him, and became, however reluctantly at first, the whistle-blower who brought Nixon down. That is certainly the image that Dean and his supporters have assiduously and successfully projected over the last three decades. As our story will show, he is, more likely, a slippery opportunist who caused the problem and then put covering his own ass above any notions of honesty or integrity.

John Dean is a midwesterner, born in Akron, Ohio, in 1938. He was sent away to boarding school and graduated from Staunton Military Academy in 1957, where his roommate was Barry Goldwater, Jr., a son of the iconic conservative Arizona senator. The slim, trim young man was a determined swimmer, and became an all-American backstroker. After a year and a half at Colgate University in upstate New York, Dean moved back home and graduated from the College of Wooster in 1961. Always an indifferent student, he ranked in the lowest third of his class.

After graduation he moved to Washington and spent a year working toward an MPA—master's of public administration—at American University. He switched to law school and was graduated from the Georgetown University Law Center in 1965.

Dean's first and only actual experience in private practice with a law firm lasted about six months, and ended badly when he was fired for unethical conduct. As a junior associate with the firm of Welch & Morgan, he was assigned to a client applying for an FCC broadcast license. The license looked like such a good deal that Dean and some of his associates got the bright idea of filing their own competing application. When this came to the attention of the firm, he was ousted.

He bounced back. It can't have hurt that he was then married to his first wife, a senator's daughter. With the sponsorship of his Ohio congressman (and fellow Wooster alumnus), he landed the plum position of minority counsel for the House Judiciary Committee. The irony of a lawyer who had just been fired for unethical conduct surfacing on the staff of the Judiciary Committee may not have gone unnoticed. He was terminated effective August 13, 1967. Six months later, Dean joined the National Commission on Reform of the Federal Criminal Laws as associate director. He also got his prior law firm to recharacterize his departure as having been over law firm policy differences.

Dean left the commission in February 1969 to join the newly inaugurated Nixon administration as one of three associate deputy attorneys general, reporting to deputy attorney general Richard Kleindienst. Dean soon became a favorite—even a protégé—of then attorney general John Mitchell. His principal job was to be the Justice Department's congressional liaison. In that pivotal position he further enhanced his connections with congressmen and senators on both sides of the aisle. He was active in opposing the Kennedy-Flug juggernaut that successfully defeated Nixon's first two Supreme Court nominations, and his work brought him to the attention of the White House. When John Ehrlichman left the counsel's office to become Nixon's assistant for domestic affairs in July 1970, Dean was tapped to replace him.

The new White House counsel was only thirty-four years old, and only several years into an already checkered career. He had overcome a badly flawed start to enjoy a meteoric rise in the Washington firmament.

Ehrlichman had used the entrée and access provided by the counsel's position to carve out a role for himself as the administration's domestic czar. In choosing his successor as counsel, he may have purposely looked for someone who would not be able to use the position in the way he had, or to create a competing power base. If he were, in fact, looking for a pliable lightweight, in John Dean he found his man. And if that is the case, it should be seen as a cautionary tale of a classic bureaucratic move that produced disastrously unintended consequences.

From the start John Dean cut an exotic figure in the buttoned-down Nixon White House. Everything about him—his looks, his clothes, his car, even his hours—proclaimed him a peacock in a paddock of workhorses. Amid an array of Brooks Brothers clones, he dressed carefully and modishly. His hair was longer and his ties were brighter and wider. No one at the time could recall having seen him in the sober suit and horn-rimmed glasses that he wore for his televised appearances before the Ervin Committee. He was clearly aware of his look—and his good looks. In fact, he stated that one of the reasons he most feared being sent to prison was that his diminutive stature and boyish surfer looks would mark him for homosexual rape.

He was, technically, between marriages, and enjoyed the life of a bachelor in a town that caters to men—particularly to those in prominent political positions.

The counsel's office functions as the president's lawyer—but the scope of its operations is really a reflection of the gravitas of its head. Under Ehrlichman it became so involved in policy formulation that he was appointed assistant to the president for domestic affairs—taking with him all his top aides to the newly created Domestic Council. One of the few functions that Ehrlichman didn't take was the responsibility for conducting background checks on presidential appointees. Results of FBI full-field investigations on prospective presidential appointees continued to be reported to, and reviewed by, the counsel's office. The other major responsibility was to handle clemency requests.

In the main, however, Dean's office relayed requests for legal advice, help, and information to the Department of Justice, where the real legal work was being done. Dean also benefited from the talents of Fred Fielding, his very capable new deputy. Years later, in addition to a notable private practice, Fielding would return to the White House in 1981 as counsel to Presidents Ronald Reagan and—in 2007—George W. Bush.

Not to put too fine a point on it, John Dean had very little that he had to do day by day. He wasn't only being self-deprecating when he later testified that he was mostly a glorified "messenger boy" from Haldeman to Mitchell, and that the title (counsel to the president) was the best part of the job.

Under Ehrlichman the office had acted as a staff resource on a number of sensitive projects, as well as for anyone who had questions about the legal aspects of something they were doing, or who needed advice about anything connected with their work. As a result, in addition to all the highly sensitive FBI background material on presidential staff and appointees, the counsel's office under Dean still possessed many files on sensitive political matters—involving both individuals and issues, and dating from the very beginning of the Nixon administration—that Ehrlichman had left for safekeeping, and to maintain lawyer-client privilege.

As we have seen, Bob Haldeman assigned John Dean the responsibility of setting up an intelligence operation for Nixon's reelection campaign.

When Gordon Liddy made his second proposal regarding bugging, Dean had said that such things shouldn't be discussed in the presence of the attorney general. His words have been construed to show that he recognized how improper Liddy's proposals were. But, as Dean's conduct clearly demonstrates, he was actually making a pragmatic political assessment rather than a moral judgment. Far from rejecting Liddy's plan, it is more likely that Dean simply wanted Mitchell, his mentor and sponsor, to have plausible deniability in case anything went wrong.

Confirmation of this version of events is secondhand, but comes from James McCord's recollections of what Gordon Liddy had told him at the time. McCord's hand-typed statement, dated March 26, 1973 (and reproduced in part in Appendix I), has Liddy telling McCord that:

> *A few days later Dean told Liddy that a way would have to be worked out to undertake the operation without directly involving the Attorney General so that he would have deniability about it at a future date.*

Dean later claimed he sought the same distance for himself. He began to claim that following the second meeting with Mitchell, he had met with Haldeman, and secured his assent that the White House shouldn't be involved in that aspect of campaign activity. As with so much of Dean's story, his claims about what he supposedly discussed with Haldeman shifted over time, as his own interests changed. There was no mention of such a meeting during Dean's first two weeks of sessions with the career prosecutors. When it was first described, it was meant to show that Dean himself had opted out of any conspiracy to break the law—and then to prove that Haldeman had known about the program from the outset. At a later point, he claimed that he had used this meeting to urge that Haldeman step in and stop the whole idea before it got started—in which case he—Dean—could not have been expected to take any further action to stop the Liddy plan.

One wonders if such a meeting ever occurred at all. Haldeman was nothing if not regimented and documented, and it is notable that no such meeting appears on his office calendar or schedule, or in any of the copious notes he made; nor does he allude to it in the detailed daily diary he wrote in longhand every night. To his dying day, Haldeman maintained that no such meeting ever occurred. Perhaps the most convincing—and consistent—reason for believing that it never happened is that Dean never appears to have reminded Haldeman of that conversation in the ten months following the break-in. Indeed, the White House tape recordings continued to show Haldeman's ongoing and unquestioning acceptance of Dean's reassurances that no one on the White House staff had been involved in any aspect of Liddy's plans.

Although both Dean and Dash try their best to fudge it in their respective books, all notes and memos from the U.S. attorney's office concerning their April meetings with Dean are consistent: His immunity negotiations with the Ervin Committee began about mid-April—which means that Dash was negotiating with Dean and/or Shaffer while Dean was still counsel to the president. No wonder they didn't want the specific dates to be pinned down.

Dash does confirm that he began a series of lengthy face-to-face meetings with Dean and Shaffer beginning on May 9. But Senator Ervin's May 8 announcement that Dean would testify before the committee under a grant of immunity means that the arrangements had been made sometime before. Dean says of that first meeting:

> He [Dash] wasn't out to prosecute anyone, but he had strong gut feelings about where the facts would take him—and he saw Richard Nixon standing at the end of the corridor that he wanted most to travel down.

The admitted Dash-Dean-Shaffer meetings continued the evenings of May 10 and 13, and then moved to Dean's home in Old Town, Alexandria, on May 15 and 16. At this point Dash's book ceases to document specific dates, but it is clear that he was in constant touch with his star witness. It is also clear that the reason for these meetings was that Dash was helping Dean with the 245-page opening statement that he read to the committee—with the national TV audience hanging on every word—revealing everything questionable about the Nixon administration that he had learned in his position as counsel to the president. Dash himself put it a bit more obliquely.

> *I limited my questioning of Dean to pinpointing the highlights of his testimony. A number of viewers, most of them lawyers, wrote to me complaining that I had not subjected Dean to rigorous cross-examination at the hearing.*
>
> *Of course, these people did not realize I had interrogated Dean for a month before his public testimony.*

No committee member seemed to care about questions of privileged information or lawyer-client privilege—the theater was too good to quibble over any citizen's—even a president's—constitutionally protected rights.

We have already seen that Ben-Veniste credits Shaffer with having prepared much of Dean's written statement. Perhaps that is the work of one's attorney. But given all the investigative journalism that was going on at the time, it is surprising that some enterprising reporter never ferreted out the fact that Dean also had considered advance help with his statement from Sam Dash. Their highly unusual and unorthodox secret meetings—continuing over the course of a full month—were truly newsworthy.

The much predicted highlight of Dean's testimony—his accusation of President Nixon—came not from his prepared statement, but during the Q & A following it. Sam Dash had reserved for himself the dramatic moment that had been so well rehearsed in advance. After taking Dean once again, step-by-step, through his testimony, Dash asked:

> *Now, after all those events, after the President having told you how Bob Haldeman had kept him posted on your handling of the Watergate case; and that he appreciated how difficult a job that*

was; and your statement to the President that you only contained it,
and that someday it might unravel; and your own statement to the
President that in a civil case, an ex parte relationship had been es-
tablished to influence the judge; and then the discussion on the Pat-
man hearings—frankly and honestly, Mr. Dean, when you left the
President on September 15, did you just have an impression as to his
knowledge of the cover-up, or did you have a conviction concerning
that?

It was time for the long-teased money quote, and John Dean delivered
big time:

> *Mr. Dash, there was no doubt in my mind that the President was*
> *aware of it and I would have to, to use your language, say I had a*
> *conviction, or I was convinced.*

There it was. The unspeakable finally spoken. The weeks of predictions that Dean would accuse President Nixon of knowingly participating
in the cover-up were confirmed. Because of the media buildup and subsequent coverage, the impact was tremendous.

Of course, the impression given the public was every bit as misleading
as the carefully crafted words were intended.

Today, we know from White House tapes released in 1974 that while
Dean met or talked with the president on twenty-two occasions, he did not
describe any cover-up activity—or even begin to reveal aspects of his own
involvement—until March 21, 1973. Nor did Dean ever receive any direct
presidential orders concerning the cover-up.

In a 1981 article—"John Dean's Memory: A Case Study"—Dr. Ulric
Neisser, now professor emeritus of psychology at Cornell University, compared Dean's testimony regarding another important conversation (September 15, 1972, the day the original Watergate indictments were handed
down) with the tapes and reached a devastating conclusion.

> *Comparison with the transcript shows that hardly a word of*
> *Dean's account is true. Nixon did not say any of the things attributed*

*to him here: He didn't ask Dean to sit down, he didn't say Haldeman
had kept him posted, he didn't say Dean had done a good job (at least
not in that part of the conversation), he didn't say anything about
Liddy or the indictments. Nor had Dean himself said the things he
later describes himself as saying: that he couldn't take credit, that the
matter might unravel some day, etc. (Indeed, he said just the opposite
later on: "Nothing is going to come crashing down.") His account is
plausible, but entirely incorrect. In this early part of the conversation
Nixon did not offer him any praise at all, unless "You had quite a
day, didn't you?" was intended as a compliment. (It is hard to tell
from a written transcript.) Dean cannot be said to have reported the
"gist" of the opening remarks; no count of idea units or comparison of
structure would produce a score much above zero.**

So John Dean had spoken the unspeakable. That's what the senators
and the media accepted and celebrated. But Dean's actual words were perhaps less forthcoming than the eager interpretations they were given. Consider them again: "Mr. Dash, there was no doubt in my mind that the
President was aware of it and I would have to, to use your language, say I
had a conviction, or I was convinced." In what thirty years later would become known as a Clintonian parsing ("that depends on what the meaning
of 'is' is"), Dean never said Nixon did or knew anything. "There was no
doubt in my mind" is a highly qualified statement, especially when the
payoff is "I had a conviction, or I was convinced."

Just as ideas have consequences, words have meanings, and there are
reasons John Dean said what he said. Had he testified accurately, he may
well have said something more like this:

---

*Dr. Neisser makes the point that although Dean's memory was almost completely
inaccurate, his testimony nonetheless conveyed much of what is now perceived as
the truth of the conversations in question (that Nixon knew about and had participated in the cover-up). But this sober ex post facto academic point (which is not
necessarily true) doesn't address the devastating impact at the time of these almost
completely fabricated conversations from the man the senators and the nation's media were celebrating because of his purportedly phenomenal and all but photographic memory.

I orchestrated the cover-up, so I knew that criminal acts were com-
mitted. I thought I was doing what was expected of me. They wanted it
contained, and that's what I thought I was doing. But now that I've
been caught, and I'm facing some very serious charges, I'm trying to get
immunity, so I won't have to go to jail. In return for immunity, the
committee expects me to finger the president. That presents a problem,
because I didn't tell him about the criminality. My hard-won immu-
nity only covers past acts, so I'm not about to add perjury to my prob-
lems by saying that I did. What I can *do is claim that upon reflection*
I now think that the president must *have known about the cover-up*
from some other source. And it's nice to know that saying this has been
sufficient to obtain at least partial immunity for me.

Dean's testimony occurred prior to disclosure of the White House taping system. Although he later claimed that some of Nixon's peculiar actions had led him to suspect that their conversations were being taped, it
must have come as quite a shock to learn that a voice-activated system had
been recording every conversation from beginning to end. When the tapes
were released months later, it became clear that many of Dean's conversations were not at all as he had described or characterized them. In fact, detailed analyses were done both by the White House and the special
prosecutor, and each confirmed at least seventeen substantive instances in
which Dean's Ervin Committee testimony either differed from, or wasn't
supported by, the White House tape recordings.

That Dean's allegations of presidential wrongdoing weren't supported
by the tapes turned out to be of small significance compared to the altered
focus of media attention that followed the release of the tapes themselves.
While the degrees of Nixon's culpability represented on the recordings continue to be debated even today, there is no question about the devastating
impact of the picture of Nixon that the tapes presented.

Like the decidedly unmighty Oz discovered posturing behind the cur-
tain, the president of the United States portrayed on the tapes turned out to
be a petty, paranoid, and vindictive man conducting himself in a manner,
and expressing himself with a vocabulary, that was patently unpresidential.
The impact of the tapes themselves—and the window they opened onto

the seamy underbelly of the Nixon White House—was so great that the Democrats' bait and switch regarding the need for their release went virtually unnoticed.

Dean's allegations had been sufficient to provide the legal basis for demanding and obtaining access to the tapes. Once obtained, it was of little consequence that his allegations turned out to be largely unfounded. Now that the tapes themselves were available, and with a precedent for access to them established, the Kennedy-led fishing expeditions could begin in earnest.

Of course, there was no thought of prosecuting Dean for perjury for his erroneous testimony. He was, after all, still the Camelot conspirators' star witness, and his credibility had to be maintained—at least, until they no longer needed him. He was simply allowed to adjust his testimony at the later trials so it would conform to any inconvenient inconsistencies that had arisen on the tapes.

10

The Ervin Committee Pioneers
the Politics of Personal Destruction

For all the credit—and adulation—the Ervin Committee and the Watergate Special Prosecution Force received, the simple fact is that the primary source of their investigatory material was the files of Silbert's U.S. attorney's office team and the FBI investigations undertaken at their direction—all of which had been done before the WSPF was created and the committee was established. With the exception of a few revelations that emerged from new inquiries, or in the course of the hearings, all the committee's most dramatic public disclosures were derived from information that was already known to the federal prosecutors. (Ironically, the major exception was the disclosure, on July 16, of the existence of the White House taping system.)

By mid-March, an arrangement had been worked out with Attorney General Richard Kleindienst to allow the four senior members of the Ervin Committee access to information from FBI Watergate interviews. (Kleindienst, who had been deputy attorney general from the beginning of the Nixon administration, had succeeded John Mitchell as attorney general; he was sworn in on June 12, 1972, five days before the Watergate break-in.) Lest there be any doubt about Weicker's reputation even among his colleagues as a publicity-seeking unguided missile, this arrangement conveniently omitted him from having such access.

Things got much easier once the WSPF was created. On June 8, Vorenberg and Neal of the WSPF met with Dash and Thompson to discuss ways of achieving greater degrees of cooperation between the two groups. Dash was a former student of Cox's at Harvard, and the atmosphere was collegial.

The fruits of this meeting did not take long to ripen. Three days later, Neal wrote (in a memo reproduced in Appendix J) that an agreement had been reached to coordinate a WSPF witness interview with Carmine Bellino of the Ervin Committee staff, noting, "I think this is an arrangement in which we can cooperate with the Committee without any danger to our operation." Given their service together on the Get Hoffa Squad in RFK's Justice Department, this conclusion should come as no great surprise.

On June 18, Philip Heymann, one of Cox's closest staff members, wrote suggesting two points with regard to the Ervin Committee: First, that full-time WSPF staff members be assigned to review all Ervin Committee transcripts for possible additional charges; and second, that a "perjury" file be started—not just for possible later prosecution, but also for bargaining purposes with potential witnesses. Heymann's memo, reproduced in Appendix K, certainly indicates the perceived value of allowing the Ervin hearings to precede any criminal indictments. The file copy of this letter that I found in the National Archives contains a handwritten note from Cox to Neal emphasizing the importance of Heymann's suggestions—which were promptly implemented.

On July 9, Ervin wrote to Cox requesting that four additional staff members (including Terry Lenzner) be given access to the raw FBI interview files, called 302 Forms. Ervin, Baker, Dash, and Thompson had already been granted such access.

Significantly, congressional access was limited to FBI interviews done *prior* to Cox's arrival—thus precluding the possibility that any Republicans would realize the full scope of the freewheeling inquiries into Nixon and his administration that Cox's army was now pursuing full bore.

On July 13, the committee confirmed an arrangement whereby it would be informed of any documents in the WSPF possession—at least, concerning Haldeman and Ehrlichman—that were not already known to the committee itself.

Given this level of Ervin Committee–WSPF cooperation, and noting the special prosecutor's daily scrutiny of Ervin Committee transcripts, and Dash's later admission that he "made sure all senators on the committee were supplied with questions that probed key issues without slowing the proceedings with repetition or going off the point"—it is fair to wonder whether the special prosecutor's staff was feeding questions to be asked of specific witnesses.

It wouldn't be surprising if they had. In fact, given the degree of symbiosis that had developed between the committee and the WSPF, it would be surprising if they hadn't. Of course, it would be an egregious violation of prosecutorial ethics to draft questions for a congressional hearing in hopes of adding additional names to a perjury file. Yet the fact remains that the WSPF did bring perjury charges against Haldeman, Ehrlichman, and Mitchell as a result of their Ervin Committee testimony. Some dots have to be connected; some dots virtually connect themselves.

Once the Ervin hearings were completed, the flow of assistance and information reversed direction. Now the committee was deluged with a near constant stream of WSPF requests for documents and information from the special prosecutor. There was no resistance or reluctance to sharing such information—even though the committee's files had been sealed from review by all other individuals and organizations.

The Ervin Committee's velvet glove treatment of John Dean stands in stark contrast to the reception accorded members of the Nixon administration who weren't as willing—much less as eager—as John Dean, although that admittedly sets an almost impossibly high standard, to cooperate with the Kennedy-coached game plan. In the words of Maurice Stans, who knew firsthand whereof he wrote.

Ervin himself played a rough game, designed to emphasize the importance of his contribution to the hearings, while at the same time piously asserting that he was only a country lawyer and hamming up his act like a medieval clown. If a witness pleaded guilty to a crime with suitable penitence to satisfy Ervin, he was extolled as a virtuous boon to society. If he sought instead to deny guilt, he was brutally attacked as a master-criminal. There was no place in Ervin's categories for an innocent person who protested his innocence. A protestation of innocence was ipso facto evidence of guilt, and Ervin made the most of that conclusion by savagely insinuating questioning that was designed to convince the television audience that he was the ringmaster whipping into line a troop of dangerous criminals.

Virtually all the adverse witnesses had already been required to appear before the grand jury. This enabled the Kennedy conspirators to have two bites at the apple, because committee witnesses were under oath, and therefore at risk of prosecution for perjury regarding prior testimony. If some point hadn't been pinned down during a grand jury appearance, the committee could revisit the same ground.

There should have been serious legal concerns about calling witnesses to testify before the committee when indictments were pending. For example, Stans and Mitchell had already been indicted in New York in the Vesco case.*

They argued that being compelled to appear before the committee presented them with the Hobson's choice of having to testify or assert their Fifth Amendment rights to silence. Taking the Fifth before the committee was sure to poison the jury pool, in violation of their inherent right to decline to testify without that being brought to the jury's attention. Further, under normal trial procedure, the government must present its entire case (which is, at its completion, subject to a motion to dismiss) before a defendant is required to choose between taking the stand in his own defense or pleading the Fifth.

---

*Robert Vesco was a controversial financier—and an international fugitive—accused by the Securities and Exchange Commission of embezzling hundreds of millions of dollars from companies he had acquired. He had made a substantial contribution to Nixon's 1972 campaign—allegedly with the hope of making his SEC problems disappear.

In the Senate hearings there was no such requirement that the committee present a prima facie case. In fact, there was no such right in general. Stans and Mitchell—along with Haldeman and Ehrlichman—decided that testifying rather than taking the Fifth was the lesser of two evils, and was also mandatory from a political point of view (precisely the opposite situation that Dean would have faced if the Kennedy cohorts hadn't succeeded, and he had been indicted prior to his Ervin Committee appearance).

There is something deeply wrong with a political investigation by Congress in which witnesses making accusations aren't held to any standard of truth, while the testimony of the accused is pored over by politically motivated prosecutors with the goal of identifying any misstatement for later accusations of perjury. Even if you don't agree that it is wrong, you can't argue that it is fair.

It is one thing to be held to such a high standard before a grand jury, whose proceedings are both profoundly serious and completely secret. But the nature of congressional hearings is something else entirely. A very few are pristine and produce important results. But most—and particularly the most prominently publicized—amount to politically driven donnybrooks; they are more like grand stands than grand juries.

Months passed and after the cherry blossoms fell, Washington settled in for another long, hot summer. But week after week, then month after month, the Ervin Committee somehow never found the time to hear any witnesses concerning the fund-raising practices and financial activities of the Democratic Party during the 1972 presidential campaign. The only item in the public record is press coverage on June 14, noting that the committee had subpoenaed financial records from five Democratic campaigns.

Apparently nothing of great moment was received—or at least thought sufficiently valuable by the special prosecutor's staff to consider reviewing further. There are records—and a number of GAO referrals for investigation—but no legal actions resulted.

There is a passage in the WSPF's final report, dated October 1975, that suggests that they were only able to investigate "Reports of pre-April 7 [1972] contributions to several Democratic candidates, which the candidates had made public." But there is no mention of any such reports being sought or obtained from Ervin Committee files, so there is no way of knowing if this was the product of shared fruit.

John Dean's riveting public testimony to the Ervin Committee was accompanied by a major behind-the-scenes committee document dump. Perhaps the reporters who examined the inventory of the mass of materials were so riveted by Dean's testimony that they neglected to notice two small inserted passages explaining that several documents (exhibits 34-5 through 34-8, and 43) had been "submitted for identification only, not for publication, and will be retained in the files of the committee." Sam Dash, who said that publication of these exhibits would serve no purpose, had locked them in the committee's safe, and wouldn't let even the staff see them.

What were these dynamite documents, and what made them so potentially volatile that they had to be locked away, even from the committee's own staff or members? One item was a memo by William Sullivan, a former head of the FBI's intelligence operations, detailing decades of bureau misdeeds at presidential behest, under prior administrations. Some of its contents were alluded to in an article published in August 1973 entitled "Team of FBI Agents Used by President Johnson as Political Operatives at the 1964 Democratic Convention."

> The memo, personally typed by Sullivan to limit its readers to an absolute minimum, had originally been classified as a top-secret document. It provided thumbnail descriptions of a dozen specific situations where the FBI had served as the political investigative arm of the White House. . . .
>
> On November 12, 1968, Sullivan wrote, President Johnson personally requested the FBI "to check all outgoing telephone calls made by the then Vice-Presidential candidate, Spiro Agnew, on the date of November 2, 1968, at the time he was in Albuquerque, New Mexico. This was done."
>
> The FBI response, considering the fact that LBJ requested the information more than a week after the calls had been placed, was remarkably detailed. Five phone calls were made in all by the Agnew team during their Albuquerque stop, Sullivan said: three from a

*phone on Agnew's plane and two from a nearby pay phone. Agnew
had talked to Secretary of State Dean Rusk, Johnson was told, and an
Agnew staff member had made two calls, one to Cal Purdy in Texas
and another to a New York sculptor named Bruce Friedel. The fourth
call went to a Jim Miller, also of New York. The fifth call was to a
telephone in the Nixon-Agnew Campaign Headquarters chargeable to
Maurice Stans.*

*After an extensive investigation, the Senate Intelligence Commit-
tee concluded that every administration from Roosevelt's to Nixon's
had permitted, and sometimes encouraged, the FBI and other federal
agencies to engage in improper political intelligence operations. . . .
The Kennedy brothers "had the FBI wiretap a Congressional staff
member, three executive officials, a lobbyist, and a Washington law
firm. Attorney General Robert Kennedy received the fruits of an FBI
"tap" on Martin Luther King, Jr, and a "bug" on a Congressman,
both of which yielded information of a political nature."*

If the Ervin Committee seriously intended to uncover abuses and recommend reforms, at least some historical context and bipartisan perspective would have been necessary. The fact that any bipartisan perspective
was not only eschewed but suppressed amply demonstrates the committee's
real purpose and intention.

Among the more troublesome—and well documented—excesses of
the Ervin Committee was the straightforward effort by Kennedy capos
Carmine Bellino and Terry Lenzner, aided by Lenzner's two associates
Marc Lackritz and Scott Armstrong, to nail Nixon's best friend, Bebe Rebozo. (Charles Gregory Rebozo was the youngest of a family of Cuban
immigrants in Florida—hence his nickname "Bebe" for the Spanish "baby.")
A self-made, successful entrepreneur in real estate and banking, he would
pay a high price for his friendship with Nixon.

Dash opens a chilling window onto Bellino's investigatory approach.
There was great frustration that despite extraordinarily aggressive investigations, nothing bad had been turned up on Rebozo. Investigators were
tantalized by a 1969 campaign contribution—one hundred thousand dollars in cash—that Rebozo had received from the eccentric billionaire

Howard Hughes. At the time such a contribution was completely legal. The money was returned to Hughes, apparently after having been discovered unused in a safe in 1973. The story was well-known, and had already been thoroughly investigated. But for the Rebozo investigators, the Hughes cash was like a pork chop trailed in front of a rottweiler, and they were not about to let it go.

The dynamic duo of Carmine Bellino and Terry Lenzner told Sam Dash that they had a way to nail Rebozo once and for all. After all, the man must be guilty of something—he was Nixon's friend, for God's sake. Bellino, the master forensic accountant, wanted access to all of Rebozo's financial records—not just the ones dealing with the Hughes contribution or his tax returns, but *everything,* including private personal records as well as business and bank material. He was convinced the audit he could then conduct could hit pay dirt.

Here is how Sam Dash—somewhat appalled despite his boys-will-be-boys tone—described the Rebozo feeding frenzy.

> *According to Bellino, this audit might uncover large cash expenditures which could not be tied to identifiable receipts, indicating Rebozo's use of a special cash fund—and the only one known to be available to him was the $100,000 Hughes money.*
>
> *Desperate for a solution, Terry drew up a subpoena which would command Rebozo to turn over to our Senate Select Committee all his private and business financial records. When Terry sent his subpoena request for Rebozo's records to me for my approval, I was amazed at its scope. It would have stripped Rebozo naked. I knew Bellino's theory and I was as eager as Terry to get at the truth of whether Rebozo had tampered with the Hughes money. However, I also realized how easy it was for investigators to allow their zeal to run away with them, especially when they believed that their cause was right and just.*

Like Gordon Liddy with his overly aggressive intel plan, Terry Lenzner was undeterred. He took a creative approach to this attempt by more clear-thinking superiors to rein him in. The resourceful Lenzner returned with what Dash described as "an alternate route." The IRS had assigned its best agents to an exhaustive audit of Rebozo; they were very close to completing their work, and they had been sharing a lot of their material with the special prosecutor's office.

Dash goes on to describe how the Ervin Committee requested all of the IRS audit records, but the IRS commissioner was only willing to share Rebozo's actual tax returns, and not all their investigatory issues and findings. As Dash notes:

> *I suspected that his decision in this regard was motivated in part by a request he had probably received from the special prosecutor's office not to supply Terry and his staff with the records. The special prosecutor's top assistants were not sympathetic with the aggressive tactics of Terry's team. They suspected him of being the source of some of the committee's major leaks, and may well have been concerned that IRS records in their hands would find their way to the* Washington Post *or* The New York Times.

Instead, Lenzner prepared a memo, dated April 14, 1974, addressed to all Ervin Committee members, complaining about the lack of IRS cooperation, and implying a cover-up in the Rebozo investigation. Lenzner's memo somehow found its way onto the front page of that same day's edition of *The New York Times*. This must have set some kind of a record—usually the ink had at least dried on Ervin Committee secret material before it was leaked.

Dash seems only mildly upset that members of his staff had so obsessively pursued something that was only tangentially related to the committee's jurisdictional mandate of 1972 presidential campaign activities. But two of the Kennedy clan's closest confidants—men known for their aggressive style and partisan commitment—were determined to get access to all the financial records of President Nixon's closest friend. The fact that Dash chose to mention it in his book indicates that he felt something wasn't right about it. Even so, he neglects to mention that at the end of two years of intensive investigations, costing $3 million, Special Prosecutor Henry Ruth conceded that they had found no evidence of any wrongdoing by Bebe Rebozo.

Barrels of newspaper ink were consumed in the outrage over the possibility that the Nixon administration had requested IRS tax audits of its enemies. Here we have a confirmed case of the Kennedy family's accountant obtaining five years of previously audited tax returns filed by Nixon's best friend, under a scarcely defensible ruse, and then complaining that the IRS wouldn't additionally release its own audit notes. What was the take of *The New York Times* on all of this? Their story's main thrust was to the effect of "here's another case of Nixon's IRS participating in a continuing cover-up by refusing to share vital information."

Despite their facade of independence and objectivity, the Ervin Committee hearings were a political witch hunt orchestrated by Kennedy Clan Democrats. The pious public promises to investigate abuses in both parties were purposefully ignored, and they carefully targeted solely the Nixon administration. Its excesses should not have been fed by Sirica or the special prosecutor, and would have been documented and exposed by a truly alert and independent press.

The one-sided view carefully nurtured by the committee was successful in undermining public support for the newly reelected president. In all, the Ervin Committee granted partial immunity to over two dozen witnesses. Some—like Jeb Magruder and John Dean—were central figures steeped in criminal conduct and knowledge. But that was hard to tell from their treatment by the committee and the coverage of them in the media, which presented them as dupes at worst, and quasi heroes at best.

By and large, the actions of the Ervin Committee weren't criminal in and of themselves. It was what it was: a supercharged partisan production by the party in power flexing its muscles. The real crime of the Ervin Committee hearings was the coordinated inaction. In order to make the committee's partisan points most effectively in the court of public opinion, the special prosecutor had to forestall the indictments that were ready to be handed down. Justice delayed is justice denied, and the fact that these indictments were deliberately postponed for months in order to gain political advantage is very wrong.

In spite of tantalizing items mentioned by Sam Dash—in his own book and as quoted in news articles—little has survived in the internal memos and documentation from committee records themselves. Perhaps little of what really went on was ever reduced to writing; perhaps it was all done by phone or in person—or simply leaked to the press—but there is a surprising paucity of analytical work now available to researchers. There was fact gathering, to be sure, but almost no written discussion of what was yet to be pursued or how it might all fit together. Those were highly charged times, filled with larger-than-life personalities. Perhaps the momentum was such that they really were making it up as they went along.

11

The Watergate Special Prosecutor and the Terrors of Prosecutorial Abuse

On a Monday morning in April 1940—April Fool's Day, in fact—the newly appointed attorney general of the United States, Robert H. Jackson, gave a speech to the United States attorneys—from each federal judicial district all across America—at their meeting in Washington.

He described the awesome power prosecutors wield, and stressed the need to use it responsibly. Prosecutors constantly have to choose which of the many possible cases they have the time and resources to prosecute. The choice should never be made based on public sentiment or personal whim; cases should be chosen for prosecution only if the offense was flagrant, the harm to the public the greatest, and the proof of guilt most certain.

Jackson continued:

> *If the prosecutor is obliged to choose his cases, it follows that he can choose his defendants. Therein is the most dangerous power of the prosecutor: that he will pick people that he thinks he should get, rather than pick cases that need to be prosecuted. With the law books filled with a great assortment of crimes, a prosecutor stands a fair chance of finding at least a technical violation of some act on the part*

of almost anyone. In such a case, it is not a question of discovering the commission of a crime and then looking for the man who has committed it, it is a question of picking the man and then searching the law books, or putting investigators to work, to pin some offense on him. It is in this realm, in which the prosecutor picks some person whom he dislikes or desires to embarrass, or selects some group of unpopular persons and then looks for an offense, that the greatest danger of abuse of prosecuting power lies. It is here that law enforcement becomes personal, and the real crime becomes that of being unpopular with the predominant or governing group, being attached to the wrong political views, or being personally obnoxious to or in the way of the prosecutor himself.

The words were eloquent and the sentiment was critical. Almost five decades later, D.C. Circuit Court judge Laurence Silberman (who had been deputy attorney general during most of the Watergate prosecutions) applied the Justice Jackson concern about selective prosecution to the newly minted phenomenon of the independent prosecutor.

Our concern is based on the self-evident proposition that the whole raison d'etre of the independent counsel is not to administer the criminal law across a whole population, but rather to focus on one individual or group of individuals targeted at the inception of the office. In effect, an entire self-sufficient government agency is created from scratch to investigate and perhaps prosecute a single individual.

When President Nixon nominated Elliot Richardson to be attorney general, he knew that he was committing himself to an independent resolution of the Watergate problem. The new attorney general was a proud—and prickly—man who had no special history with Nixon, and could not be considered a Nixon ally, much less a Nixon partisan.

Elliot Lee Richardson (Harvard, '41; Harvard Law, '44) was "Mr. Résumé" and a card-carrying member of the Eastern liberal wing of the Republican Party. He had clerked for Judge Learned Hand on the Second Circuit, and then for Supreme Court justice Felix Frankfurter. Then he worked on the staff of Massachusetts Republican senator Leverett Saltonstall. From 1956 to 1959 he was an assistant secretary in the Department of Health, Education and Welfare that had just been established by President Eisenhower. He left to become U.S. attorney in Massachusetts. He was elected lieutenant governor of Massachusetts in 1964, and in 1966 he was elected as the Commonwealth's attorney general.

In the Nixon administration, Richardson began as undersecretary of State in 1969. In 1970 he was named the secretary of HEW. Following Nixon's reelection in 1973, he had been appointed secretary of Defense; he had been at the Pentagon only three months when Nixon tapped him to take over as attorney general.

Richardson had had no connection whatsoever with Watergate, and there could not have been a more qualified choice than this distinguished, accomplished, erudite, and (not least important, given the nature of the times in Washington) eminently confirmable man.

Before he would accept the new appointment, Richardson insisted on the right to appoint, if he decided it was necessary, a special prosecutor—an independent and respected individual to assume the decision-making role with regard to any Watergate indictments. The request seemed reasonable, and even if it hadn't, at that point Nixon had almost no leverage. So he acquiesced.

The Senate Judiciary Committee, which would hold the confirmation hearings for the newly nominated attorney general, was chaired by an ag-ing grandee, James Eastland of Mississippi. In reality, as we have seen, the committee was hugely influenced, if not controlled outright, by Senator Edward Kennedy and his top assistant, Jim Flug. Kennedy and Flug pre-sumably already knew something that neither Richardson, nor Haig or anyone else on the president's staff, knew. They knew that John Dean was willing—indeed, was eager—to point the finger at his former White House colleagues, including the president, if it would gain him the immunity from prosecution that he so desperately wanted. If they could only prevent Dean's indictment, and prolong the ongoing investigations, they could weaken Nixon—and pave the way for Teddy Kennedy's expected 1976 presidential bid.

The first step was to remove Richardson from any role overseeing the

Watergate investigations, in order to neutralize any possible Republican influence or involvement in the creation of a special prosecutor's office to mount their assault on the Nixon presidency.

As Teddy Kennedy's biographer Adam Clymer writes:

> *Now Kennedy and Flug got heavily involved, telling Cox and Richardson that the charter proposed for Cox did not promise enough independence. With Richardson and his aides, they rewrote some key sections to enhance the counsel's ability to deal directly with Congress and to get the money he needed for his inquiry.*

As noted by the Democratic chief counsel of the House Judiciary Committee, "When Nixon first nominated Richardson, Kennedy was opposed, but Kennedy's opposition to Richardson evaporated as soon as Richardson agreed to appoint Cox as independent prosecutor."

The "Duties and Responsibilities of the Special Prosecutor" ("Guidelines") are reproduced in Appendix L and are well worth reading at this point. What seems startlingly likely in hindsight is that they were drafted with the benefit of Shaffer's insights into what Dean was willing to say—to assure that the special prosecutor would be able both to prevent Dean's indictment and to assemble and direct a Get Nixon Squad along the lines of Bobby Kennedy's Get Hoffa Squad. The fact that they didn't control the executive branch—that the attorney general's brother was not the president—required an assumption by the legislative branch of the investigatory and prosecutorial powers inherent within the Department of Justice, yet one entirely without any limit from its oversight or supervision.

The Guidelines gave Special Prosecutor Cox truly staggering power. In addition to all the prosecutorial authority possible, he was also guaranteed unlimited budget and manpower resources. He alone would decide what information was shared with Congress. He was granted authority over all other organizations within the Department of Justice—and not only for Watergate matters, but for "all offenses arising out of the 1972 presidential election for which the special prosecutor deems it necessary and appropriate to assume responsibility, allegations involving the President, members of the White House staff, or presidential appointees." Given the immediate threat of Dean's indictment by the Silbert team, authority over the offices of U.S. attorneys was also specifically included.

In short, by fiat of Kennedy Democrats on the Senate Judiciary Committee, Archibald Cox got ownership and control over all the prosecutorial powers of the executive branch. Whenever any question arose of reining in the full-scale assault later launched by Cox, it became clear that such a possibility had been contemplated and precluded in advance by those who had drafted the Guidelines. And that Richardson, without even realizing it, had given away all the powers of the presidency during his confirmation process.

It was an act unprecedented in our nation's history: Teddy Kennedy and his Senate Judiciary Committee cohorts caused the creation of a Get Nixon Squad within the Nixon Department of Justice, whose staffing was dominated by former members of Robert Kennedy's Justice Department, and whose focus was predominantly if not entirely political. Cox was the perfect person to head it—a card-carrying member of the Kennedy clan who had served in all three previous Democratic administrations, but who brought all the seeming independence, prestige, and Ivy-covered distinction of the Harvard Law School.

On Friday, May 26, 1973, Elliot Richardson was sworn in as America's sixty-ninth attorney general. The ceremony, hosted by the president and Mrs. Nixon, was held in the East Room of the White House. Chief Justice Warren Burger administered the oath. In his speech, Richardson said that a "kind of sleaziness" had undermined the processes of government, and he said he planned to eliminate it.

Later that same day, several blocks down Pennsylvania Avenue at the Department of Justice, another swearing in took place. In the fifth-floor office of the U.S. solicitor general—the office he had occupied during the Kennedy administration—Archibald Cox was sworn in as special prosecutor.

Although his hometown paper, the *Boston Globe,* buried his swearing in on the jump page of the Richardson story, it provided some particularly pertinent details.

> Cox, a Harvard Law School professor with long-standing ties to the Kennedy family, was sworn in by Senior Judge Charles Fahy of the US Circuit Court of Appeals here.

Ethel Kennedy, Senator Edward M. Kennedy, Kennedy aide James Flug and Samuel Dash, once Cox's student at Harvard and now chief counsel to the Senate Watergate investigating committee, joined Richard and his aides in applauding Cox's brief remarks. . . .

[Cox] said he was satisfied that "I have been given all the powers and independence any man could wish to perform the task that's been given to me."

The coverage in *The New York Times* identified Cox as "a lanky Harvard University law school professor with long-standing ties to the Kennedy family," and considered it pertinent to point out that Nixon had lost Massachusetts in the 1960, 1968, and 1972 presidential campaigns.

While some invitees clearly enjoyed themselves—the *St. Louis Post-Dispatch* reported that Ethel Kennedy "beamed" as she watched the swearing in—others thought it was in bad taste. Former solicitor general Erwin Griswold later said, "There were at least ten members of the Kennedy family present. And I thought it was a terrible mistake."

Only two weeks before his appointment, Cox had told an interviewer that he had serious philosophical and ideological differences with the Nixon administration. Henry Kissinger, who had known him at Harvard, told Nixon: "Cox will be a disaster. He has been fanatically anti-Nixon all the years I've known him."

Although the White House was officially silent on Cox and his swearing-in ceremony, there can be little doubt that Richard Nixon was starting to wonder just what the hell he had agreed to by signing off on Richardson's Kennedy-imposed choice for special prosecutor and his unprecedented guidelines.

Chapter 7 detailed some of the specific actions taken by the special prosecutor beginning May 29, 1973, his first official day in office. But let us also examine his actions of the prior week—after being publicly identified as Richardson's choice for special prosecutor but before being sworn in. Cox clearly was primed, even before assuming office, to take all possible steps to prevent any indictment of John Dean. Dean may have been guilty, he may have confessed, he may have reneged on his agreement to testify before the grand jury, but the Kennedy clan was not about to allow him to be indicted and ruin their plans for him before they even got started.

While Cox may have initially assumed that he would have a clean slate from which to begin his Watergate investigations, it soon became apparent that he was in imminent danger of been one-upped by career prosecutors in the U.S. Attorney's office, who were racing to wrap up the cover-up case they had broken.

It was going to take some pretty fancy footwork to change over from the idea of a single supervising special prosecutor to a prosecutorial staff of almost a hundred strong—but this is the week where that approach began to germinate, even as Cox could also see that opportunity slipping away because of the determination of the career prosecutors.

Thus, he must have been a very unhappy camper the morning Cox picked up the *Washington Post* and read that the three prosecutors were threatening to resign unless he consulted them about their case. Unnamed sources said that the prosecutors' plans to hand down additional Watergate indictments would be delayed for months if the special prosecutor insisted on starting everything from scratch. Cox called U.S. Attorney Titus and told him to bring his three loquacious prosecutors to a meeting in his temporary office that very afternoon.

Press secretary Doyle conveys the chilly atmosphere that prevailed.

> *The meeting lasted two and a half hours. The demands of the three men were never stated as demands but they were clear. Unless Cox gave them a quick vote of confidence and announced publicly that they would remain in charge of the cover-up case, they planned to resign.*
>
> *Cox told the three men [the prosecutors] he expected them to stay at their posts until relieved. To make sure that there would be no mis- understanding, he put it in writing.*
>
> *"The public interest requires you as honorable and responsible public officials to carry on while I am familiarizing myself with all that has been done; and at that time we can see what is the most ap- propriate for the future."*
>
> *When the next day's* Post *carried a story saying the three men had*

been given Cox's vote of confidence, Cox made public his letter to them. His private response was to call Jim Neal in Nashville.**

Doyle's spin is a little hard to swallow, especially in light of what we now know about Deep Throat, grand jury activity during April and May, Silbert's prosecution memo, the Titus exchange, and the whole series of steps being taken to prevent John Dean's pending indictment. Indeed, in Henry Petersen's August testimony before the Ervin Committee, he asserted, "The case was snatched out from under us when we had it 90 percent complete."

What is clear is that at this meeting, Cox had specifically ordered Harold Titus not to predict the timing of any indictments. But Titus, aware that his prosecutors had all but completed their case and not wanting to give up credit or control, went ahead and issued a press release stating that comprehensive indictments could be expected in as little as sixty days. His statement is reproduced in Appendix M and confirms the competition between the career prosecutors, who felt they had already solved the case, and the yet-to-be sworn in special prosecutor, who very much wanted to control when and how all that would come about.

The Cox side of this competition is revealed in the draft of a memo he sent Titus the following week. This draft, recently discovered in files Cox had left to the Harvard Law Library, contains a paragraph omitted from the final version—reproduced in Appendix N—that not only confirms he had "explicitly disapproved" any Titus statement, but also displays a decidedly unwelcome attitude toward the career prosecutors.

Three other actions within the Department of Justice on May 24 give some indication of the importance placed by the Kennedy clan on being absolutely sure that Dean would not be indicted.

First, an inventory of all pending cases anywhere within the Department

---

*Neal was Shaffer's cocounsel in the 1984 case that resulted in Hoffa's conviction for jury tampering and put the labor leader in jail. According to Doyle, Hoffa had called Neal "the most vicious prosecutor who ever lived." Given the fast moving circumstances of Cox's arrival and reaching out to Neal (who could only commit to two weeks of work), it is hard not to speculate that Neal's name had somehow been suggested by his former colleague.

involving political corruption was demanded. Second, Cox, determined to leave no base uncovered in this regard, wrote U.S. Attorney Titus that he expected all future actions to be cleared with him in advance. Third, Cox demanded copies of any prior authorizations for Titus to seek indictments. The abrupt nature of this memo is so telling that it is reproduced in Appendix O.

The most likely explanation for all of this is that Cox or his top two lieutenants had been put in touch with Charles Shaffer, either directly or through the Kennedy-Flug connection, and were buying time by moving forcefully to prevent Dean's indictment, while RFK's Get Hoffa Squad alumni were being reassembled for their new mission.

Now officially sworn in, and having taken steps to assure himself that no indictments would be issued over the Memorial Day weekend, Cox flew back to Boston to spend his first weekend as special prosecutor at home in Cambridge.

Archibald Cox didn't write a book about his six months as special prosecutor, so the only semiofficial record we have is that of his press officer, James Doyle. As Doyle relates, Cox had invited two of his fellow Harvard Law professors, James Vorenberg and Philip Heymann, to join him over the Memorial Day weekend in Cambridge to help think through his new responsibilities as Watergate special prosecutor. In fact, they had already been working during the previous week on staffing for his office. Doyle also suggests that Cox spent much of the weekend reading grand jury transcripts—which is strange, considering that John Dean, the president's principal accuser, had yet to appear before any grand jury.

Doyle describes two meetings on that Memorial Day Monday that involved outsiders.

On Monday, Cox accepted an invitation from a group of journalists, who were attending a reunion of the Society of Nieman Fellows at Harvard, to hold an off-the-record session with them. Among the papers represented in the faculty lounge of the deserted law school that holiday afternoon were *The New York Times,* the *Washington Post,* the *Boston Globe,* the *Los Angeles Times,* and the *Washington Star* (whose representative, reporter James Doyle, became Cox's press secretary, and whose later book provides the only description of this meeting).

The Nieman Foundation was begun in 1937 with a $1 million gift from Agnes Wahl Nieman, in honor of her late husband, the founder of the *Milwaukee Journal.* Its stated purpose is "to promote and elevate the standards of journalism in the United States and educate persons deemed especially qualified for journalism." By 1973, the program had evolved into a program of fellowships, whereby groups of some fifteen midcareer journalists get to spend a year at Harvard, doing pretty much as they please.

In the 1960s and '70s, when *The New York Times* dominated the newspaper business, and the three TV networks' evening news broadcasts dominated (and, arguably, dictated) the national agenda, rising journalists would be brought to Harvard not only for exposure to the latest left-liberal thinking, but also for the opportunity of making excellent contacts for the future sharing of interests. Exploring the Nieman Fellows program is not the purpose of this book, but that Cox would meet in a private session with a select group of them is highly suspect and disturbing as a first step in his newly assumed position heading a sensitive investigative operation where prosecutorial choices soon would have to be made.

While Doyle doesn't mention it, the meeting with Cox was most likely arranged by Anthony Lewis of *The New York Times,* a Nieman Fellow of the class of 1957, who, perhaps not coincidentally, wrote the introduction to Doyle's book. Lewis was known for having spent almost his entire fellowship year attending classes at the Harvard Law School—especially those taught by Archibald Cox. Subsequently, he had maintained an intimate relationship with Cox throughout the time he was RFK's solicitor general.

Is it purely coincidental—the result of everyone happening to be in Cambridge over the Memorial Day weekend—that Cox's first meeting after being named special prosecutor was with members of the press? Coincidental or not, it set the precedent for his subsequent conduct. While most prosecutors consider it proper—if not obligatory—to avoid the press until court filings make such exchanges appropriate, Cox was a professor who loved to talk. While his comments were almost always off-the-record— and usually involved responding to hypothetical situations posed by reporters—his accessibility provided the grist and background information for an endless stream of Watergate stories in the daily newspapers and on TV, many if not most of them highly prejudicial to those under investigation.

The other meeting that Memorial Day weekend was a detailed briefing for Cox, Heymann, and Vorenberg from Jim Flug. As we have seen, Flug had been instrumental in drafting the Guidelines that gave the special prosecutor his unbridled jurisdiction and authority; he had also attended Cox's swearing-in ceremony the previous Friday at the Department of Justice.

By now the message Jim Flug brought to Cambridge will sound familiar to the reader. He urged his audience of three not to concentrate solely on Watergate—what they were supposed to investigate—but rather, to cast the widest possible nets over other aspects of Nixon and his administration. The professors made notes and tried to draw diagrammatic representations of the topics and individuals Flug told them about. As James Doyle noted, "Flug was describing interrelationships but he had not suggested a clear and definable pattern." Doyle noted that one of the attendees saved his notes, and "they contained a tangle of lines that looked like a spider web, with the names of the various principals and suspected criminal activities slicing back and forth like the lines on an organization chart—for an organization gone mad."

Doyle, of course, is describing a meeting he didn't attend, and his description was written after all the Watergate trials had concluded. The chart that he describes isn't to be found in the special prosecutor's papers at the National Archives—but then neither are many papers from Archibald Cox, Philip Heymann, James Vorenberg, or James Doyle himself. Perhaps they just didn't generate any documents to speak of—which would make them the first lawyers and journalists in history not to generate documents to speak of, or otherwise. Or perhaps they thought it prudent to take their papers with them when they left government service.

Nonetheless, it doesn't take much imagination to figure out what Flug's briefing of the new special prosecutor and his top aides would cover. In those days before PowerPoint, Flug's points would not have lacked power. Not a man known for his diplomacy or politesse, his no-nonsense briefing could have gone something like this:

- From Charles Shaffer and others we know a lot about what Dean is willing to say that you may not yet be fully privy to—or fully appreciate. Dean is the most important guy in the picture, and it is vital that he be handled very gingerly. Let's examine what we have learned—and figure out the steps we think could best exploit this opportunity.

- Let's also go over the Guidelines, so you can fully appreciate the scope of the authority we crafted for you, including the unlimited nature of your budget. Let's examine, too, the expectations of your friends and admirers on the Senate Judiciary Committee and the Ervin Watergate Committee that you will work closely with in pursuing investigations. Don't get bogged down investigating the cover-up itself. That work is all essentially done. It is far more important that you exercise the authority we have given you to investigate every aspect of the Nixon presidency. Watergate should be only the tip of the iceberg. You should leave no stone unturned in looking into everything else that could be actually incriminating or even just embarrassing for the president and members of his administration.

This is, admittedly, pure speculation. But it is based on some known facts. First, it is hardly likely that Flug traveled to Harvard on a holiday weekend in order to meet for over two hours with Cox and his two most trusted advisers just to shoot the breeze; the circumstances indicate the need for urgency and privacy. Second, Sam Dash recorded Flug's advice at the time he was planning the activities of the Ervin Committee, and nothing had changed in the intervening two months as far as Flug's interests were concerned. Finally, because Flug had been instrumental in crafting the Guidelines, he would be the ideal person to conduct a tutorial on their unprecedented scope and nature.

Separately, well hidden within Cox's personal papers left to Harvard's Law School library is a May 31, 1973, memo from fellow professor John Hart Ely, the first page of which is reproduced in Appendix P, which begins following up their earlier conversation (which must have occurred the week prior), beginning with an analysis as to whether Cox could require President Nixon to appear before a grand jury. The remainder of Ely's analysis is not essential to conclude that Nixon was the target of the Harvard crew from the very outset.

Then, too, we have already examined the actions that Cox, Vorenberg, Heymann, and their staff started taking when they returned to Washington the next morning and began their first week on the job.

That Memorial Day weekend in Cambridge marked the end of the Camelot Conspiracy's planning phase. On Tuesday morning Cox and his two top aides returned to Washington ready, willing, and able to begin its implementation. His first step was a public statement, reproduced in Appendix Q, saying Cox alone was in charge and would be making all the decisions; and specifically noting that "the U.S. Attorney and his aides have been instructed to refrain from any kind of statement, comment or speculation about any aspect of the investigation."

12

Cox's Army of Ivy Leaguers

The Watergate Special Prosecution Force has been described as "Cox's Army." And an army it was, in terms of discipline, motivation, and, not least, its sheer size. Special Prosecutor Archibald Cox quickly assembled a staff of lawyers that was larger than eighty-eight of the ninety-six U.S. attorneys' offices all across the country.

The general attitude prevailing at Army HQ was captured in the meeting between Cox's administrative deputy, James Vorenberg, and Justice Department administrator Glen Pommerening, the assistant attorney general for administration who was in charge of establishing the WSPF's budget and staffing. Vorenberg described how they planned to organize task forces that could handle the currently known cases as well as anything else that arose in the course of their investigations. He outlined the numbers and qualification levels of the attorneys they would need.

Pommerening estimated that the price tag would be $1.2 million per year—a sizable amount for the Justice Department's budget. Vorenberg told him to add 50 percent. By one account Pommerening, whether reacting to the unprecedented size of the operation or the unmitigated attitude with which he was confronted, winced as he wrote down $1.8 million. Then Vorenberg told him to add another million dollars for office expenses.

A few weeks later, the WSPF's $2.8 million budget had passed Congress and Cox's Army very quickly got used to never hearing the word "no."

In a press conference on June 15, Vorenberg told the assembled reporters that the WSPF would probably hire between fifty and seventy-five people. Perhaps he was just tired out from all the heavy negotiating with Pommerening, and forgot that the budget he had established was based on ninety hires—the number that he had been projecting from day one, and that he eventually exceeded.

Some of the ninety staff slots were supposed to be filled by investigators, but the special prosecutor soon found that there was a virtually unlimited supply of FBI and IRS agents available for that purpose. With this constraint removed, even more lawyers could be hired to supervise even more investigations. By the end of the summer, the WSPF had filled eighty of the ninety intended slots. Publicly they admitted to having thirty-eight lawyers, a number carefully adhered to in all subsequent public statements.

When Nixon agreed to the appointment of a special supervising prosecutor, he had envisaged it as a good-faith gesture—a token of his willingness to let Richardson's investigations be carried on independently. It was likely that some senior administration officials would be indicted, and a respected lawyer, placed over both the U.S. attorney's office and the Criminal Division of the Justice Department and reporting directly to the attorney general, could be very useful for making those sensitive calls.

Nixon, whose political antennae were highly sensitized, and whose survival skills were legendary, was clearly blindsided by the transformation of this kind of supervising prosecutor into a special prosecutor leading an army of politically motivated lawyers intent on aggressively investigating every aspect of his administration. Crimes had clearly been committed in connection with the Watergate break-in and cover-up. But they were now being used as the pretext for investigating everyone and everything involved with every aspect of the Nixon administration's first five years—all on the chance that additional actions of a questionable nature might be uncovered, and the reputations of additional Republicans tarnished.

The growth of Cox's Army to almost a hundred strong puts the twenty special assistants on RFK's Get Hoffa Squad in the shade. It also provides an idea of the sheer size of the Kennedy clan's Get Nixon initiative. A review of WSPF personnel files suggests at least sixty lawyers served in some capacity during the WSPF's four-year life.

At the time, few outside of the Kennedy clan really knew what Dean had done during the cover-up, or what he was now willing to say. Only in retrospect can we appreciate the magnitude of the transformation of the idea of a supervising Watergate prosecutor into an in-house Get Nixon Squad.

Nixon's aversion to Ivy Leaguers was long-standing and based on personal experience. Throughout his career he had been all but uniformly condemned—and his character all but uniformly aspersed—by the traditional Eastern elite products of the Ivy League universities and the establishment institutions. This became particularly acute during Nixon's term as president. Opposition to the Vietnam War radicalized many students at the elite Eastern Ivy League schools, whose protests already had driven President Lyndon Johnson from seeking a second term. Nixon, whose methods of ending the war—especially the midnight bombing of Cambodia—made him in their eyes a war criminal, was hated with a vitriol of historic proportions.

The disdain was fully reciprocated. As the president put it on tape, "The guys from the best families are most likely to develop that arrogance that puts them above the law. If they're from any Eastern schools or Berkeley, those are particularly the potential bad ones."

Of course, Nixon wasn't alone in this regard. William F. Buckley, Jr., made the same point when he famously quipped that he would "rather entrust the government of the United States to the first four hundred people listed in the Boston telephone directory than to the faculty of Harvard University." Richard Nixon was determined to place his non-Ivy mark on Washington. As president he made a point of (and took pride in) appointing administration officials from non-Ivy schools. One aide compiled a list of the educational backgrounds of U.S. ambassadors as a preliminary to purging any Ivy from the ranks.

In 1973, while meeting with Governor Ronald Reagan of California, Nixon received a call from a former Vietnam POW, colonel Robinson Risner, who had spent four of his seven years of captivity in solitary confinement. After the call Nixon emotionally said to Reagan, "Compare these fine men with those sniveling Ivy Leaguers," who, in the ultimate put-down from the meat-and-potatoes president, "played with each other in frilly sports—squash and crew."

We already know most of the senior WSPF staff from their work in RFK's Department of Justice—and the contrast is startling:

Office of the Special Prosecutor

ARCHIBALD COX (Harvard, '34; Harvard Law, '37; clerk for Judge Learned Hand) was a Triple Crown Kennedy clan confidant. He had headed JFK's issues analysis and speech-writing teams during the 1960 campaign; he was second in command in RFK's Department of Justice as solicitor general; and he had worked closely with Teddy Kennedy on numerous matters, particularly the campaigns to defeat Nixon's Supreme Court nominees (including Haynsworth and Carswell, who were defeated, and Berger, Powell, and Rehnquist, who were confirmed). The most recent exchange of Cox-Kennedy correspondence—concerning the landmark Supreme Court abortion ruling *Roe v. Wade*—had occurred less than a month before Cox was named special prosecutor.

Cox's first two appointments were his closest colleagues from the Harvard Law School: Philip Heymann (Yale, '54; Harvard Law, '60; clerk for Justice John Marshall Harlan), his former student, who had served with him in RFK's solicitor general office; and James Vorenberg (Harvard, '49; Harvard Law, '51; clerk to Justice Felix Frankfurter), who had headed RFK's Office of Criminal Justice and written position papers for George McGovern's 1972 presidential campaign. These two were instrumental in completing the staffing and establishing the direction of the fledgling special prosecutor's office before they returned to Harvard in the fall of 1973. Vorenberg came back to Washington in August 1974 to help with the possible indictment of Richard Nixon following his resignation, and again in the fall of 1975 as primary author of the *Watergate Special Prosecution Force Report*.

According to Doyle:

> The special prosecutor, Vorenberg, and Heymann had been working on the staffing problem from the day Cox was named, relying at first on people they knew personally. They wanted lawyers to start work

immediately, long before the FBI could finish background checks on them. The best way to avoid embarrassing mistakes would be to have people known to be trustworthy. Cox had one confidant screen West Coast applicants and another examine the large pool of attorneys practicing in Manhattan. Vorenberg spent most of his time on the personnel problem.

It is certainly reassuring to know the reason why vast numbers of WSPF hires were from RFK's Department of Justice and/or Harvard and other Ivy League law schools was in order to avoid "embarrassing mistakes." One might otherwise worry that they were recruiting their friends to be sure there would be a uniform understanding and appreciation of the potential and purpose of the WSPF's Get Nixon agenda.

PETER M. KREINDLER (Harvard, '67; Harvard Law, '71; clerk for Justice William O. Douglas) was hired as Cox's executive assistant.

HENRY S. RUTH, JR. (Yale, '52; Penn Law, '55), deputy special prosecutor, had served as a special attorney in the Organized Crime section of RFK's Department of Justice, as well as in the Office of Criminal Justice in the deputy attorney general's office.

CARL B. FELDBAUM (Princeton, '66; Penn Law, '69), hired as Ruth's executive assistant, had been his student at Penn.

PHILIP A. LACOVARA (Georgetown, '63; Columbia Law, '66), WSPF counsel, was deputy solicitor general, having joined the Justice Department in 1966.

JAMES S. DOYLE (Boston College, '56; Harvard Nieman Fellow, '65) was Cox's special assistant for public affairs. He claimed he was hired as press secretary with the understanding that he would write about his experiences. Perhaps this is why there are virtually no records of his work in files at the National Archives—he took them with him to write his book, *Not Above the Law: The Battles of Watergate Prosecutors Cox and Jaworski: A Behind-the-Scenes Account*, published in 1977.

Task Force Heads

JAMES F. NEAL (University of Wyoming, '52; Vanderbilt Law, '57; Georgetown Masters of Law '60), head of the Watergate Task Force, had been personally hired by RFK onto the Get Hoffa Squad, and had been cocounsel (with Dean's lawyer, Charles Shaffer) in two of the key Hoffa trials.

RICHARD H. BEN-VENISTE (Muhlenberg, '64; Columbia Law, '67), Neal's deputy on the Watergate Task Force, came from the U.S. attorney's office in the Southern District of New York, where he had specialized in organized crime and racketeering cases, including the *Sweig* case.

THOMAS F. McBRIDE (NYU, '52; Columbia Law, '56), head of the Campaign Contributions Task Force, was another former member of RFK's Criminal Division. His deputy was Charles Ruff (Swarthmore '60, Columbia Law '63), who had been a member of the Organized Crime Section of RFK's Criminal Division.

WILLIAM H. MERRILL (Dartmouth, '47; Yale Law, '50), head of the Plumbers Task Force, had been chief assistant U.S. attorney in Michigan under Robert Kennedy and Lyndon Johnson, had run for Congress in Michigan in 1966, and was chairman of Michigan Citizens for Robert Kennedy in the 1968 campaign.

RICHARD J. DAVIS (Harvard, '65; Columbia Law, '69), head of the Political Espionage Task Force, had worked with Ben-Veniste and Peter F. Rient in the U.S. Attorney's office in New York.

JOSEPH J. CONNOLLY (Penn, '62; Penn Law, '65), head of the ITT Task Force, was the son of a congressman from the Philadelphia suburbs. He was the WSPF's most prominent Republican, but his work history included time at the Pentagon under Robert McNamara and as a staff member on President Lyndon Johnson's Crime Commission (Commission on Law Enforcement and Administration of Justice). Connolly was the only task force head to resign in protest—when his indictment recommendations were not followed.

Other WSPF Staff Counsel

Although arguably the principal reason for WSPF's creation, the Watergate Task Force itself consisted of only six other lawyers: George T. Frampton, Jr. (Yale, '61; Harvard Law, '69; clerk to Supreme Court justice Harry Blackmun); Gerald Goldman (Harvard, '65; Harvard Law, '68; clerk to Supreme Court justice William Brennan); Jill Wine Volner (University of Illinois, '64; Columbia Law, '68), who also had spent five years in the Organized Crime and Racketeering Section of the DOJ's Criminal Division, joining under then attorney general Ramsey Clark; Peter F. Rient (Harvard, '60, Harvard Law, '63), former chief appellate attorney in the U.S. attorney's office in New York, where he worked with Ben-Veniste; Lawrence Iason II (NYU Law School, '71); and Judith Ann Denny (George Washington Law, '72).

The rest were assigned to other investigators.

A determined effort was made to claim great diversity among WSPF attorneys, but this was either wishful thinking or outright prevarication. In addition to the twenty key staff members described above another eighteen held degrees from Harvard, Yale, or Columbia:

HARVARD
John F. Barker, '63
Mary E. Graham, '71
Janet Johnson, '67
David H. Kaye, '69

HARVARD LAW
Nathaniel H. Akerman, '72
Philip J. Bakes, Jr., '71
Charles R. Breyer, '63
Stephen G. Breyer, '64
Kenneth S. Geller, '71
Sidney M. Glazer, '48

Stephen E. Haberfeld, '70
Henry L. Hecht, '73
Jay S. Horowitz, '67
John G. Koeltl, '71
James L. Quarles III, '72
Roger M. Witten, '72

YALE LAW
Hamilton P. Fox, '70

COLUMBIA LAW
Robert L. Palmer, '71

The Watergate Special Prosecution Force took great umbrage at White House accusations that their group consisted primarily of partisan Democrats. Yet Sam Ervin himself acknowledged that seven (Cox, Heymann, Vorenberg, Ruth, Neal, Miller, and McBride) of its eight senior attorneys had served in Robert Kennedy's Department of Justice. It also is instructive that the only WSPF attorneys who have served in subsequent presidential administrations have only done so in those of Democratic presidents.

We have already noted Attorney General Robert Jackson's and Judge Laurence Silberman's warnings about the dangers of selective prosecution. Let's take a look at a sample of the WSPF's actions that should arouse such concern.

The WSPF's initial approach—set by Cox, Heymann, and Vorenberg, apparently under Flug's tutelage—was to undertake a full-scale review of every allegation of wrongdoing lodged against the Nixon administration. This was confirmed in press conferences by Cox and Vorenberg—who even invited members of the public to send in allegations of wrongdoing, and promised that each and every one would be investigated.

Only eight of the Watergate special prosecutor's attorneys were actually assigned to the Watergate Task Force. The remaining two score and more were assigned to other areas of investigation. This lopsided allocation of resources reflected two facts. First, the Watergate case had already been made by the federal prosecutors; at this point it was more of a mopping-up exercise than an ongoing operation. Second, with the Kennedy element now factored into the equation, there was a higher priority on uncovering additional areas that might be ripe for prosecution, and would allow the onslaught against the Nixon administration and the Republican Party to continue as long as possible into the 1976 presidential election cycle.

Some of the headings from the WSPF 1975 Report indicate just how wide the nets were cast:

- "Dirty Tricks" Investigation
- Investigations Relating to International Telephone and Telegraph Corporation (ITT)
- "Plumbers" Investigation
- Other Break-in Investigations
- Wiretap Investigations

- Alleged Abuse of Federal Agencies
- Investigations of Alleged Mistreatment of Demonstrators
- Investigations of President Nixon's Tax Returns
- Investigations of 1972 Campaign Financing and Related Matters
- Investigations of Alleged Sale of Ambassadorships
- "Townhouse" Investigation
- Milk Fund Investigation
- Hughes-Rebozo Investigation
- National Hispanic Finance Committee Investigation

This list identifies only those investigations the WSPF acknowledged publicly. As we shall see, there were many others.

The grand jury was originally conceived as a protection for ordinary citizens. Before subjecting the accused to an actual trial, a prosecutor would have to convince a group of laymen that sufficient evidence existed to prove that a crime had been committed. The intention was noble, but the practice, inevitably, led to abuses.

David Burnham succinctly expresses the problem.

> *Despite the homage repeatedly paid to grand juries, lawyers have long joked that any prosecutor worth his salt could get a grand jury to indict a ham sandwich. More than twenty years ago, in an analytical article based on his years of experience as a federal prosecutor and judge in Chicago, the late William J. Campbell put it well: "Today, the grand jury is the total captive of the prosecutor, who, if he is candid, will concede that he can indict anybody, at any time, for almost anything, before any grand jury."*

Burnham also cites Stuart Taylor, an attorney and former Supreme Court correspondent for *The New York Times*, who summarized the situation succinctly:

> *"Would this license to rummage through anyone and everyone's papers on demand, without probable cause and virtually without*

limitation, in total secrecy and without judicial supervision, sound reasonable if rephrased to describe what is going on?" Taylor asked. *"Try crossing out 'grand jury' everywhere those words appear, substituting 'the politically appointed federal prosecutor,' and read it again."*

Being summoned before a grand jury must be a terrifying experience, especially if criminal conduct is known to have occurred in your workplace. You testify alone, because your own lawyer—and you should have retained your own lawyer if you fear that any of your former colleagues have become suspects—cannot accompany you into the grand jury room. It is a cumulative nightmare comprising the cost of your lawyer quietly probing, for hour after billable hour, everything you have done, seen, or said, in order to determine if you could somehow be at risk by indirection or association; the sleepless nights worrying that you might actually know something significant without realizing it; the research and brain wracking to be sure that you remember anything that might possibly be the subject of the prosecutor's questioning; and testifying with the possibility that you might later be accused of perjury.

Judge Learned Hand, dissenting in *U.S. vs. Remington,* in 1953 observed: "Save for torture, it would be hard to find a more effective tool of tyranny than the power of unlimited and unchecked *ex parte* examination."

But surely, you may be thinking, distinguished men from the Harvard Law School faculty wouldn't think of abusing grand jury investigatory powers—and certainly not for political purposes. Three internal memos from the WSPF's files may trouble you in this regard.

The first is one from Philip Heymann to William Merrill and James Neal, and dated July 24, 1973, reproduced in Appendix R, which urges development of a list of all staff assistants, special assistants, or other personnel associated with principal Watergate or Plumbers figures, so they can all be brought in for interviews. Given the scope of Haldeman's and Ehrlichman's responsibilities, this would have included Nixon's entire White House staff.

That's right, he's arguing: Let's go after all the young staff assistants we can find, and squeeze them to see what they might tell us about their bosses. Who knows what might turn up about Watergate, about the Plumbers, or about anything else that might pop out? It seems clear from Neal's memo quoted below that "being interviewed" was rather clearly a WSPF euphemism for a grand jury summons—so what this proposal amounted to was organizing a pogrom of Nixon staffers.

A week later, on July 30, 1973, Neal wrote a memo to Ben-Veniste, Frampton, Goldman, Haberfeld, Iason, Geller, and Volner that put some flesh on the Heymann memo's bare bones:

> *The first list below [naming 47 people] identifies those individuals I think should be interviewed or re-interviewed and/or taken before the grand jury. The information I recollect the individual is alleged to possess relevant to our investigation [many contain only the notation "De-brief generally"].*
>
> *The second list [of about 24 names, with many redacted] below contains those individuals we need to put before the grand jury either without an interview in advance or following an interview.*

Finally, there is Neal's advice to this same group the following week, dated August 6, 1973:

> *I will be in the office only intermittently over the next two or three weeks. During this period you should interview and/or put before the grand jury those individuals listed on my memorandum of July 30, 1973, as well as the following [6] additions.*
>
> *In the course of an office interview you may have some question whether the interviewee should be put before the grand jury. You may conclude that it is a matter for the grand jury, because it adds an important bit of evidence to our case or because you may question whether the witness is telling the truth. In all events if there is any question in your mind, put the interviewee before the grand jury.*

Richard Ben-Veniste, self-described in his own book (*Stonewall: The Real Story of the Watergate Prosecution*) as hard-nosed and cocky in court, would have been in high dudgeon (and hog heaven) grilling Nixon associates in the secrecy of the grand jury, where no opposing counsel or effective judicial supervision could curb his aggressive instincts. Here, at last, away from prying eyes, he could really tear into people foolish enough to have accepted jobs in Nixon's White House, or with his reelection committee. These memos, and Ben-Veniste's prior known conduct, might lead others to conclude that Archibald Cox's office of special prosecution had become an office of special persecution.

At least American citizens can depend on having their rights protected, because grand jury investigations are held in absolute secrecy. No one will ever know that you were called, much less what you said. Unfortunately, the WSPF's operation was run differently. There were frequent and massive leaks of grand jury testimony. Muckraking columnist Jack Anderson printed grand jury transcripts in his syndicated newspaper column. We also know that Special Prosecutor Cox confided grand jury information to Senator Kennedy. It finally reached the point where even Judge Sirica, a man with many friends in the press, felt it necessary to convene a special meeting of all district court judges to reemphasize the importance of maintaining grand jury secrecy.

13

Friends in High Places:
The Strange and Unusual Handling
of William O. Bittman, Esq.

As we have seen, a primary focus of John Dean's cover-up initiative was directed toward convincing the seven original Watergate defendants to plead guilty, in order to avoid a trial that might uncover the real story behind the break-in.

His principal avenue of approach to these defendants was through their lawyers. Howard Hunt was the leader of the group, and his lawyer was William O. Bittman. As a young man recently out of Fordham Law School, Bittman had enjoyed fifteen minutes of fame that brought him favor with the Kennedy clan by stepping in at the last minute to join the prosecutorial team that chalked up one of the two convictions that sent Jimmy Hoffa to jail. Nailing Hoffa—especially after such a "battle-field promotion"—assured Bittman a platinum life membership in the Kennedy clan. Bill Bittman was now a made man, and RFK soon rewarded him by assigning him as lead investigator on the Bobby Baker case. This required considerable discretion and finesse, because the spectacularly corrupt Senate aide Baker was a long-standing Texas crony of LBJ's who had helped out many Democrats over the years. (In fact, Robert Kennedy was pursuing such a risky investigation partly to keep Johnson in line, by reminding him who held the cards.) Baker resigned under pressure. The Kennedys admired—and owed—Bill Bittman, big time.

Now, after a decade in private practice as one of Washington's power lawyers, at the respected firm of Hogan & Hartson, Bill Bittman found himself in big trouble, thanks to Watergate. He had crossed a line and become involved in the cover-up himself. He had relayed Howard Hunt's demands for money to John Dean, Chuck Colson, and CRP officials; he had received and distributed the monies paid in response to his demands; and he had worked with and among lawyers for the CRP and the other Watergate defendants, encouraging them to enter guilty pleas. In November 1972 he had been given a memo from Hunt to deliver to Colson, and then actually met with him on Hunt's behalf on January 3, 1973. He had clearly gone well beyond representing his clients' interests, by actually participating in the cover-up himself—and everyone in the special prosecutor's office soon knew it.

One indication of the degree to which Bill Bittman had crossed the line are the twenty-two boxes of WSPF investigatory files on him at the National Archives. What to do with Bill Bittman—and the serious problems he raised involving legal ethics, fairness, credibility, and consistency, balanced against loyalty to the Kennedy clan, with its past glories and ongoing interests—became the subject of considerable discussion and debate within the WSPF offices.

Here are a few examples from internal WSPF documents that detail the kinds of questions raised and considerations applied to the Bittman dilemma.

- Details of Bittman's involvement with the cover-up were enumerated in Silbert's transition memo of June 7, 1973.
- In Peter Kreindler's memo to Neal of June 14, 1973, the last item deals with Bittman.
  "Bittman—Bittman's involvement in the collection and distribution of funds from CRP appears suspicious. It was decided to call him in for an interview. He will be told no decision has been reached as to whether an indictment against him will be sought."
- James Neal's memo to Cox of August 16, 1973, urges.

Friends in High Places   149

"Finally, we should begin to give thought to complicated problems
such as the method of handling John Dean and Gordon Strachan
and such problems as whether Bittman, [Kenneth] Parkinson and
Kalmbach are witnesses or defendants." [Everyone else mentioned—
except Bittman—was subsequently indicted.]

- Ben-Veniste memo to his prosecution team of January 8, 1974, notes:
"The Watergate Task Force is scheduled to meet with Mr. Jaworski
on Friday, January 11, at 4:00 to discuss Mr. Bittman."
- Frampton memo to Jaworski of January 11, 1974, states:
"Bittman was a key figure in two of the most important areas of the
cover-up: the payment of cash to the defendants in exchange for the
silence regarding both the Watergate operation and other possibly
illegal activities; and the extension of assurances to Hunt concerning
the time he would have to spend in jail, also in consideration of his
continued silence."
- Ben-Veniste memo to Jaworski of January 28, 1974, states:
"The Watergate Task Force would like to meet with you on the
afternoon of Thursday, January 31, 1974 to discuss the status of
Gordon Strachan, William O. Bittman, Kenneth Parkinson,
Charles Colson, Herbert Kalmbach, and John Caulfield." [Again,
everyone else mentioned—except Bittman—was subsequently indicted.]
- Frampton memo to Ben-Veniste of January 29, 1974, notes:
"Since our discussions two weeks ago with Mr. Jaworski about the
status of William Bittman, we have been attempting to pinpoint
with some precision the elements of the Government's direct case
against Bittman. In the course of this effort, we have developed important new evidence against Bittman."
- Watergate Task Force status summary of March 4, 1974, notes:
"Bittman attorney-client litigation? Consider charges against Bittman."
- Lacovara memo to Ben-Veniste of February 6, 1974, entitled "Possible
Charges Against William Bittman," also makes an explicit case. The
memo is reproduced in Appendix S and is well worth reading because its
single paragraph makes a most persuasive case—and puts the full weight

of Lacovara's considerable reputation behind the effort to include Bittman in the comprehensive cover-up indictment.*

- Ben-Veniste, Jill Volner, and George Frampton memo of February 7,
  1974, to Bittman witness file, memorializing points covered in that afternoon's meeting with Bittman and his counsel, Herbert Miller.
- Frampton memo to Bittman witness file of February 12, 1974, memorializing the conversations that he and Ben-Veniste had that day and the
  day before with Silbert, Glanzer, and Campbell about Bittman's role—or
  lack thereof—in attempting to secure Hunt's cooperation with prosecutors.
- Neal memo to file of November 2, 1974, recounting communications
  with Hogan & Hartson firm.

Bittman was not included in the Watergate cover-up indictments un-
sealed on March 1, 1974, but he did testify before the House Judiciary
Committee impeachment inquiry hearings on July 9, 1974, and was a witness at the cover-up trial itself later that fall. Shortly after Bittman's trial
testimony, the special prosecutors were approached by Bittman's partners at
Hogan & Hartson, his former law firm, stating that they were aware of the
Hunt memo to Colson of November 13, 1972, but now realized that it had
been removed from their files prior to being microfilmed. Knowing of this
communication, Bittman approached the special prosecutors later that
same afternoon and provided them with a copy of the secreted memo. Realizing Bittman's subterfuges, the special prosecutors again considered
whether he should be indicted for false statements and perjury. (The memo
itself, never actually delivered to Colson, was seen by prosecutors as clear

---

*Lacovara and Ben-Veniste are both graduates of Columbia Law School—not the
Kennedys' Harvard—and do not appear to have bought into the idea of limiting
cover-up indictments solely to Nixon loyalists. They are legitimately making the
case that Bittman's criminal involvement is part and parcel of the conspiracy. Their
senior colleagues, most of whom had worked with and knew Bittman, realized that
including him in the indictments would confuse the jury—and the public—by allowing the impression that there had been criminal activity that wasn't directly related to Nixon and the Republican Party. Separately, Lacovara's analysis regarding
separate motives within a single conspiracy is also instructive with regard to any
Kennedy conspiracy.

evidence that Hunt himself viewed the CRP payments as an exchange for his continued silence.)

- Neal, Ben-Veniste, Volner, and Frampton memo to the file of the same date, recounting a subsequent meeting with Bittman (apparently without his own counsel present). Bittman was advised of his rights, and allowed to make a statement. The memo continues:

  "After this Mr. Bittman and I [Neal] had a frank conversation in which I told Mr. Bittman he had repeatedly misled us during the summer of 1973 because I had repeatedly asked him during that summer in the presence of a number of people if he had any information that Mr. Hunt thought the matter of commitments was a two-way street, that is, that Mr. Hunt was remaining silent in exchange for funds and he repeatedly assured me he had no such information. I also pointed out that Mr. Bittman never at any time disclosed the contents or existence of this memorandum to me even though he was admittedly aware of it in the summer of 1973. Mr. Bittman stated that he did not believe he had misled me and he wished to make a review of the files and a complete statement of this matter at some later time as soon as possible to do so. I also reported to Mr. Bittman my frank opinion that from the time he was aware of the contents of this memo he must have known no attorney-client privilege attached because it indicated an on-going offense at the time he received it and at the time he became aware of its contents. I further stated to him that I could not see any reasonable person believing this was a privileged communication in view of its contents and that I thought he was guilty of withholding relevant information at best."

- Ben-Veniste memo to Henry S. Ruth (who had become the special prosecutor when Jaworski resigned) of January 6, 1975, entitled, "Additional Prosecution," detailing reasons for prosecuting Bittman.
- Frampton memo to Ruth of the above date, also recommending Bittman's prosecution.
- Volner memo of March 4, 1975, summarizing the details of Bittman's proposed prosecution.

- Volner memo to Ruth of April 15, 1974, entitled, "Addendum to Bittman Pros Memo of 3/4/75," expanding on the most promising counts that had been identified in their meeting of March 10, to review and discuss a possible Bittman prosecution.
- Draft Bittman indictment for perjury dated May 7, 1975, by WSPF attorney William J. Gilbreth.
- Analysis of count 2 against Bittman dated June 26, 1975, by Kenneth Geller.
- Kenneth Geller memo to files dated June 1975, entitled, "Bittman Investigation—Expected Proof."*

In the end, however, Bittman was never indicted—neither along with the original Watergate cover-up conspirators, nor later when, despite his attempts to conceal it, a fuller understanding of his unique role had become clear. There are memos by Jaworski and Ruth stating their conclusions as to why no such indictments were sought, but they read as somewhat less than candid and as having been written with the record in mind—especially when compared with the extensive description of the intense internal debates recounted by Doyle:

> Bittman particularly became the focus of a spirited debate. He was strongly recommended for inclusion in the cover-up charges by all the lawyers on the Watergate Task Force and by counsel Philip Lacovara. . . .
> Bittman had been inextricably involved in the passing of requests from Hunt and the passing of money to Hunt. His evasive testimony, his demeanor, and gradually developing information contradicting his story on small points made him a more and more suspicious figure.

---

*It is also important to appreciate that since Bittman was never indicted, all investigative records remained under seal. Thus, none of the above memos could be reviewed by National Archives staff, let alone be made available to the public, until after his death in March 2001. In point of fact, none of them had been reviewed by anyone until my Freedom of Information Act (FOIA) request was submitted in late 2005.

Doyle himself must have felt the decision was exceptional enough to require some kind of explanation. He lists two possible considerations: first, that Bittman was a partner in Hogan & Hartson, Sirica's former law firm, and his indictment might have forced Sirica to recuse himself from presiding at the cover-up trial. Having to choose between keeping Sirica on the bench and bringing one of the most pivotal cover-up conspirators (and a bent attorney, at that) to justice would have been a no-brainer for the Kennedy cohorts. Given Sirica's consistent pro-prosecution rulings, this wouldn't even have been a close call—only an unethical one.

Second, Doyle speculates that because Bittman was Neal's friend and former colleague, his indictment would have precluded Neal from assuming his expected role as lead prosecutor at trial. But if this were the case, it should have had the reverse effect, and Bittman should have been included precisely to avoid charges of favoritism, and even the appearance of impropriety.

But these memos are after-the-fact justifications. One suspects that there were two at least equally persuasive reasons for omitting Bittman from the indictments. First, he was not only a member of the Kennedy clan's inner circle, but one of its bona fide idols. The clan's ethos required standing up for fellow members right or wrong; in fact, solidarity was all the more important when they were wrong. It is more than likely that this is the principal reason Bill Bittman got a pass from RFK's old boy network.

Second, from the point of view of the Camelot conspirators, including Bittman would have complicated their scenario for the cover-up trial. The carefully crafted case to be presented had been streamlined of complexities, and simplified for a jury to understand: Nixon and his men did it, and John Dean's testimony proves it. The unexpected appearance of a Kennedy clan member among the indictees might have led to uncomfortable questions or unwanted paths to follow. Given Bittman's documented and undeniable role in supplying hush money, what might prevent a jury from deciding that his actions were far more culpable than those of Haldeman or Ehrlichman, whose connections were far less certain and far more circumstantial—and, perhaps more important, far more difficult to prove? The Kennedy Clan Democrats wanted juries to see Haldeman and Ehrlichman at the guilty end of the spectrum, not somewhere in between that could require them to apply interpretations and make judgment calls.

Interestingly, Ben-Veniste and Frampton, in their book, recount what they admit was their brilliant and tough direct examination of Bittman as the government's witness in the cover-up trial, but somehow neglect to mention the part they played in the WSPF's great internal struggle over whether to indict him. This glaring omission of their unsuccessful efforts to indict Bittman not only undermines the forthrightness and credibility of their book, but also raises the question of what further steps members of the Watergate Task Force might have taken, given their uniform advocacy of Bittman's indictment.

Another interesting case is that of Gerald Alch (Harvard, '54; Boston University Law, '57), who was Watergate burglar James McCord's lawyer.

McCord concluded fairly early on that Alch was far more interested in getting him to plead guilty—as a result of pressure from Dean and Bittman—than in defending his interests, so much so that McCord fired Alch just shortly after the trial's conclusion. When he wrote his letter to Judge Sirica, McCord undoubtedly thought that he would get a break for his candor and honesty—specifically, the new trial that he requested. Postponing Dean's indictment was the Kennedy clan's goal, and allowing McCord (as well as Hunt and the Cubans, who filed similar new trial motions) to have a new trial could only serve to stir things up, so Cox vehemently opposed McCord's motion, saying he could have spoken up sooner. McCord then revised his argument to claim that he would have spoken up sooner but for the fact that his attorney, Gerald Alch, had led him astray. His request was once again rejected. Much later—in November 1974, roughly in the middle of the cover-up trial—his persistent belief that he had been wronged culminated in a second letter to Judge Sirica.

The second McCord letter, which represented scarcely less of a bombshell than its predecessor, was ignored by Judge Sirica, and received no known attention from the media.

In McCord's view, Alch and Bittman had not only been passive participants in the cover-up conspiracy by having encouraged him to plead guilty; they had, in fact, double-teamed him on January 8, 1973, the first day of the break-in trial. McCord's second letter makes several significant charges. Because it is so pertinent, and because its existence has been completely ignored, I will quote its numbered paragraphs at some length:

1. *Perjury was committed by my former attorney, Gerald Alch, before the Senate Watergate [Ervin] Committee on May 23, 1973, in matters involving him and Mr. William O. Bittman on January 8, 1973, in connection with discussions about executive clemency by Alch with me that day, at Bittman's request according to Alch. . . .*

3. *I believe that both Alch and Bittman perjured themselves before a federal grand jury on this subject—otherwise had they admitted the true events and discussions which had occurred with me on January 8, 1973, and between themselves on that date, both would have been indicted. . . .*

7. *It is interesting to note that none of the men involved in this conspiracy on that day, January 8, 1973, have been indicted by the Special Prosecutors—not Bittman, not Alch, not Caulfield [who also had contacted McCord in an attempt to convince him to plead guilty].*

Yet their acts were a part of the conspiratorial chain of overt acts of that day, and of Caulfield and Ulasewicz's illegal contacts with McCord which were to follow. Ulasewicz in fact admitted before the Senate that his contact with McCord on January 8, 1973, was an obstruction of justice. [Like Caulfield, Tony Ulasewicz was a former New York Police Department officer used by the White House for various private political matters.] SSC Book I, p 291. . . .

13. *My allegations in the above paragraphs both about Alch and Bailey and about Bittman have always fallen on deaf ears with the Special Prosecutors. [Bailey was F. Lee Bailey, who was Alch's partner.]*

The Special Prosecutors have in fact undertaken to defend in writing before the Court of Appeals the actions of Gerald Alch [probably a reference to WSPF opposition to McCord's motion for a new trial], rather than to probe the conflicts between his sworn testimony and my own.

Never have the Special Prosecutors called me before the grand jury either to prove these conflicts, and the involvement of Bittman, or about anything else. They appear to want to keep the grand jury record free of anything I might say. . . .

15. Special Prosecutor Richard Ben-Veniste indicated to me during his pre-trial interviews of late August 1974 that he wanted me to conceal the role of Gerald Alch as the first person from whom I had heard the words executive clemency mentioned in early October, 1972, immediately after Alch had come from a meeting in Bittman's office.

Ben-Veniste indicated further in October 1974 during a telephone call with me that he had no interest in the origins of the mention of executive clemency to me in early October 1972. My words to Ben-Veniste at that time were to the effect that I did not trust Ben-Veniste and that it appeared he was covering for Alch (and therein Bittman). I had refused to talk further in person with Ben-Veniste after August 1974; his call to me in October 1974 was to persuade me to do otherwise, or rather to unsuccessfully attempt to do so. . . .

25. Since the Special Prosecutors have chosen not to call me as a prosecution witness, nor plan to do so as a court witness, they would apparently rather lose certain counts in the charges in the indictment rather than to have McCord's information disclosed to the jury. It can only appear to me that they are thus trying to protect Bittman and Alch, and possibly Bailey, from indictment. My testimony on these issues can implicate no others, other than the prosecutors themselves.

What are we to make of this letter and these charges? It certainly is troublesome that McCord seems to be claiming that Ben-Veniste won't let him appear before the grand jury because Ben-Veniste did not want the jury to hear McCord's claim that Bittman and Alch had improperly pressed him to plead guilty.

While this letter was publicly finessed, the question still remains about how it was treated behind the scenes. And the short answer is that we simply don't know. McCord, who so far had been batting a thousand as far as whistle-blowing was concerned, was making some very serious allegations of impropriety against not only Bittman and Alch, but also against Ben-Veniste. If such a complaint had been made to the Department of Justice, an independent review would have been required. But the WSPF was, literally as well as figuratively, a law unto itself, and McCord's second letter struck out on three counts: It received no notice, no response, and no press coverage. Like the tree falling in an empty forest, McCord's second letter made no sound in the special prosecutor's offices. Having served his purpose as far as they were concerned, the Kennedy clan relegated McCord to the ranks of one-hit wonders.

There may be others like Bittman and Alch who were similarly given a Kennedy-stamped pass, but we will never know until they die, and the National Archives is allowed to open their files.

There is a tantalizing memo from James Neal to WSPF attorneys William Merrill and Philip Bakes, dated August 15, 1973, and reproduced in Appendix T. Neal's memo states that one of the individuals scheduled for interview by the Plumbers Task Force has admitted committing perjury, and will probably be indicted. Neal writes: "I simply ask that you coordinate his appearance with Rick Ben-Veniste and keep in mind that he has committed perjury and that we will probably want to indict him somewhere along the line." Since no such indictment ever occurred, the individual's name must always remain undisclosed, and we must remain curious as to whom it might have been and why no indictment was ever forthcoming.

14

The Denny/Rient Memo:
The Special Prosecutor's Own "Smoking Gun"

Readers still in doubt about what was going on during this time frame will be intrigued to learn about the existence of a previously undisclosed internal WSPF memo that covers the period of Dean's changing story, between April 2 and May 5, 1973, in some detail. Dated November 15, 1973, it summarizes statements made by the federal prosecutors Seymour Glanzer and Donald Campbell during meetings held on September 18 and October 10 with Judy Denny and Peter Rient of the WSPF Watergate Task Force.

These meetings were held in anticipation of formalizing Dean's plea agreement, which was to be presented before Judge Sirica on October 19, 1973. The focus of their discussions covered how events had unfolded during the critical period between April 2 and May 5, 1973.

The Denny/Rient memo details changes from Dean's initial version of events, as well as confirming the prosecutors' knowledge of Dean's own criminal acts. It also contains disclosures in several areas that might well be characterized as constituting a smoking gun from within the WSPF's own files.

I found the Denny/Rient memo (see Appendix U) in the files of the

WSPF that I gained access to as a result of filing an FOIA request in 2004. The memo provided extensive background and made many telling points about John Dean's career as a witness to Watergate. Because it is being printed here for the first time, I will quote a number of its troublesome notations.

>   *Glanzer and Shaffer are close friends and have known each other since Shaffer worked in the Department of Justice. . . . (Glanzer notes Shaffer is a brilliant and resourceful attorney.) . . .*
>   *Late in the evening of April 5, Shaffer called Glanzer at home, saying there was an emergency that he needed to discuss immediately. The two met alone at Glanzer's home. There was a mutual understanding that the discussion was in confidence. Shaffer began by asking Glanzer how far the prosecutors were willing to pursue the case. Glanzer replied that there were no restraints and they would go wherever the evidence led. Shaffer then expressed concern that since he (Shaffer) was known as a friend of the Kennedys and Glanzer was a Democrat, there might be accusations of scheming against the Administration, but Glanzer told him not to worry. . . .*
>   *Shaffer even preferred that Glanzer not talk to Silbert. (Shaffer also expressed uncertainty about an attorney-client privilege, and there was some discussion of work product privilege and executive privilege.) . . .*
>   *Shaffer thought Dean would make a valuable witness and hoped to obtain immunity for him. . . .*
>   *Shaffer offered Dean's cooperation in return for immunity, stressing Dean's value and reliability. . . .*
>   *Shaffer talked only of Dean's knowledge regarding Mitchell and Magruder. There was nothing said about Ehrlichman, Haldeman, Colson, or Nixon. . . .*
>   *Dean's disclosures were very diffused and of little substance and he hedged considerably because of the attorney-client privilege and the fact that the President had not been told everything yet. Dean said that it was "about time someone bit the bullet and I'm willing to." However, Dean wanted to tell Nixon first and he was afraid he couldn't get through Haldeman. . . .*

Dean told about the January and February meetings in Mitchell's office, but did not tell about the hiring of Liddy or of talking to Liddy before the January meeting. . . .

Dean did not mention his subsequent meeting with Haldeman at this time. He gave no information at all about Haldeman or Ehrlichman. . . .

In order to preserve feelings of mutual trust, Glanzer would from time to time tell Shaffer who was appearing before the grand jury and how leads to those persons came from a source other than Dean. . . .

Dean never acknowledged a cover-up or conspiracy or paying the defendants for silence until after he was fired (April 30, 1973). . . .

After the February 4th meeting, Dean told Haldeman about the meeting and Haldeman replied that the White House should not be involved. . . .

Glanzer and Campbell agree that Dean's receiving the FBI 302 reports was not mentioned on the 8th or 9th of April. . . .

Dean said that at some time [counsel to CRP Kenneth] Parkinson and [Mitchell's CRP aide Fred] LaRue had come to Dean's office with a sheet of paper with money requests from Hunt on it, but Dean never said that the money was for Hunt's silence.

Dean mentioned the McCord letter complaining about a CIA defense being contemplated. Ehrlichman told Dean to "stroke" McCord. Also Bittman visited Colson and discussed clemency. Again the response by Ehrlichman and Haldeman was that Colson should "stroke" Bittman, but make no promises. . . .

Campbell remembers that Dean told of the March 21 meeting where Dean attempted to tell the President about the situation, but that the President didn't understand. Dean would not divulge his exact words because of attorney-client privilege and executive privilege. . . .

Shaffer and Glanzer had three telephone conversations and one meeting on April 14th. Glanzer cannot remember who called who the first time, but in any event Shaffer came to Glanzer's home as a result of the call. This was probably in the early morning [that is, after midnight]. . . .

In the early evening on the 14th, Glanzer called Shaffer from the

Department of Justice while meeting with Titus and Petersen. Later in the evening, Glanzer called Shaffer to inform Shaffer of the prosecutors' disclosures to Kleindienst. . . .

On the evening of April 23, Shaffer met with Silbert and Glanzer. Glanzer says that by this time, the discussions had turned into a political game. Dean was bargaining with the Senate for immunity and the prosecutor's attempts at agreeing on a plea were in vain. . . .

On April 29, Shaffer called Glanzer at home to discuss the Vesco case. (It was not unusual for Shaffer to call Glanzer to discuss things generally.) . . .

After April 15, the situation was in a state of flux. The appointment of Cox and the preparation for Senate hearings changed the outlook from all sides. . . .

By the end of April, Dean had become much more antagonistic toward Haldeman and Ehrlichman in his discussions with the prosecutors and also in public, issuing the "scapegoat" statement. [After Dean was fired on April 30, he issued a public statement saying that he would not be a "scapegoat in the Watergate case."] Before that, the impression he gave of Haldeman was of a "great devoted public servant," clean and hard working. He had been restrained in his praise of Ehrlichman. . . .

[Referring to the May 2 meeting] Initially, there were some procedural discussions about listening to Dean tell about Presidential involvement, including the problem of executive privilege and attorney-client privilege. The prosecutors decided to listen to whatever Dean had to say. . . .

[Dean] said Colson could corroborate the meeting on June 19th where Ehrlichman gave the order to tell Hunt to leave the country. (Dean became hostile to Colson when Colson did not corroborate.) . . .

At a meeting in Haldeman's office between Haldeman, Ehrlichman, Dean and Mitchell, Ehrlichman asked Mitchell about Hunt's money problem. Mitchell replied that he didn't think it was a problem any more. . . .

On May 3, Dean began focusing on Presidential involvement, thus changing dramatically from his previous stance. . . .

Among the procedural matters discussed [on May 3] were the question of whether Dean would go to the grand jury as a witness (this was left undecided) and the possible filing by Shaffer of an inter-pleader concerning documents which Shaffer said would destroy the President. Dean was somewhat concerned about being arrested for turning over the documents since he never had control of them. [This is an apparent reference to counsel files taken by Dean when he jumped ship.] . . .

Months before Dean's March 21 conversation with Nixon, Dean had discussed the cover-up with [White House special counsel] Dick Moore. Although Moore suggested going to Nixon then, Dean did not do so. . . .

Glanzer originally wanted to give Dean immunity because of his value as a witness, but was persuaded by Silbert and Campbell that Dean should not be granted immunity. In hindsight, Glanzer thinks this was a good decision.

Glanzer thinks that the prosecutors' effect was neutralized by the appointment of a special prosecutor and the Senate Committee coming into being, and that they began to lose control over the case.

What can we conclude from this very candid memo?

First, it details an extraordinary—and troubling—closeness between Seymour Glanzer, who is one of the federal prosecutors investigating the case, and Charles Shaffer, Dean's lawyer. Both are Democrats; both are alumni of Bobby Kennedy's Department of Justice; both view the Nixon White House as their real target.

Second, it's point-by-point documentation of the evolution of Dean's story ought to be extraordinarily troubling—then and now: There is no allegation of a conspiracy, no initial inclusion of Haldeman and/or Ehrlichman (let alone mention of the Haldeman meeting in which Dean later claims to have tried to turn off Liddy's plan), and certainly no allegation of presidential wrongdoing.

Third, it is clear that Dean's main objective is to obtain immunity from criminal prosecution—and that his story and the people he inculpates—changes substantially over the month of April, as he continues to be denied immunity. In their own words: "changing dramatically from his previous stance."

Fourth, it is possible that Glanzer may have violated his own oath of office by improperly keeping Shaffer abreast of the unfolding of the cover-up collapse, confiding confidential information as though Shaffer were a member of the prosecution team, thereby thwarting the criminal investigation and helping further deliver Dean into the hands of the Ervin Committee.

Finally, one can only wonder how WSPF attorneys could have written their sentencing recommendation letter on behalf of John Dean (which alleged that virtually all of his criminal acts were at the direction and behest of Haldeman and Erhlichman), or why such a revealing memo was not disclosed to counsel for the defendants in the cover-up trial that began a full year later, as seemingly required of the prosecution by Supreme Court rulings.

The use of prior inconsistent statements to impeach a witness's credibility is a well-known and highly effective trial technique. The documentation of Dean's dramatically changing story—by the very federal prosecutors conducting the original investigation—would have shredded his credibility as the government's primary witness.

Indeed, on the first day of trial, lead WSPF prosecutor Jim Neal suddenly begins to worry that such a course of inquiry might be pursued by defense counsel. In a memo reproduced in full in Appendix V, he directs one of his assistants to prepare—that very day—a day-by-day summary of Dean's early revelations to the career prosecutors. Apparently also worried that if defense counsel appreciates the extent of Dean's changes, they may ask why they were not so informed in advance of trial, he helpfully provides his own ideas of just how such changes might be minimized or rationalized.

15

The Media Invents a "Massacre"

The American public has been led to believe that what happened in the White House on October 20, 1973, stands as one of the single most egregious abuses of power ever committed by a sitting president. This isn't surprising, given what is supposed to have happened on that night, when the president fired his attorney general because he refused to fire the special prosecutor—just when it appeared that the special prosecutor was about to discover proof positive of presidential wrongdoing.

But let's look at what really happened, so that we can better understand how the hysterical press coverage converted a partisan outcry into conventional wisdom.

FRIDAY, OCTOBER 19. Two major events occurred—one in late morning, the other in the afternoon. In the morning John Dean appeared in Judge Sirica's courtroom to enter a plea to a single felony count, with sentencing postponed until after the expected cover-up trial. Not only was Dean being let off with only a single felony—which amounted to a slap on the wrist, given his central role in the Watergate events—but the indictment that was released to the public in connection with the plea had been specifically drafted in order to soft-pedal Dean's wrongdoing, and to present the WSPF's view that his role had been to implement a conspiracy con-cocted and directed by more senior Nixon aides.

Most Watergate commentators have underestimated (and many have simply ignored) the significance of Dean's plea that Friday morning. To Nixon, it was confirmation that Cox intended to let Dean off in exchange for his help in making a case against Haldeman and Ehrlichman, and per-haps even Nixon himself.

But Dean's plea, no matter how directly threatening it might be, was only the first part of a one-two punch delivered that Friday by the special prosecutor. The second part, later in the afternoon, was the WSPF's dis-avowal of the so-called Stennis Compromise on the White House tapes. From Nixon's point of view, Cox had suddenly and publicly rejected an ap-proach that he himself had urged in the first place.

To understand why this seemed so ominous, at least a little backstory is required.

In the first attempt to obtain copies of the recently revealed White House tape recordings, Cox had subpoenaed nine different conversations, mostly involving John Dean and based on his allegations. Judge Sirica had ruled in his favor, and the Court of Appeals had upheld Sirica's decision. Prior to reaching its decision, however, the appellate court had asked the parties to try reaching some kind of compromise regarding access to the tapes. The subsequent discussions, although they produced no agreement, appear to have centered around the idea of tape summaries being pro-duced after being authenticated by an independent third party. The Ap-peals Court's ruling also contained the idea of a middle man operating between the White House and the WSPF, in that it called for the tapes to be turned over to Sirica to see if any parts of the subject conversations had evidentiary value in the Watergate case.

Nixon's lawyer, Fred Buzhardt, had listened to the subpoenaed tapes and found no evidence of any wrongdoing by the president. So, backed by Charles Alan Wright, perhaps the nation's foremost expert on federal courts, who now was acting as counsel for the White House, Buzhardt de-cided to take a firmer stand, and he tried to reopen the earlier discussions, during which Cox himself had suggested that tape summaries could be authenticated by an independent third party. The attraction of this compromise was that the prosecutor would get the benefit of knowing what was on the tapes, while the president would still be able to claim that he had preserved the principle of executive privilege.

Searching for someone who would be acceptable to both sides as an authenticator, the White House suggested Senator John Stennis of Mississippi.

Cox had indicated all week that he was willing to consider an authenticator compromise on the nine tapes in question, but he wouldn't renounce the possibility of requesting additional tapes or White House documents in the future. In the course of intense jockeying and negotiations over this point, Richardson had indicated, perhaps unintentionally, that Cox would resign if he were ordered not to seek further White House materials.

It all came to a head on this Friday afternoon, the last day the White House could file an appeal of the adverse tapes decision to the Supreme Court. Cox felt that this was a false deadline that could easily be extended so negotiations could continue at everyone's leisure. But these latest negotiations had been going on when John Dean walked into Judge Sirica's courtroom that morning, and the White House wanted closure. Thinking they had Cox's concurrence, Senators Ervin, Baker, and Stennis were invited to the White House that afternoon for the official announcement of the Stennis Compromise.

According to my understanding of James Doyle's version of events (admittedly one-sided but the only inside source we have for WSPF actions), Cox had actually changed his mind and reneged on the core element of the compromise—the willingness to accept tape summaries authenticated by an agreed-upon third party—that he himself had suggested earlier. Doyle claims Cox did so after a phone conversation with his daughter (who was then in law school) and reading an article by Anthony Lewis in *The New York Times* (which Doyle takes credit for having facilitated). Whatever the reasons, Cox wrote a letter stating that he would never accept a situation in which he did not have direct access to the nine tapes in question.

After speaking with Cox, Richardson also informed the White House that he could not order Cox not to seek further documents. At 8:00 P.M. that Friday evening, the White House announced that Cox had rejected the Stennis Compromise, and released a letter instructing Richardson to "direct Special Prosecutor Archibald Cox of the Watergate Special Prosecution Force that he is to make no further attempts by judicial process to obtain tapes, notes, or memoranda of Presidential conversations."

SATURDAY, OCTOBER 20. Special Prosecutor Cox took the extraordinary step of calling a weekend press conference for 1:00 P.M. at the National Press Club. He announced that he would not abide by the president's decision; in fact, he would ignore it. In dramatic terms, he posed the issue as one of whether or not the rule of law would prevail in America. The press conference, although hastily summoned over the Columbus Day weekend, was well covered. Cox's remarks were carried without any response from a White House that had been caught completely off guard, without any staff available to respond on the Saturday afternoon of the three-day holiday.

Nixon felt publicly double-crossed by Cox and his Kennedy clan partisans. Added to the Dean pleading, it seemed clear that the White House was now seriously under siege by the Camelot conspirators. He determined to get back to the original idea of a special supervising prosecutor—as conceived before Cox and the Kennedy clan hijacked it—as a nonpartisan lawyer sitting above Henry Petersen (at the Department of Justice) and Earl Silbert (in the U.S. attorney's office) and identifying and recommending to Attorney General Richardson those administration officials who should be indicted.

So Richard Nixon took what turned out to be a fateful step. He ordered Attorney General Richardson to fire Special Prosecutor Cox. It was a completely proper and legal order for the president to issue; he was the head of the executive branch, and therefore the boss of everyone in it. He undoubtedly hoped that Richardson would agree that what Cox had done was unacceptable and would agree that firing him was the proper course of action. But whether he agreed or not, the president had every reason to expect that his attorney general would respect his authority and carry out his order.

Richardson undoubtedly realized that the order to fire Cox, regardless of what Cox had done, had suddenly placed him in the very public position of having to choose between being a media hero or a media villain. That is the kind of choice that no man—and certainly no politician—would welcome. Whatever the reason or reasons behind his decision, Richardson chose to submit his own resignation instead, saying that the Guidelines precluded him from firing Cox.

The deputy attorney general, William Ruckelshaus (Princeton, '57; Harvard Law, '60), also refused to carry out the president's order, and was terminated by the White House before his proffered resignation was received. The next in line in the Justice Department's statutory hierarchy was the solicitor general of the United States. Former judge and Yale professor Robert Bork had been solicitor general for only about seven months. Bork decided that it was his constitutional duty to execute the president's order; the fact that he had opposed the appointment of a special prosecutor from the outset would later be used to muddy his motives in this regard. He both fired Cox and abolished the WSPF as an independent entity, folding its responsibilities back into DOJ's Criminal Division, under Henry Petersen.

When news of these events reached the major newsrooms, the national media went absolutely berserk. The TV networks frantically broke into the regularly scheduled programs (CBS's *Mary Tyler Moore Show, NBC Saturday Night at the Movies,* and the *ABC Suspense Movie*) to announce what it soon styled "the Saturday Night Massacre." John Chancellor was the widely respected anchor of NBC News. With his typically skillful concision and clarity, he presented what would become the generally accepted tone taken by the media:

> *Good evening. The country tonight is in the midst of what may be the most serious Constitutional crisis in its history. The president has fired the Special Watergate Prosecutor, Archibald Cox. Because of the president's action, the attorney general has resigned. Elliot Richardson has quit, saying he cannot carry out Mr. Nixon's instructions. Richardson's deputy, William Ruckelshaus, has been fired.*
>
> *Ruckelshaus refused, in a moment of Constitutional drama, to obey a presidential order to fire the special Watergate prosecutor. And half an hour after the special Watergate prosecutor had been fired,*

agents of the FBI, acting at the direction of the White House, sealed off the offices of the special prosecutor, the offices of the attorney general, and the offices of the deputy attorney general.

All of this adds up to a totally unprecedented situation, a grave and profound crisis in which the president has set himself against his own attorney general and the Department of Justice.

Nothing like this has ever happened before.

Chancellor signed off that night with a chilling statement. "In my career as a correspondent," he said, "I never thought I'd be reporting these things."

Kennedy family speechwriter Theodore Sorensen asked House speaker Carl Albert for permission to draw up a secret "comprehensive contingency plan" for Democratic action, in case Nixon was forced from office. (The Speaker of the House is third in line of succession to the presidency, but after Agnew's resignation, Albert had been bumped up to number two, pending the naming and confirmation of Agnew's successor.)

In the face of the media firestorm of protest that followed, the White House did a complete about-face. It announced that the president would not only turn over all the subpoenaed tapes to Judge Sirica, but would also rescind his decision to abolish the WSPF, and would appoint a new special prosecutor.

When this announcement was made in Sirica's courtroom on Monday morning, the media was caught flat-footed. In less than forty-eight hours all of their dire predictions about the virtual coup d'état Nixon was attempting were shown to have been totally unfounded. And without losing a beat, the story now shifted; apparently it had been the fearless reporting by the media that had made the White House retreat from overturning the Constitution.

That the White House was not necessarily wrong on the merits of its arguments, and had conducted itself properly and in good faith throughout the private negotiations over the Stennis Compromise, was completely lost in the firestorm. It was a PR battle, not a legal one—and the media, following the Kennedy Clan Democrat's game plan, saw to it that Nixon lost decisively.

With Cox's departure, any vestige of restraint or prosecutorial discretion was lost completely; a Kennedy clan hero had been taken out and there would be hell to pay in retribution. Understandings, tentative agreements, and any concept of even-handed administration of justice went by the boards; Nixon aides only peripherally involved would pay with their reputations and with their freedom for Nixon's audacity in thinking he could protect himself from the Kennedys' onslaught. Leon Jaworski replaced Cox but he never got control of Cox's army. He had a tiger by the tail and could only barely hang on.

One early example involves the sensitive files John Dean had removed from the counsel's office in mid-April 1973. The month following Cox's departure, but well after Jaworski was appointed as his successor, Dean decided the files should no longer be in his own possession, so he arranged for his WSPF friends to subpoena them. The memo circulating the draft subpoena, as well as a follow-up clarifying its rationale, are reproduced in full in Appendix W. The scope of the subpoena indicates the extent of his removals; the fact that the draft subpoena was circulated to the deputy special prosecutor and all affected task force heads—but not to Leon Jaworski—speaks volumes about the scope of his control.

16

Impeaching a President:
The House Judiciary Committee
Joins the Camelot Conspiracy

A nother reaction to the Saturday Night Massacre came four days later, on October 23, when the House Judiciary Committee announced that it would conduct an inquiry into whether grounds existed to impeach the president.

The House Judiciary Committee consisted of thirty-seven members—twenty-one Democrats and sixteen Republicans—virtually all of whom were lawyers. The impeachment inquiry staff comprised forty-three lawyers. Their average age was thirty-three, and a great many of them were recent law school graduates. As with the WSPF, there was a concentration of Ivy Leaguers, with eighteen coming from Harvard, Yale, or Columbia law schools.

From all outward appearances, the impeachment inquiry staff did little for its first five months of existence except follow the remainder of the Ervin hearings and the evidentiary hearing that Judge Sirica held in advance of the cover-up trial. Like the rest of America, they were waiting for indictments. Staff director John Doar wasn't even hired until two months later, and the public hearings didn't begin for almost half a year—until May 9, 1974.

After examining the question, the WSPF was fairly certain that it wasn't constitutionally enabled to help the impeachment inquiry in any explicit manner. But the Kennedy Clan Democrats were hardly to be deterred at this point, and they hit upon a rather ingenious solution to enable them to circumvent the Constitution. When the cover-up indictments were finally announced, on March 1, 1974, they were unusually detailed, cataloging some forty-two specifically alleged "overt acts." That alone would have been of considerable help to the impeachment inquiry, but there was something even better. A fifty-five-page document "prepared" by the grand jury, and known as the Roadmap, was delivered to Judge Sirica in a sealed leather briefcase addressed to the House Judiciary Committee. While patently obvious that this Roadmap had been drafted by the WSPF staff, it had technically originated with the grand jury, and therefore didn't constitute executive branch involvement with the Judiciary Committee's impeachment inquiry. Problem solved; mission accomplished.

As a product of the grand jury, the Roadmap remains secret to this day, and we have to deduce its contents from what others have said about it. The consensus is that it consisted of a series of citations of publicly known events that might indicate that impeachable offenses had occurred. It also, apparently, included specific instructions on which items deserved closer scrutiny.

The impeachment inquiry staff set about reviewing and confirming the existence of all of the Roadmap's landmarks. They assiduously, and independently, reconfirmed all of the public incidents. Large notebooks of news clippings and congressional and court testimony were assembled. It is hard to imagine a more pointless expenditure of such high-powered staff time. But once again, as was so often the case where the Camelot Conspiracy was concerned, the object of the exercise was to prolong the questioning rather than answer the questions.

Skipping five months ahead for a moment, the House Judiciary Committee began its historic votes on July 27, 1974, and over the next three days approved three separate Articles of Impeachment. They were never taken up by the full House of Representatives, because Nixon resigned on August 9. The committee then disbanded its impeachment inquiry staff and sealed its records for fifty years, confident that there would be no second-guessing its approach or procedures for a very, very long time.

That confidence was justified for two decades, until 1995, when the Judiciary Committee's longtime chief counsel, Jerry Zeifman, published his diaries from that era in a book entitled *Without Honor: Crimes of Camelot and the Impeachment of President Nixon*. Zeifman, a lifelong Democrat, had served on the Judiciary staff for some seventeen years. He will never be accused of carrying any water for Richard M. Nixon; his attitude seems to be that Nixon was such a liar and thief that he should have been impeached shortly after assuming office in 1969. His book, however, tells the strangest of tales—and backs it up with some rather persuasive contemporary documentation.

For example, Zeifman appears to believe:

• The impeachment inquiry staff was controlled by Burke Marshall (Yale '44; Yale Law, '51), a Yale Law professor, and the former head of the Civil Rights Division at Bobby Kennedy's Department of Justice, and longtime Kennedy family counsel. Marshall, as we have seen, was one of the first people Teddy Kennedy tried to call after Chappaquiddick—and was one of his on-site advisers during those critical days in Hyannis Port. By 1974, as Zeifman tells it, Marshall was understood to be the attorney-general-in-waiting, and was already providing Kennedy with advice and counsel from that perspective.

• John Doar (Princeton, '44; University of California–Berkeley School of Law, '49) was nominally the head of the impeachment inquiry staff. He had been Marshall's longtime protégé and deputy in Robert Kennedy's Civil Rights Division, and had succeeded him as its head when Marshall returned to Yale. Marshall identified a handful of recent Yale Law School graduates, and encouraged Doar to hire them for the impeachment inquiry staff. Among these Marshall scholars were two young women who later achieved some prominence: Renata Adler (Bryn Mawr, '59; MA Harvard, '62; Yale Law, '73) and Hillary Rodham (Wellesley, '69; Yale Law, '73). They were part of the Yale-heavy core group of insiders around Doar, which also included Bernard Nussbaum (Columbia, '58

Harvard Law, '61), the senior associate special counsel who directed the staff's Watergate investigation. Zeifman claims that they were, in fact, coordinating everything with Marshall at Yale—who could be expected to be coordinating everything with Teddy Kennedy.

- The Doar-Marshall strategy was twofold, according to Zeifman. First, to slow down the impeachment process and keep Nixon in office as long as possible, in order to further weaken the Republican Party, in anticipation of Teddy's expected presidential run. Second, to make sure that no attempts were made to compare Nixon's misdeeds with those of prior presidents. The last thing Teddy Kennedy's campaign needed was a national airing of Camelot's dirty linen as a way of getting Nixon off the hook.

- In furtherance of this Kennedy-inspired and -directed strategy, Zeifman claims that the impeachment inquiry staff purposely did nothing for the first six months of its existence. No witnesses were interviewed; no hearings were held; no independent investigations of Nixon administration officials were undertaken. Doar and his intimates, who were taking the lead from Burke Marshall, went to great pains to keep this nonaction hidden, not only from the public and the members of the committee, but even from other staff members who weren't in the know. Hence there was a vast amount of busywork generated, such as reassembling from scratch all the press clippings and other publicly available materials that were cited in the grand jury's Roadmap. While the clueless staff members were assiduously spinning their wheels, Judiciary Committee members were being assured that the staff was moving slowly in order to leave no stone unturned in its search for the truth.

- When demands from some committee members for a study of abuse allegations during prior administrations could no longer be ignored, Doar gave the assignment to one of his Yale insiders—Hillary Rodham. She turned to the distinguished Yale historian C. Vann Woodward, who helped identify twelve scholars who were then given the task of identifying and documenting all prior claims of abuse of presidential powers. Their report, edited by Professor Woodward, was given a somewhat cumbersome (although undeniably descriptive) title: *Responses of the Presidents to Charges of Misconduct (Including Accusations of High Crimes and Misdemeanors from George Washington to Lyndon Johnson): An Authoritative History Requested by Counsel John Doar for the Impeachment Inquiry Staff Investigating Charges Against Richard M. Nixon.*

When the professor's report was completed it showed other presidents had been accused of similar abuses—and Doar directed Ms. Rodham to suppress it. She was so effective that committee members were later taken completely by surprise when the volume, which they had never seen, was published commercially two months after Nixon resigned. Charles Wiggins, a Nixon defender who had been particularly vocal in requesting that the study be prepared, discovered its existence when he happened across a copy of the paperback version in an airport bookshop.

Faced with such a number of serious charges, especially from such an inside source, it's hard to know exactly how to react. The essentials of his story are demonstrably true. Jerry Zeifman really was chief counsel of the House Judiciary Committee during the impeachment inquiry; Hillary Rodham Clinton's 2003 book *Living History* confirms her Yale Law professor Burke Marshall had fed her name, along with others, to John Doar; the Woodward study of misconduct by previous presidents does exist in published form; and Congressman Wiggins's September 26, 1974, letter is a matter of public record. There also is independent confirmation of sorts from Renata Adler, another recent Yale graduate recommended to Doar by Burke Marshall. In an article in the *Atlantic Monthly* ("Searching for the Real Nixon," December 1976), she undermined the entire basis for Nixon's impeachment:

> *In view of the Church Committee's account of the conduct of previous administrations, including violations of law and abuses of power since at least 1936, the first two Articles [of impeachment] seemed to dissolve; as to [the third Article], there had been a disagreement about it from the start.... The problem with all three Articles, and with their accompanying Summary of Information and Final Report, and with the thirty-odd volumes of Statements of Information [Doar's scrapbooks] ... is that ... all those volumes never quite made their case or any case.*

Zeifman comes across as a complex man and not without axes of his own to grind. But even if what he writes is only partially accurate, he exposes and confirms the hidden hand of Teddy Kennedy and his supporters also operating behind the scenes of the House Judiciary Committee's impeachment inquiry.

The Liberal Media:
Long-term Enablers of the Kennedy Clan

The role of the media is to keep politicians honest by keeping the public informed. This is why freedom of the press is central to our First Amendment rights.

During the 1960s, motivated by the ongoing struggle for civil rights at home and opposition to the developing war in Vietnam abroad, many reporters were no longer content with providing objective accounts of the stories they were assigned. They began to get involved personally; some only subtly shaped the stories they filed, but some actually worked hand in glove with subjects and sources they considered progressive. Because such involvement might well be seen by the public as being inconsistent with their function as reporters, it was best kept quiet.

Let's take a brief look at some of the media mavens who were at the center of reporting on Watergate.

Ben Bradlee (Harvard, '42), was the snappily dressed and calculatedly profane executive editor of the *Washington Post,* one of whose cub reporters was Bob Woodward (Yale, '65).

In an earlier incarnation, as *Newsweek'*s Washington bureau chief, Bradlee and his wife, Toni, had been personal friends of John and Jacqueline

Kennedy. During the 1960 Democratic primaries Bradlee sent at least one confidential memo that we know about to candidate Kennedy, based on inside information he had gathered while covering his rival, Lyndon Johnson, for the magazine.

When Kennedy was in the White House, Bradlee continued to pass information to him. In one memo to the president's secretary, Bradlee wrote, "The boss asked for the enclosed last night. Can you slip it noisily on his desk with me compliments?" As David Burnham noted, "Bradlee's attempt at Irish dialogue—'me compliments'—was bad enough. But the reporter's reference to the President as his 'boss' is worse."

Burnham, a former reporter for *Newsweek* and *The New York Times*, describes how Bradlee once submitted a *Newsweek* article to the Kennedy White House for clearance, as a condition for being shown confidential FBI documents.

A separate event occurred early in 1963, when *Newsweek* was preparing a cover story on Robert Kennedy; Bradlee acceded to Bobby's request not to publish two important stories he had been told by the president. One involved a hoodlum who claimed he had been hired by the Teamsters to kill Bobby Kennedy. Again, former *Newsweek* reporter Burnham summed up the unhealthy aspects of this buddy-buddy relationship between his magazine's Washington bureau chief and the first family:

> *Some years later, with President Nixon's 1974 resignation, the* Washington Post's *hard-nosed investigation of the burglary of the Democratic National headquarters quickly became the stuff of myth. Thousands of smart young reporters dreamed that one day they could work for an editor like Ben Bradlee. Unfortunately, to the extent that articles of Woodward and Bernstein contributed to the downfall of Nixon, the record shows that this famous investigation was very much the exception. Much closer to the national norm of leaks and cronyism was the Kennedy-era reporting by Ben Bradlee and Tony Lewis, in which journalists allowed themselves to become a part of the government's team. The press; some watchdog.*

During the early days of the WSPF, several newspapers ran stories about it that were clearly based on inside leaks. Archibald Cox and his Kennedy cronies were greatly annoyed—not because of the leaks (they had themselves been leaking)—but because they didn't know who was doing the rogue freelancing.

In fact, there hadn't been any leaks; reporters had simply been sorting through the office garbage at night. It is telling that Cox felt at ease calling his old friend Ben Bradlee to ask for confidential help, and that Bradlee was equally at ease betraying his craft. After Cox described his problem and his frustration, Bradlee said, "If you ever tell anyone I told you this, I'll deny it. But Archie, you've got a trash problem." The WSPF immediately invested in shredders for each office.

Anthony Lewis (Harvard, '48; Harvard Nieman Fellow, '57) had a brilliant legal mind and a lucid prose style. During the Kennedy administration he covered the Supreme Court for *The New York Times* and was very supportive of RFK's efforts to bring Hoffa to justice. He won a Pulitzer Prize (his second) for his Court reporting in 1963. The following year he published *Gideon's Trumpet,* about the landmark ruling regarding an impoverished defendant's right to an attorney. During Nixon's first term he was in London as the paper's bureau chief. According to Burnham, while he was there in 1968, he drafted a campaign speech for Robert Kennedy. When the paper's Washington bureau chief found out about what to some would be a stunning breach of journalistic ethics, he ordered an immediate stop to any such involvement.

In 1972, Lewis returned to Washington as one of the *Times*'s weekly columnists. As a columnist, of course, he was free to express his strongly held personal opinions concerning the inadequacy and errors of Republican attorneys general, Justice Departments, and Court appointments. But during the Kennedy years, while covering the Supreme Court as a reporter, and without informing either his editors or his readers, he had already crossed the line from coverage to advocacy.

Both Victor Navasky and David Burnham have described how Lewis worked to influence the Supreme Court's 1964 decision on the one-man one-vote case, *Reynolds v. Sims.* As Burnham writes, Lewis "became intimately engaged in an organized behind-the-scenes effort to persuade the Supreme Court to rule in a way that he, the Attorney General, and the administration's top political advisers had decided was best for the nation and the long-term political interests of the Kennedy family." Lewis obtained a copy of a brief written by Solicitor General Archibald Cox that the Justice Department was getting ready to file. A regular reporter in possession of such a document would have written a story based on it to inform the paper's readers of how the government viewed the case.

But Tony Lewis wasn't a regular reporter. He was an advocate, and he decided that Cox's brief wasn't strong or pointed enough to be sure of influencing the Court's ruling. So he drove to Cox's house and told him about his concerns. When the brief was filed a few days later, it incorporated many of Lewis's points.

Clark Mollenhoff of the *Des Moines Register* was another reporter who played a prominent role during the Kennedy era. Like Lewis, Mollenhoff had been intimately involved as a reporter in Robert Kennedy's efforts to convict James Hoffa. In this effort (and in his own book, *Game Plan for Disaster: An Ombudsman's Report on the Nixon Years*), he characterized himself as Kennedy's "soul mate."

The relationship of the media to the Ervin Committee, the WSPF, and the House Judiciary Committee impeachment inquiry set new lows for advocacy, leaks, and cronyism.

Sam Dash admitted that he sought—and received—off-the-record help from the *Washington Post*'s Bob Woodward. As Dash described it, he proposed "an unusual arrangement in which he would provide tips to the Committee without receiving any information from us in return." Since the committee, its staff, and its members were responsible for daily tsunamis of leaks—particularly to Woodward—this statement is disingenuous, and presumably included only to maintain the public image of probity.

Senator Weicker, who had a reputation for monumental amounts of leaking, gloats about his own press relations, his closeness with reporters, and his willingness to confirm stories so that they could be published. It isn't surprising that the ambitious Connecticut senator found time to meet personally with Ben Bradlee.

I also met with Ben Bradlee, executive editor of the Washington Post. *I wanted to know him a little better because the* Post *had made more Watergate disclosures than any other news organization; he was interested in me because of the views I had started to express and because I was moving into a key investigative position. I mentioned to Bradlee that from information I had gathered, I was convinced that Haldeman knew about Watergate-type campaign activities that violated the letter and the spirit of the law.*

Perhaps the paradigm of the media's attitude is provided by what might otherwise seem an insignificant and meaningless gesture. During John Dean's testimony, which lasted for hours and was characterized by degrees of detail that were, as we have seen, taken to indicate an almost photographic memory, he suddenly faltered and stumbled over remembering the name of a restaurant in which an event had occurred.

Daniel Schorr, who was there covering the hearing for CBS News, sent a note with the correct name to Dean's lawyer. When Dean smoothly corrected his mistake by apologizing for his lapse and supplying the correct name of the restaurant, the audience actually applauded. As Dean reports, "The crowd's support, which I hadn't expected, did more to repair the dents [Republican Senator Edward] Gurney had made in my credibility than anything I could possibly have said or done."

Does anyone think Dan Schorr would have sent that note if the faltering witness had been Bob Haldeman or John Ehrlichman?

Jim Doyle, the WSPF's press officer, records an example of collusion on the part of the nationally syndicated and ostensibly incorruptible muckraker Jack Anderson.

George Clifford, who has ghostwritten some of Anderson's books, gave us an invaluable lead. He had gotten a tip that Maurice Stans was spotted at a New York storage warehouse removing and shredding documents stored there by the Committee to Re-elect the President. By the time Clifford got to the warehouse the owners were saying nothing and the elevator operator was too scared to talk. Without confirmation

Anderson could not use the story. Clifford turned over the details to the prosecutor's office, and by subpoenaing witnesses and questioning them under oath, Cox's staff was able to verify that Stans had indeed entered the warehouse and that a number of documents had been shredded. No crime was proved, but the information was valuable when a case was being prepared against Stans.

You have to read between the lines very carefully to realize that the witnesses never said that Stans himself had shredded documents, as Doyle clearly implies. One might also wonder about the secrecy of grand jury testimony if the WSPF press officer had such easy access to it—and felt free to print information from its deliberations.

Perhaps it was because his book had already run to a couple of hundred pages that Doyle didn't have room to mention that Stans was acquitted in this case. But Doyle didn't let the rigors of limited space prevent him from mentioning the outcome when a Nixon supporter was found guilty, or from casting an aspersion on the judge who recognized the relatively minor nature of a first offense.

James Polk, then of the Washington Star, *gave the campaign contributions Task Force its first leads into the activities of George M. Steinbrenner III, the American Ship Building Company owner and part-owner of the New York Yankees. Polk's information helped uncover one of the more flagrant violations of the campaign finance laws, and Steinbrenner eventually pleaded guilty to a felony. An accommodating judge in Cleveland let him off without jail time.*

Perhaps Doyle was so intent on praising Polk, his former colleague at the *Star,* that he didn't notice the ethical question raised by a reporter passing tips to a government source instead of writing about them.

In the 1970s, there was a media establishment, and it had clearly chosen sides. Even before Vietnam, Nixon had been seen by the American elite as a bad man who was consistently on the wrong side of events and history.

Where Watergate was concerned, Ervin, Sirica, Cox, and even Dean (whose self-serving and self-aggrandizing account of events was uncritically accepted because it was anti-Nixon) were cast as the heroes. When Cox was fired there was unrestrained outrage expressed in print and on television, and the cumulative effect on the public was absolutely devastating for the White House.

One might assume that given the unique and sensitive nature of his position, Special Prosecutor Cox would have devoted the vast portion of his time to supervising the many investigations being undertaken by his rapidly expanding office. Instead, he met almost constantly with writers and reporters. While many such sessions were "off-the-record," as his press secretary had advised him, "Nothing in Washington is ever really off the record. They won't write about it, but they'll gossip about it, and eventually it will end up in print, probably distorted."

Cox was an old enough Washington hand to know this full well. Both men knew what they were doing when Cox was made readily available to the media:

> *We had breakfast, luncheons, or dinners with the editors of the* Washington Post *and* The New York Times, Newsweek *and* Time; *with John Chancellor and David Broder, Peter Lisagor and Robert Novak. Cox held background sessions with reporters who covered the office, but they were of a different kind, with legal issues often discussed in detail, Cox wearing his professor's cap a bit too obviously. The sessions with the high priests and priestesses were more basic; these powerful men and women were allowed to challenge Cox directly and make up their own minds about his capacity to do the job.*

Perhaps it is appropriate at this point to mention that—for understandable reasons regarding justice and fairness—prosecutorial leaks are neither proper nor legal.

For WSPF attorneys on the Get Nixon Squad, however, such restraints were theoretical at most. Although Leon Jaworski lacked the professorial garrulousness of his predecessor, the cozy relationship between the WSPF and the media survived the transition with hardly a hitch. Jaworski cultivated a special relationship with three journalists in particular: *Washington*

Post columnist Philip Geyelin (Harvard Institute of Politics, '66), Meg Greenfield (Smith College, '52; Cambridge University, Fulbright Scholar, '52–'53), the *Post*'s editorial page editor and *Newsweek* columnist; and, of course, Tony Lewis of *The New York Times*.

James Doyle noted that:

> *Lewis would frequently fly down from Boston to see Jaworski and while he would write well-informed columns (and sometimes drop hints to reporters in the Washington bureaus about matters to be pursued), he did not try to scoop his colleagues with perishable news items which would have spoiled in a day or two and ruined his relationship with Jaworski as well.*
>
> *"Tony," I said, "can you come down some time in the next week or so? It would be very useful to interview Leon." Lewis asked if there were particular subjects to be pursued. "You might be thinking about the arguments of prejudicial publicity preventing a fair trial in notorious cases and how a prosecutor should respond to that problem," I said. That puzzled him, since the question of pretrial publicity was considered the exclusive concern of the judge, but Lewis promised to think about the issue before he arrived.*

It is interesting to contemplate just how much inside information was being made available to friends in the media by Kennedy Clan Democrats. Doyle is not shy—or seemingly concerned—about revealing how the media was included in the most confidential of internal discussions. Indeed, he takes great pride in his belief—naive in the way that only a reporter can be naive when his own profession is involved—that information acquired in this way was never published immediately following its receipt.

Stage One of the Camelot Conspiracy:
Destroying the President

The Kennedy clan's strategy had been implemented during the summer of '73. By the summer of '74, Nixon was reduced to the desperate options and actions of a cornered animal. The details of the endgame are well enough known. It is the attitudes of Nixon's opponents as their total victory nears that are the most revealing.

The precedent for whether an impeached president could look to the Department of Justice for a defense was limited and ambiguous. When Andrew Johnson was impeached he was defended by his attorney general, but he had resigned in order to defend the president as a private citizen. For Nixon, the question was settled when the possibility of help from the Justice Department was opposed by Cox and precluded by Richardson. The White House asked at least to be allowed to post notices at the department's main building, and in U.S. attorneys' offices on the East Coast, asking for volunteers to join the president's legal defense team. Following grudging consent, the notices were posted, and about a dozen young lawyers responded and were hired onto the White House legal staff.

Several lawyers from private practices also came forward to assist the

White House—including Samuel Powers, J. J. Sullivan, and H. Chapman Rose. But they only stayed briefly; no one seemed able to withstand the media onslaught or professional pressures that accompanied being identified with Nixon's defense.

Lest anyone—at any level—not understand the risks of associating with the president at this point, the WSPF approved an ominous action with regard to legal secretaries in the White House counsel's office. In their eagerness to discover who was responsible for an $18\frac{1}{2}$ minute gap that had been discovered on one of the subpoenaed White House tapes, they directed the FBI to interview these secretaries in secret, and without giving them any prior notice. These conditions were to be achieved by showing up unannounced at their homes at night. Needless to say, this technique had a somewhat chilling effect on any concept of lawyer-client privilege. But to WSPF attorneys, with their Get Hoffa mentality, this was just one of the necessities when you took on the mob.

Thus were White house lawyers and staffers served notice that any action taken in defense of the president was in danger of being characterized as "another overt act in the continuing cover-up."

Even after legal heavyweight James St. Clair arrived in December 1973 to head Nixon's courtroom defense, there remained a substantial risk that the president would be driven from office without having benefit of adequate counsel. Given the fifty men and women working for the Ervin Committee majority staff (including seventeen lawyers), the ninety staff members of the WSPF (ultimately including over sixty lawyers), and the unified House Judiciary Committee's impeachment inquiry staff (including forty-three lawyers), the president's legal team of fewer than a dozen lawyers was ludicrously outmanned and outgunned.

On the night of Thursday, August 8, Nixon announced that he would resign the following day. On August 9, at noon, Gerald Ford was sworn in at a ceremony in the East Room of the White House. Nixon returned to California and holed up in his San Clemente house. Some said he had been robbed of the fruits of his recent 61 percent landslide; others said it was a fate he had richly earned and deserved.

Before Nixon was gone even a few hours, the Washington handicappers were at work. *Time* magazine identified Teddy Kennedy as "President

Ford's likeliest rival in the 1976 Presidential campaign," and summarized the conventional wisdom.

> *Loyalists of Massachusetts Senator Edward Kennedy insist that their favorite has emerged a winner from the resolution of Watergate. Kennedy, they argue, has the personal magnetism needed to unseat Ford in 1976. "Ford's going to run a personality campaign," says one Democratic strategist, and "I've been hearing people say that Ted's the only candidate we have with a personality strong enough to move people."*
>
> *Other Democrats agree that Kennedy is most capable of unifying the various elements that can be rallied to the party's side—liberals, the labor unions, big-city ethnics, Catholics, blacks, the Spanish-speaking.*

Veteran journalist Jules Witcover confirmed the Massachusetts senator's standing (which he thought predated Nixon's resignation):

> *1973 saw a seemingly inexorable drift in the party back to the dream of another Kennedy candidacy, with all of the political magic it promised . . . National polls showed him far ahead of all prospective contenders; local and state politicians who came to Washington for party meetings and other affairs adopted an attitude of resignation. . . . They shared doubts about the man's electability, but accepted the inevitability of his nomination.*

No question about it. The Kennedys had won—and won big. They had unseated a president and opened the path to the presidency. How did they celebrate now that Nixon had resigned? They got right back to work on the question of whether Nixon should be indicted for his participation in the cover-up.

James Vorenberg returned from Harvard to help, although it is not clear whether he was invited by Jaworski or just assumed that the on-site Harvard crew at the WSPF would need guidance now that Nixon was gone; he may well have worried (and rightly, as it turned out) that Jaworski would lack the intensity (much less the vindictiveness) that Cox would have brought to the exercise. "Sleepy Jim," as generations of Harvard Law students have affectionately called him, must have been reassured to find that at least success had done nothing to reduce the fervor of the Kennedy cohorts. After all, they had signed up for the Get Nixon Squad, and why should they let the technicality that Nixon was no longer there stop them now? Allowing Nixon to escape simply by resigning just wasn't good enough. They wanted to see him in jail—just like Jimmy Hoffa.

Special Prosecutor Jaworski found himself facing a near mutiny because of his perceived hesitancy to pursue Nixon into retirement. Tired of sitting through endless heated debates on the subject, he asked all those with strong views about a criminal indictment—whether they were on the Watergate Task Force or not—to submit their views and recommendations in writing.

There are some fifteen of these memos submitted to Jaworski from WSPF staff members that survive in WSPF files, each and every one strongly recommending indictment and prosecution.

There are also two nonlegal memos. One analyzes newspaper editorial reaction, and the other describes recent public opinion polls on the question of indicting the now former president. The main thrust was that since there was some diversity of editorial and public opinion, the special prosecutor had a free hand to decide on his own. Even Doyle, the press officer, got into the act—suggesting that Jaworski might wish to poll Congress to see how members felt.

These memos reveal more of a lynch mob mentality than anything resembling evenhanded judgment or prosecutorial discretion. Cox's firing had so outraged the Get Nixon Squad that all sense of proportion or prosecutorial discretion had been cast aside. The staff's principal argument was that equal protection of the laws required prosecution: It's not nearly enough that he has resigned; it is our manifest duty to put him in jail. The sentiment was so one-sided that Jaworski felt that he had to assign a lawyer the task of articulating the reasons why Nixon should *not* be indicted.

Afterward, many people asserted that Nixon was never really in danger of being pursued and indicted, that cooler heads would have prevailed—

even within the special prosecutor's office. In his book Jaworski states that he wouldn't have authorized prosecution. But the vituperative tone of WSPF internal memos is too filled with hatred and vengeance for Jaworski to have withstood for very long before he had a mutiny—and the media disaster for his reputation that would have invited—on his unwilling hands.

No, Nixon was going to be indicted and dragged from courtroom to courtroom with his reels of tapes while various lawyers in a multitude of other cases tore him apart on the witness stand. Most concerned observers—including people with no love for Richard Nixon—feared that this process, which might last for years, could worsen the national trauma and continue to divide the country, and prevent moving past the mire of Watergate and beginning the healing most Americans wanted so badly. For the Kennedy clan, of course, the greater the dysfunction and the deeper the divisions, the more the country would look with longing and nostalgia to the Camelot days of yore, and rally around another Kennedy candidacy.

On September 8, President Ford surprised and shocked the nation— not to mention the Kennedy conspirators—by granting a "full, free and absolute" pardon to Richard Nixon. It is well-settled law that the constitutional provision providing for presidential pardons is so clear and unambiguous that there is no reasonable ground on which its exercise might be challenged. A recent example of this was the furor over the pardons issued by President Clinton during his last hours in the White House. Although they were universally condemned, their validity was never questioned.

In the WSPF's offices, however, the Kennedy cohorts were not about to let even a presidential pardon stand in their way. When Jaworski made a pro forma request for an analysis of the scope of the Nixon pardon, his staff took it as an invitation to suggest ways the pardon might be challenged in court. Their submissions are instructive to the point of being downright scary. One suggested that since the constitutional power of the president to pardon had not been tested in court, it remained completely vulnerable. Another posited that it could only be exercised following indictment and conviction—and was therefore invalid in Nixon's case (because Ford's pardon had intervened before any Nixon indictments). Another recommended indicting the president because, instead of precluding indictment, the pardon should be viewed as a defense that could be invoked only after indictment, and during a trial. In other words, if the president didn't wish to try to clear his name by offering a full defense, he could invoke the pardon.

Another staffer urged that, while a "full, free and absolute" pardon might bar criminal prosecution, it might not prevent a civil suit brought by the government to recover damages caused by the Nixon presidency. Another analyzed the possibility of publication of a grand jury report that might detail Nixon's criminal culpability even if no indictment were forthcoming. (Of course, WSPF attorneys would be the ones to draft such a grand jury report.) Another argument suggested that the pardon be challenged for lack of specificity, on the grounds that the constitutional language describing a "full, free and absolute" pardon was too vague to be valid.

One memo, submitted by Phil Lacovara on September 13, was as ingenious as it was tortuous—and is therefore reproduced in Appendix X. In an argument that either demonstrated the WSPF's delusions of grandeur or exposed the author's desperation at the prospect of losing Nixon—or both—Lacovara claimed that Ford's constitutional power to pardon had actually been usurped by the WSPF Guidelines. The argument went something like this: The Guidelines agreed to by Attorney General Richardson during his confirmation had granted the special prosecutor full and unreviewed independence to prosecute whomever he wished. Because the president must have concurred in Richardson's action, the Guidelines thus not only precluded Nixon from interfering with indictments, but also from granting pardons (which could be seen as interfering with WSPF prosecutions). If Nixon were precluded from granting pardons, so was his successor, because Nixon's presumed concurrence in the Guidelines would have been an institutional decision, not a personal one. In other words, Richardson's acceptance of the Guidelines would have been a decision that bound the presidency, not just a president. Creative, yes—but not really a persuasive argument of how a condition of confirmation that was never enacted into law by either house of Congress could trump a constitutionally explicit presidential power.

Jaworski, confronted with this kind of logic from an able and trusted aide, confided to his deputy that he would be too embarrassed even to raise such arguments in open court. His memo, also reproduced in Appendix X, suggests the extent to which Jaworski was prisoner of Cox's army: Here he was begging for support in rejecting the presented logic; he had earlier sent a handwritten note asking for his deputy's views; and now he was being forced to actually express his own with no apparent support.

Kennedy Democrats in Congress were equally outraged with the idea that their innings might be coming to an end before they beat Richard Nixon into the ground. Rumors began to circulate that the "fix was in," and that Nixon had made the promise of a pardon a precondition for his resignation. The House Judiciary Subcommittee on Criminal Justice decided to pursue these rumors, and demanded all relevant White House documents from the new president. The long nightmare of Watergate was not to be allowed to end, and a determined effort was being made to taint President Ford—who had now emerged as the most likely Republican candidate to run against Teddy Kennedy in 1976.

Ford's response was an act unprecedented in American history. He voluntarily appeared before the House Judiciary Committee on October 17 to read a forty-five-minute statement and respond to questions. This was the first (so far the only) time a sitting president formally testified before a congressional committee.

In recent years the Kennedys have surprised many of their supporters (and, perhaps, more to the point, disarmed many of their critics) by embracing the Nixon pardon as a consummate act of statesmanship on the part of President Ford. In 2001 he was awarded a Profile in Courage Award by the John F. Kennedy Library Foundation. Teddy Kennedy finessed his bitter opposition to the pardon and denunciation of the pardoner: "Unlike many of us at the time," he said, "President Ford recognized that the nation had to move forward, and could not do so if there was a continuing effort to prosecute former President Nixon." Almost three decades after the event, with most passion spent, it wasn't a bad gambit for Teddy to give some belated props to the short-term but long-lived and popular thirty-eighth president. That the Kennedy clan's orchestrated reaction to Ford's pardon had ruined his election chances in 1976 was now ancient history—and, they hoped, forgotten. Of course, it's possible that Teddy was sincere, and that his thinking had changed. But it's also possible that it was more of a feint to the right—a masterstroke of disinformation—to discourage any profiles of the distinctly uncourageous role the Camelot Conspiracy had played in driving a recently reelected president from office to serve its own partisan purposes.

Stage Two of the Camelot Conspiracy:
Crippling the Republican Money Machine

For the GOP, the postresignation 1974 midterm congressional elections were a ballot-box disaster approaching the magnitude of the 1964 Goldwater wipeout 10 years earlier. The Democratic margin in the Senate (only one third of which was up for election) increased from 22 to 30 votes, and in the House it tripled—from 50 to 150 votes.

Things were looking up, indeed, for Teddy Kennedy's expected presidential run in 1976. But there was still work to be done—and other opportunities to be explored. Nixon's 1972 election victory had been neutralized, and Nixon himself, along with his presidency, had been removed. Now the certainty of a Kennedy victory in 1976 could be significantly advanced with the achievement of the Camelot Conspiracy's two other goals: decimating the superior Republican fund-raising apparatus, and undermining any potential Republican presidential candidates through investigation and intimidation.

For some reason the WSPF's Campaign Contributions Task Force seemed only to focus on Republicans: Republican fund-raisers, Republican contributors, and Republican candidates. Because that unbalanced and unfair approach could never be admitted, decidedly different language was used in the Vorenberg-authored official WSPF report (*Report of the Watergate Special Prosecution Force on Campaign Contributions, Investigation of 1972 Campaign Financing and Related Matters*), which may well have been drafted purposely to mislead the public, by going out of its way to create the false impression that the inquiry had been even-handed.

The Campaign Contributions Task Force originally was headed by Thomas McBride, another stalwart from the Criminal Division of RFK's Department of Justice. The entire introduction to their section in WSPF *Report* is reproduced in Appendix Y. It begins with a patently untrue assertion that:

> Beginning in June 1973, the Campaign Contributions Task Force systematically examined the campaign finances of major 1972 Republican and Democratic Presidential candidates.

This would seem to describe a thorough, evenhanded, and appropriately nonpartisan approach to the question of campaign finance. But, as so often where the Kennedy Clan Democrats are concerned, it is necessary to look beneath the well-composed exterior to find out what was really going on. Thus the quoted sections below are followed by a reality check:

> This examination included the investigation of several hundred separate transactions, including corporate and labor union contributions.

In fact, the only labor unions that were examined were the Carpenters and Seafarers unions—which just happened to be the only unions that contributed to Nixon's reelection campaign. In spite of the opposite implication, and the fact that the WSPF had received GAO prosecution referrals involving at least three other unions (the United Rubber, Cork, Linoleum & Plastic Workers, the Amalgamated Meat Cutters & Butcher Workmen, and the International Brotherhood of Electrical Workers), no other unions were even contacted. Union campaign support of Democrats has been—and remains to this day—a serious area of concern not only among Republicans, but also for those interested in transparent political finance. Despite the exactly opposite impression the WSPF's *Report* was clearly intended to give, the WSPF Campaign Contribution Task Force investigation was a one-sided, politically motivated exercise from its outset.

Report of pre–April 7 contributions to several Democratic candidates, which the candidates had made public.

Why does the WSPF have the *complete* Nixon list, but only lists that have been *voluntarily* disclosed from Democratic candidates? Of course, this is just where the "Task Force began its inquiries"—the implication being that efforts were made to obtain comparable lists from all Democratic candidates. But that implication is misleading. The letters that were, indeed, sent to Democratic presidential candidates only requested contribution information on a voluntary basis, and specifically confined the request to corporate contributions—carefully excluding any inquiry involving union contributions.

Information obtained in the Watergate investigation about the sources and disposition of campaign funds used in the Watergate break-in and cover-up.

The only Democrat indicted was Duane Andreas, who had made a legal pre–April 7 twenty-five-thousand-dollar contribution to Nixon. Apparently the ensuing investigation was so thorough that it actually managed to turn up *one* non-Republican transaction of concern, and the WSPF distributed the resulting indictment to the press. While the WSPF was thus able to produce one Democrat who was indicted for breaking campaign contribution laws, the Andreas example held a sobering lesson: Don't dabble with giving to both sides—Democrats who also support Republicans should expect to be exposed and made examples of. Duane Andreas was tried in July 1974—in Minneapolis—and acquitted on all counts, but his indictment remained as a cautionary tale for Republican contributors.

The prosecutors interviewed major Republican and Democratic fundraisers, including Herbert Kalmbach of FCRP, who cooperated with the office under an agreement involving his guilty plea to two charges (described elsewhere in this section).

Naming Kalmbach, Nixon's personal lawyer, at this point in the report is a gratuitous slap at the Finance Committee to Re-elect the President. No Democratic counterpart is named; that, of course, would smack of McCarthyism.

Agents of the FBI and IRS examined the campaign financial records of the major Presidential candidates and those Congressional candidates whose campaign finances, for various reasons, became relevant to matters directly within the jurisdiction of the Special Prosecutor.

This is a reference to the Townhouse Project, an effort undertaken by the White House to support certain congressional candidates in the 1970 midterm elections. (The Townhouse Project was named for the place it was conceived: one of the restored federal townhouses on Jackson Place across the street from the White House.) It constitutes the only WSPF investigation of any congressional campaign. The specific violation—having a campaign committee without a treasurer—was pursued under a law that had not been enforced even once since 1934. Although it was on the books when the Townhouse Project was set up, it had been repealed in conjunction with the new disclosure laws that came into effect in April 1972.

The Campaign Contributions Task Force's Charles Ruff submitted a memorandum in August 1974—two weeks after Nixon's resignation—recommending prosecution, even going so far as to point out that *scienter,* the criminal intent normally necessary for conviction, would not be absent just because none of the defendants even remotely suspected their actions might be illegal. All that was necessary under "modern case law" would be to show that the defendants acted intentionally rather than negligently.

The Campaign Contributions Task Force efforts involved

interviews and investigations of some eleven individuals with connections to the Nixon White House, two dozen financial contributors,
and campaign donations made in thirty-two states. A thorough
investigation, indeed, but one in which, just coincidentally, all
those investigated were Nixon supporters. Perhaps it was also
coincidental that all of the Republican senators receiving contributions in connection with the 1970 Townhouse Project would be up
for reelection again in 1976, and thus could be more vulnerable to
possible allegations of improprieties.

*FBI agents interviewed hundreds of employees and financial offi-
cers of corporations and unions and examined bank and corporate
records; IRS agents took similar steps in cases that seemed to involve
possible tax violations.*

This is the second reference to FBI and IRS support, and it
seems that the WSPF actually sent FBI and IRS agents to interview substantial Republican contributors. This could reasonably be
expected to have at least a dampening—if not a downright chilling—
effect on any campaign contributions they might be considering in
the next presidential election, the one in which Teddy Kennedy
was expected to run. Realistically, the arrival of FBI or IRS agents
on a contributor's doorstep could be expected to blow a giant hole
in any party's fund-raising apparatus. And such housecalls, at least
as far as I have been able to ascertain, were solely confined to Republican donors.

*In some cases, particularly when there was a suspicion of an ex-
plicit quid pro quo relationship between contributions and Government actions, WSPF attorneys conducted interviews of contributors,
fundraisers, and Government officials.*

By definition, this would only have involved investigation of
the Nixon administration, since only the 1972 campaign was reviewed. One can only wonder what might have been uncovered
with regard to prior administrations. As with the Ervin Committee's investigations, however, they were specifically exempted from

review. When a series of these cases came before Judge George Hart of the D.C. District Court, the prosecution was forced to admit that this was the first time the government had ever brought suit over such campaign contributions—characterizing the situation as a prior policy of nonenforcement. WSPF press secretary Doyle noted that Judge Hart had the temerity to ask, albeit in a private conversation with WSPF counsel, just when he might expect to see a case brought against any Democrats or labor unions. The true answer, although not the one given to the judge, was somewhere around the twelfth of never.

Witnesses were also called before the grand jury, especially when it appeared that attempts were being made to obstruct an investigation.

There is simply no way of knowing how many Republican fund-raisers and contributors were actually called before grand juries. No obstruction of justice cases were ever filed, so this particularly egregious activity remains forever sealed from public review.

There is no question that there were a handful of illegal corporate campaign donations that came to light, but usually all did so when Cox announced a policy of amnesty for those coming forward voluntarily. When coupled with the absence of any investigation of the Democrat-supporting unions—and with no FBI or IRS agents sent to call on them—the investigatory focus was completely one-sided.

Campaign Contributions Task Force head McBride left the WSPF staff in October 1975, when the WSPF's final report was issued, as did Henry Ruth (originally Cox's deputy, who had been elevated to the special prosecutor position following Jaworski's departure in October 1974). The fourth, and final, special prosecutor was Charles Ruff, another RFK Justice alumnus from the organized crime division, who had been a senior member of the Campaign Contributions Task Force from its outset. Already a full year had passed since Nixon's resignation. It had been over a year since the Plumbers defendants had been convicted, and over ten months since conviction of the cover-up defendants. What remained was the continued prosecution of campaign finance violations—which only ended when the special prosecutor's office finally closed up for good in June 1977, after the White House had been restored to Democratic control.

Let's look at the overall scorecard of what was achieved by the WSPF's Campaign Contributions Task Force efforts:

- There are investigatory files on 158 companies and some 131 private citizens, including such prominent Republican contributors as Walter Annenberg, Donald Kendall, Ross Perot, Richard Scaife, C. Arnholt Smith, and W. Clement Stone.
- The largest number of legal actions brought involved the Associated Milk Producers. This was a dairy cooperative owned by thousands of farmers in the Upper Midwest; it was hardly the kind of evil megacorporation—presumably some kind of bovine Halliburton—that the media had been led to expect. If anything, its multitude of misdeeds would make the actions of public corporations look inconsequential— which is probably why the WSPF Report went out of its way to disguise the connections between these cases—by treating them as individual prosecutions. In fact, the milk cooperative received the largest fine of any organization ($35,000); it was also responsible for the greatest number of individual indictments (three full trials, albeit one resulting in an acquittal, plus guilty pleas from five others, three of whom were not only fined, but each also sentenced to four months in jail).
- Guilty pleas were obtained from only two other companies of any significance: American Ship Building Company was fined $20,000 (and its head, George Steinbrenner, was fined $10,000), and Ashland Oil was fined $25,000 (with one individual fined $1,000).
- There were a handful of what might be termed nuisance cases: Guilty pleas were obtained from sixteen companies, none of which was fined more than $5,000. Guilty pleas also were obtained from seventeen individuals in connection with these improper corporate contributions. All but two were fined $1,000 or less; those two were fined $2,000.

- In noncorporate matters, guilty pleas were obtained from eleven individuals. Three received suspended sentences, and all but three were fined $1,000 or less. Herbert Kalmbach was fined $10,000, with six months in jail; Maurice Stans was fined $5,000, as was 1 other corporate officer.
- It also should be noted that the task force "investigated over 30 allegations of improper influence on Government actions by contributors to the President's 1972 campaign." After detailing the agencies investigated, the WSPF report concluded, "None of these Inquiries developed sufficient evidence to support criminal charges."

That's it; that's all. After all the turmoil, after all the press speculation, all the leaks, all the headlines and tut-tutting op-eds, after all the investigations and all the WSPF/FBI/IRS interviews—that was the result. Here's how Maury Stans nailed the truth of the matter in his 1978 book, *The Terrors of Justice*, saying these reports

> *turned out to be pure fiction, absolute hogwash. The Watergate Special Prosecutor investigated "several hundred" such accusations, through thousands of interviews and subpoenas for thousands of documents, using his own organization, the Internal Revenue Service, the FBI, the computerized records of data gathered by the Senate Watergate [Ervin] Committee, and information from members of Congress. After two years of ferreting out the facts, he announced in his final report that he could not find evidence adequate to take to court a single instance within this entire range of alleged corrupt practices.*
>
> *Insofar as the Nixon money-raising in 1972 was concerned, there were only a handful of nonwillful technical violations and these were less significant individually and in the aggregate than similar oversights and violations by a number of other candidates who were not prosecuted.*
>
> *That was the surviving sum and substance of all of the alleged financial corruption in the 1972 Nixon campaign. Not a single proved case of corrupt action. No favors granted. No contracts awarded. No cases fixed. No ambassadorships sold. No illegal contributions from foreigners. No overseas laundries. No illegal solicitations. No list of*

companies in trouble with the government. No enemy lists. No fund-raising by government officials. No extortion or coercion. No intentional circumvention of the law in a single instance. That is precisely what the Department of Justice, the Special Prosecutor, and the Courts found.

In prosecutorial terms, the Watergate Special Prosecutor's Campaign Contribution Task Force labored mightily to produce a mouse. But the task force investigations themselves had produced a more significant victory as far as the Kennedy conspirators were concerned: They had helped to paralyze the Republican fund-raising machine for the 1976 elections.

In an interview in June 1977, in connection with closing down the WSPF offices, Charles Ruff, the Campaign Contribution Task Force's senior member who became the last special prosecutor, as much as predicted that someday the truth would begin to emerge. In an article printed on June 19 in the *Washington Post,* Bob Woodward wrote that Ruff expected his work on Watergate to be questioned someday. He said, "There are judgment calls that were made that people can legitimately question." Admitting that it might all look different to future congressional investigators, Ruff said that if called to testify,

I'd say, "Gee, I just don't remember what happened back then," and they won't be able to indict me for perjury and that, maybe, that's the principal thing that I've learned in four years. . . . I just intend to rely on that failure of memory.

Maury Stans may have been the greatest fund-raiser in Republican history—but his effectiveness ended with the Watergate investigations, when he was indicted in the Vesco case and had every contribution scrutinized by the WSPF in hopes of putting him behind bars. Though acquitted in Vesco, they found three technical violations to which he ultimately pled guilty in March 1975—followed by a considerable battle, which Stans won, over whether he could be sentenced to jail.

20

Stage Three of the Camelot Conspiracy: Eviscerating Potential Opponents

The third goal of the Camelot conspirators—after hobbling Nixon and drying up the deep wells of Republican fund-raising—was to decimate the ranks of potential opponents. Teddy Kennedy had been spoiled in Massachusetts by not having any serious opponents since his first Senate race. The appetite grows with eating, and Teddy had become used to running without having to worry about the opposition.

Easily the most prominent opponent to be taken out was John Connally. Before Nixon resigned and Ford became the incumbent president, "Big John" Connally, the former Democratic governor of Texas, was the most likely Republican candidate to run for president in 1976. He had been JFK's secretary of the Navy before returning to Texas to win the governorship in 1962 (and then serving three terms). He and his wife were in the front seat of the president's car in Dallas—and he was seriously wounded—when JFK was assassinated. Losing faith as his own Democratic Party moved to the left under Kennedy influence, he became Nixon's secretary of the Treasury in 1971, and formally joined the Republican Party in 1973. Many believe he was Nixon's choice to replace Spiro Agnew as vice president, both on the ticket in 1972, and then when Agnew had to resign in 1973. He was passed over in the first instance because of opposition from the conservative Republican base, with whom Agnew was popular, and in the second because of the anticipated Kennedy-led opposition in a Senate confirmation battle.

Any Connally candidacy in 1976 was effectively aborted by a WSPF indictment charging him with accepting an illegal payment, perjury, obstruction of justice, and two charges of making false statements to the grand jury—all in connection with contributions made by the Associated Milk Producers. Materials concerning this case had been among those purloined by John Dean when he left the White House, and subsequently were shared with prosecutors in his attempt to negotiate immunity.

Connally chose to stand trial and was acquitted on all charges—but he was ruined personally and politically in the process. Theodore H. White's description is the most vivid and telling about how it ended Connally's political career.

> *Finally, he was tainted by his association with "Watergate." In the public mind, Watergate had blurred within a cloud that includes break-ins, wiretaps, laundered money, shakedowns—and also the so-called milk scandal. In 1974, John Connally had been indicted by a federal grand jury for having taken ten thousand dollars from the Associated Milk Producers, Inc. in exchange for persuading President Nixon to support a hike in milk price support. The trial, in 1975, lasted eleven days but was meaningless; the jury cleared him after five and a half hours of deliberation. But the smear stuck.*

The WSPF Campaign Task Force then apparently decided to play its own small part in an untoward and undemocratic exercise. How else to explain the files I discovered in 2006 upon gaining access to those available in the National Archives? In the task force's defense, I suppose it can be said that if what they did was undemocratic, at least it was bipartisan—they were equally willing to use their absolute power in order to gain information to harass Teddy Kennedy's potential Democratic rivals for the presidential nomination, as well as his Republican opponents in the general election.

Let's begin with a review of prominent Republicans, potential 1976 opponents all, but having no known connection with Watergate whatsoever—each of whom became the subject of a WSPF investigation.

Potential Republican Candidates with WSPF Files

GERALD FORD. Ford had no connection with Watergate, yet there are indications that portions of the raw files from the FBI's full investigation of him—done in connection with his confirmation hearings—somehow ended up in the WSPF files. This kind of unedited and unevaluated material in such files can be political dynamite in the wrong hands.

A separate campaign finance investigation regarding President Ford was launched by the WSPF in July 1976—in the middle of the Presidential campaign. The issue involved the possibility of prior campaign finance violations—while Ford was in Congress—in connection with contributions from the Maritime Union (which already had endorsed Ford's opponent Jimmy Carter, and was working hard in support of his campaign). There was considerable press speculation about the issues involved. Ford's necessary response to these allegations required detailed financial reconstructions from his earlier campaign— which was both time consuming and distracting for him and his staff—especially in the midst of his own 1976 campaign. It took three months—until less than a month before the November election—for the WSPF to graciously announce that there was not sufficient information on which to base a prosecution; their press release announcing that no case would be brought was typically understated.

NELSON ROCKEFELLER. Rockefeller was the former governor of New York, before being named vice president by Gerald Ford after Nixon's resignation in August 1974.

An all-out full field investigation of his entire political career was undertaken by the FBI—but this time with a twist. A newspaper column claimed that Roy Sheppard (a mysteriously ubiquitous courier who had transported file boxes for the CRP—following the break-in—and for John Dean—when he departed the White House) had information secreted in a safety-deposit box that could confirm rumors that Rockefeller had contributed money to George McGovern's campaign. The WSPF's very top echelon swung into immediate action: A full week of frenzied activity followed, with the FBI interviewing several Sheppard family members—a few of the interviews conducted after 10:00 P.M. at night. Two safety-deposit boxes were identified, and search warrants were obtained. Nothing relevant to Rockefeller, or to any WSPF investigation, was found in either of them.

The WSPF Rockefeller files also contain copies of a series of FBI reports on the soon-to-be vice president. There were once other files of a more sensitive nature, but they have been redacted or removed, and therefore remain unidentified and unavailable to researchers.

BOB DOLE. Rockefeller withdrew from consideration as Gerald Ford's vice presidential running mate in the fall of 1975. Ford settled on Kansas senator Robert Dole. WSPF files indicate an uptick of interest in Dole right about this time.

In early February of 1976—just weeks prior to the New Hampshire primary—the WSPF interviewed Dole in his Senate office. Their ostensible concern involved some questionable corporate contributions from Gulf Oil's Washington lobbyist to certain other senators. The question, which appears to have become important only with the prospect of Bob Dole becoming Gerald Ford's vice president, was whether Dole had ever knowingly received any of this illegal corporate cash, forwarded by his Senate colleagues.

Not surprisingly, news of WSPF interest in Dole was leaked to the media, and inspired considerable speculation, and generated many articles questioning Dole's honesty.

Unlike with President Ford's case, there was no press release or other public resolution of these amorphous suspicions about Bob Dole, and the extent to which they adversely affected his campaign and the fate of the Ford-Dole ticket can never be determined.

The only further entry in the Dole file is a rather bitter letter he sent to Charles Ruff several months after losing the election, asking that he be "advised what disposition will be made of the investigation." Ruff kindly replied that Dole was not then the subject of any investigation.

RONALD REAGAN. How, you might well wonder, could California's governor Reagan—then three thousand miles away in Sacramento—possibly be connected to Watergate? The answer is that he wasn't—but it was not for lack of trying on the part of the WSPF. He was, after all, among the leading Republicans assessing their chances in the 1976 presidential race—which, in fact, he eventually entered.

No formally identified WSPF file has been found at National Archives on Ronald Reagan, but his investigation is the central focus of McBride's one-page transmittal memo of August 19, 1974, forwarding Charles Ruff's prosecution recommendations regarding the Townhouse Project. Reproduced in Appendix Z, here's the operative paragraph:

> *The only other information of any possible consequence relates to Reagan. In 1970, Ross Perot, head of a large Dallas-based computer firm, was solicited by Kalmbach for a contribution to the 1970 mid-term congressional campaigns. He was also solicited for contributions to Reagan's 1970 gubernatorial campaign. According to Kalmbach, Perot did not ultimately contribute to the congressional races. He may, however, have contributed to the Reagan campaign. In May, 1970 Perot asked Kalmbach to set up meetings with Reagan and with Harry Dent, John Ehrlichman and possibly other administration figures. Perot says the purpose of these meetings was to complain about certain policies and actions of the Social Security Administration in requiring approval of contracts between medicare insurers . . . and Perot's computer firm. In the case of Reagan the particular issue was the substitution of one private carrier (with whom Perot had computer contracts) by another (with whom Perot was not a subcontractor) as medicare carrier in several California counties. Perot did meet with Reagan and later (perhaps through Reagan's intervention) with HEW Secretary Finch and Undersecretary Veneman. Perot did not get the relief or remedy he sought. We have not, as yet, learned whether Perot did, in fact, contribute to Reagan's 1970 campaign.*

This is a prime example of just how far afield the WSPF willingly wandered from its supposed mission. The reasoning was tendentious and tortuous; the connection, which would have been tangential even had it existed, was unproven. But seeking proof wasn't the purpose here; the purpose was investigating and possibly raising suspicions regarding potential Kennedy opponents.

Although Campaign Contributions Task Force chief McBride doesn't come right out and say it, it is not hard to conclude that his purpose is to alert Special Prosecutor Jaworski to their intention to continue their investigation into Reagan's conduct as governor. Note especially that McBride clearly didn't think he needed Jaworski's blessing to launch the investigation of Reagan in the first place. This memo was merely a courtesy report on a lead that was being checked out, perhaps following up something Jaworski had overheard in a hallway conversation.

Aside from any sense of outrage over the self-appointed scope of WSPF investigations, this gives a fair picture of the situation following Cox's removal: His teams of Kennedy Clan Democrats remained in place, well beyond any possibility of being controlled by Jaworski, whose chosen role was to sit in his office waiting for Cox's staff to bring him their indictment recommendations. If he had even suggested curtailing one of their many investigations, he would no doubt have read about his suspicious behavior in the next day's newspapers.

As with many WSPF investigations, the Reagan line of inquiry simply faded away. Perhaps worse, because no actual file has been located, we can't know how far the investigation was pursued in an attempt to tar yet another potential Republican opponent.

Potential Democratic Opponents

Because Ted Kennedy hadn't been a candidate for president in 1972, there was no possibility that any WSPF investigation would produce embarrassing information about him. The same couldn't be said for most of his potential competitors for the 1976 Democratic presidential nomination, including Hubert Humphrey, Scoop Jackson, Wilbur Mills, George McGovern, and Edmund Muskie, each of whom had tested the presidential waters in '72.

Pro forma WSPF files were opened on each of them. Of course, there was little danger of any actual prosecution. But once again, neither justice nor fairness seem to have been the objects of this particular exercise. Had any derogatory information been developed, it would have been readily available to the Kennedy cohorts for possible future use.

The Weakest Link: Teddy Kennedy Self-Destructs

By the summer of 1974, the Kennedy Clan Democrats had achieved their multiple goals more completely than they could ever have imagined back in the fall of '72, when Ted Kennedy had geared up his subcommittee to see if they could somehow tie Nixon to the hinky doings surrounding the Watergate break-in.

Indeed, they may even have succeeded not wisely but too well. The original idea had been to negate Nixon's phenomenal reelection victory by keeping him on the ropes throughout his second term; as a pitiful, helpless incumbent, Nixon would only be able to keep the seat warm for Teddy Kennedy. At the outset, few if any imagined that Nixon would actually be forced to resign only two years into his second term. And given the choice between a crippled president serving out his full term, or that president resigning and being succeeded by his scandal-free vice president, who could then run for election with all the advantages of incumbency, as well as the gratitude of the nation—given that choice, many of the Kennedy Clan Democrats might very well have chosen to keep the crippled Nixon around through '76.

But instead of being merely hobbled, Nixon had been forced from office. The foundations of the once mighty Republican fund-raising apparatus had been effectively undermined by the passive/aggressive threat of public scrutiny and judicial inquiry, and, in some cases, with the active disincentive from IRS and FBI interventions. The potential presidential candidates in both parties had been investigated; files of possibly embarrassing or damaging information had been assembled, ready for strategic use once the campaign got under way.

The Kennedy Clan Democrats and their media supporters had done everything possible to pave the way for Teddy's 1976 run for the roses, for Camelot's restoration, and for the Harvard elites' return to what they knew to be their rightful places: in power, and in charge. Now they waited for him to reserve Boston's historic Faneuil Hall and announce his candidacy.

And waited.

And waited.

But their great expectations were met by only a few halfhearted sallies, followed by silence. The putative president was AWOL.

Where was Teddy? What had happened? We will never know for sure. Perhaps he just wasn't ready; perhaps he felt America just wasn't ready for him; perhaps he considered his son's and wife's physical and mental wellness to be his principal priorities—or his most serious vulnerabilities. Perhaps he feared, as he sometimes confided to friends, being assassinated. Perhaps the internal poll results weren't sufficiently encouraging. Perhaps he feared the possibility of a backlash, if his candidacy suddenly threw a spotlight on his role in driving Nixon from office. Perhaps the absence of his father's commanding presence and indomitable will removed the pressures that had led this always relatively reluctant Kennedy to consider running at all.

Or perhaps he considered that Chappaquiddick, however much it may have receded over the intervening six years, remained an insurmountable problem.

Or perhaps all of the above.

Whatever the reasons, in the end there was no public announcement. Teddy Kennedy simply declined to run, and decided not to talk about it.

In November 1976, although the star failed to show up and perform, the show still went on, and was a great success. Jimmy Carter defeated Gerald Ford, and his administration brought new waves of executive branch

Democrats back to Washington. But these Carter Democrats were night and day different from the Kennedy Democrats, and after the initial honeymoon that fact increasingly presented problems for both sides. Jimmy Carter and his inner circle gloried in the simple values of his dirt-poor hometown of Plains, Georgia. They had their own ideas and their own distinctive style—neither of which were congruent with Camelot. Plains on the Potomac prided itself on having no time for fancy ways or airs. It was a classic clash of styles and tastes. From the Kennedy point of view, it was like *Deliverance* had taken over 1600 Pennsylvania Avenue; instead of Pablo Casals playing Bach's Suites for Unaccompanied Cello in the East Room, the Carter White House danced to the tune of "Dueling Banjos."

The Kennedyites were kept from power; and the Carterites didn't have a clue about how to run things. Jimmy Carter came and went in four years—the most inept president and administration of our lifetime—humiliatingly defeated by a conservative Republican.

Teddy was AWOL in 1976, but by November 1979, things had changed. Perhaps he had just had enough of both Jimmy Carter's incompetence and his lack of respect for, or interest in, perpetuating the Kennedy memory, furthering the Kennedy agenda, or taking care of the Kennedy Clan Democrats.

Whatever the reasons, he finally bestirred himself to run for the Democratic Party's presidential nomination. But unlike in 1972 or 1976, when he would have been squaring off against a Republican, in 1980 he had to commit political apostasy by first challenging the incumbent president of his own party. When Bobby Kennedy decided to challenge Lyndon Johnson, it was because he reflected the widespread and deeply principled opposition to the Vietnam War, and a lot of Democrats respected him for it. But when Teddy Kennedy decided to challenge Jimmy Carter, it was because he had finally decided he wanted his job, and a lot of Democrats were turned off by his opportunism and disloyalty. Carter was generally acknowledged to be a disaster, but for the Democrats, he was "our disaster."

In the words of presidential chronicler Theodore H. White, who had long been one of the Kennedy family's greatest fans:

> *The Kennedy campaign was, from the beginning, historically preposterous. What the senator proposed to do was to destroy the chief of*

his own party, the President of the United States. Having undermined
the President, he would then have to pull the Democratic Party to-
gether again and face the Republicans, defending a record he spent a
year denouncing. If he succeeded in destroying the President, that
would come at the convention in August. Thus, Jimmy Carter would
be castrated—yet officially remain as commander in chief of the
United States Armed Forces, national spokesman on foreign policy, for
another six months. He would be the silhouette of impotent authority,
not even a lame duck, but a limping capon.

The astute reader of White's description of what Kennedy proposed to
do to Carter may see the similarity to Richard Nixon's situation during his
last months in office, when he was a limping capon before he became a
dead duck.

Some Kennedy Clan Democrats may have thought that Teddy's decision was unworthy, but most welcomed it as a case of better late than never.
It quickly became clear, however, that it was, in fact, a case of too little too
late. He was still able to mobilize the old guard and the hard core, those
men and women who had been inspired by JFK and RFK, and who had
stayed loyal to the Kennedy cause for almost twenty years. But even the
most ardent loyalists had to admit that Teddy was not the man his brothers
had been; he lacked Jack's grace and Bobby's intensity; his main character
trait seemed to be indecisiveness. And besides, times had changed. Kennedy clan veterans had aged; even those who were still able to were no
longer inclined to hit the streets in an uphill campaign. And with the absence of vigorous leadership, the youngsters jumping on the bandwagon
soon sensed the absence of the fabled Kennedy magic.

The press, too, was dismayed. Since JFK first ran for the Eleventh
Congressional District in 1947, a Kennedy could count on dealing with a
friendly press. But even a slam dunk has to go through the basket, and
Teddy Kennedy turned out to be almost shockingly maladroit in his dealings with the media. To launch his presidential campaign, Kennedy arranged an interview with a friendly newsman—Roger Mudd of CBS—that
would be broadcast in prime time a few days before he would publicly announce his candidacy.

Sitting on the porch of the senator's house in the Kennedy compound at Hyannis Port, Mudd quoted the presiding judge at the Chappaquiddick trial, who had publicly expressed the opinion that Kennedy had lied. The veteran CBS newsman asked Kennedy if he thought "that anybody will ever fully believe your explanation of Chappaquiddick." Kennedy's answer to a question that should have been anticipated and planned for deserves quotation in full.

> *Oh, there's, there problem is, from that night, I, I found their conduct, the behavior almost beyond belief myself. I mean, that's why it's been, but I think that's the way it was. Now, I find that as I have stated, that I have found the conduct that in, in that evening and in, in the, as a result of the accident of the, and the sense of loss, the sense of hope, and the, and the sense of tragedy, and the whole set of circumstances, that the behavior was inexplicable. So I find that those, those, types of questions as they apply to that, questions of my own soul, as well. But that happens to be the way it was.*

The senator and his staff knew they were staring disaster in the face, so they asked Mudd for a do over, another chance at bat. Perhaps the only thing more extraordinary than their request was the fact that it was granted. A week later, in Kennedy's Senate office in Washington, Roger Mudd delivered what should have been the all-time softball of candidate questions. He asked: "Why do you want to be president?"

Once again, Kennedy's answer defies paraphrase:

> *Well, I'm, were I to make the announcement, and to run, the reasons that I would run is because I have a great belief in this country, that it is, there's more natural resources than any nation in the world; there's the greatest educated population in the world; greatest technology of any country in the world; and the greatest political system in the world. And yet I see at the current time that most of the industrial nations of the world are exceeding us in terms of productivity, are doing better than us in terms of meeting the problem of inflation; that they're dealing with their problems of energy and their problems of unemployment.*

It isn't an exaggeration to say that the Mudd interview, appearing before the Kennedy candidacy was even declared, represented the beginning of the end of any chance Teddy Kennedy had of occupying the White House.

Kennedy lost in every one of the first ten primaries he entered. When his campaign finally found traction, it was just as Carter clinched the necessary votes to put himself over the top. The highest point of Teddy's abortive campaign was his stirring, and uncharacteristically well delivered, speech at the Democratic convention withdrawing his candidacy.

So the last surviving son of the Kennedy political dynasty went down in ignominious and stinging defeat to an unpopular and incompetent incumbent—whom America soon replaced with Ronald Reagan. In many ways Reagan was everything Ted Kennedy wasn't: articulate, charismatic, disciplined, and deceptively able. And in its own way, the Reagan presidency inspired and captured the vision of the majority of Americans like no other president since JFK.

With Reagan's 1980 victory, the rightward swing of American politics that had been derailed by Watergate was resumed. Republicans actually gained control of the Senate for the first time since 1952 (achieving a six-vote majority), and the Democratic majority in the House was reduced to the 1972 level of fifty votes. With the more conservative Southern Democrats factored in, the GOP could sometimes claim conservative voting control.

All the efforts of the Camelot Conspiracy—all the legal corners cut, all the intellectual firepower brought to bear, all the reputations ruined and lives destroyed—in the end could not motivate their candidate sufficiently to run for president, and they could only postpone the inevitable emergence of America's right-center voting majority.

Even Republican money, after being dried up by the conspirators' depredations, returned big time under Reagan. Republicans were once again able to out fund-raise their opponents—both in dollar totals and in numbers of small-amount donors.

Even though they only turned out to be temporary, the results achieved by the Camelot Conspiracy shouldn't be dismissed lightly. Abating the national conservative tide for eight years was not an inconsiderable achievement. Nor was the training and launching of a whole new generation of activist liberal politicians and lawyers who, based on their experience with Watergate, would be willing to use anything and everything at their disposal to advance their cause. Indeed, many of the young lawyers and staffers from the WSPF, the Ervin Committee, and the House impeachment inquiry who cut their teeth on Watergate have played prominent roles in many of the attacks on Republican presidents and politicians over the last three decades.

Not the least of the Camelot Conspiracy's successes has been that until now its very existence was all but unknown. I trust that this book corrects that oversight. Indeed, of the many ironies connected with the Camelot Conspiracy, the greatest by far is that the only thing it failed to accomplish was what it actually set out to achieve: the restoration of a Kennedy to the White House.

22

The Camelot Conspirators Today:
From Edward M. Kennedy to Hillary R. Clinton

E ach passing decade has brought retrospective books and articles reliv-
ing anew all the heroic Watergate stories, including updates on what
happened to the scandal's major figures. It almost seems as if there is an
interest in being sure that no one has managed to climb out of the hole in
which they were buried. With the passage of time, death has claimed all
but a few of the principal players, but the fascination with the whereabouts
of those who survived remains undiminished.

Our inquiry should be no different—except our focus will be on those
who had a hand in destroying Nixon and his fellow Republicans, rather
than on those who were destroyed.

Let's review what became of the leading Kennedy clan coconspirators.

Senator Edward Kennedy and Staff

Ted Kennedy never became president, but has remained a liberal stalwart in
the Senate.

Although he frequently used surrogates (like his old roommate,
Senator John Tunney, and his old prowling pal, Christopher Dodd),

Teddy Kennedy has remained a master of the politics of personal destruction.

In 1987, from his senior position on the Senate Judiciary Committee, he memorably sank Robert Bork's nomination to the Supreme Court.

On July 1, he made a three-minute speech on the Senate floor. He began with an up-front statement: "The man who fired Archibald Cox does not deserve to sit on the Supreme Court of the United States."

Unlike his earlier Nixon-nominated targets—Haynsworth and Carswell—Reagan nominee Bork was an indisputably qualified lawyer and jurist with an impeccable intellectual pedigree. It was certainly possible to disagree with him philosophically, but he was unassailable professionally. Teddy Kennedy's solution was to savage him immediately and personally in what some Kennedy supporters felt was an over-the-top ad hominem attack. Kennedy warned:

> *Robert Bork's America is a land in which women would be forced into back alley abortions, blacks would sit at segregated lunch counters, rogue police could break down citizens' doors in midnight raids, and schoolchildren could not be taught about evolution, writers and artists could be censored at the whim of government, and the doors of the federal courts would be shut on the fingers of millions of citizens for whom the judiciary is—and is often the only—protector of the individual rights that are at the heart of our democracy.*

Kennedy's speech set off a fiercely partisan confirmation battle from which Bork never recovered. When the vote came four months later, Bork was rejected, 58 to 42. The bitterness still lingers today.

Four years later to the month, President George H. W. Bush nominated Judge Clarence Thomas to fill the Supreme Court seat vacated by Justice Thurgood Marshall's retirement. Despite the attempts of many liberal politicians and activists to "bork" him, it appeared that he was on his way to being confirmed.*

---

*Robert Bork's name had already become a transitive verb (in the definition supplied by the Urban Dictionary): "Borked means literally to get stuck or screwed."

One of Kennedy's staffers received a "tip" that Anita Hill, a law professor at the University of Oklahoma, was willing to claim publicly that Thomas had harassed her sexually when she worked for him, when he was chairman of the U.S. Equal Employment Opportunity Commission.*

With Bork's scalp already on his belt, Kennedy decided that going after Thomas would be overkill, so he tried to shop the charge around to some of his committee colleagues. After several senators declined the dubious honor (perhaps understandably uncomfortable with the dynamics of borking any qualified nominee, much less an African American), he finally found a taker in Ohio's quirky Howard Metzenbaum. Thomas survived the onslaught and was narrowly confirmed, but his reputation and standing have never recovered from these personal attacks.

As recently as 2006, Teddy Kennedy was still practicing the politics of personal destruction on Supreme Court nominees. His questioning of Judge Samuel Alito was among the reasons that Mrs. Alito finally gave way under the barrage of personal attacks on her husband and broke down in tears during the hearings.

That night on his show, *Hardball,* Kennedy admirer Chris Matthews, while demonstrating an insider's knowledge of media methods, tried to do some damage control by implying that Mrs. Alito's agony would be blown all out of proportion by conservatives: "They'll put the camera right on Ted Kennedy and show how he was the guy who molested her, basically. That's the way they'll play it"

Carmine Bellino, the Kennedy family loyalist who was chief investigator for both EMK's Subcommittee on Administrative Practices and Procedures and the Ervin Committee, was appointed chief investigator of the Senate Judiciary Committee in 1979, shortly after Ted Kennedy became its chairman. He died in February 1990.

James Flug built much of his reputation as Teddy Kennedy's enforcer blocking the confirmation of Republican Supreme Court nominees. Having helped orchestrate the defeat of Haynsworth and Carswell during the

---

*This staff member, hired only days after Thomas was nominated, was Ricki Seidman, who had been research director at People for the American Way during the anti-Bork campaign.

Nixon administration, he helped block the confirmation of Robert Bork—and nearly sabotaged the confirmation of Clarence Thomas.

In 2004, aged sixty-five, after three decades teaching and lawyering, he rejoined Ted Kennedy's Senate staff, with the express purpose of thwarting President George W. Bush's Supreme Court nominations. Hoping to "bork" nominees John Roberts and Samuel Alito, he talked trash and tried to corral votes with predictions of embarrassing disclosures and nonstop filibusters. But it was not as easy as it had been with Haynsworth and Carswell, when the Democrats held a fifteen-vote majority. Both Bush nominees were confirmed by comfortable margins, and Flug was seen as being too old and out of touch.

Charles Shaffer, while not an official member of Ted Kennedy's staff, certainly provided lots of help to his expected candidacy. Shaffer was every bit the brilliant and resourceful lawyer described by Seymour Glanzer. Following Dean's release in January 1975, he returned to his small suburban law practice, concentrating on white-collar defense work—never again to have a client at the center of a national scandal. Perhaps that is just as well: His efforts got John Dean off virtually scot-free, but the nation paid a huge price.

ERVIN COMMITTEE AND STAFF

Lowell Weicker remained a senator from Connecticut—and an exceedingly close friend of Teddy Kennedy, who counted on his support to control the Senate Labor Committee, even after Republicans assumed the majority in 1980. Weicker lost his seat in 1988 to Democrat Joe Lieberman, an outcome partially attributable to the fact that he received scant support from the Republican Party, from which he had become increasingly estranged. After his defeat he promptly quit the GOP.

James Hamilton, the one senior associate counsel on the Ervin Committee who came from Yale Law School instead of Harvard, later represented Senators DeConcini, Durenberger, and Talmadge before the Senate Ethics Committee and was consulted by Vincent Foster concerning the White House travel office actions some nine days before Foster committed suicide. Hamilton successfully argued that lawyer-client privilege survived

Foster's death—all the way to the Supreme Court (*Swindler and Berlin v. US*), thereby keeping his three pages of notes of their conversation (which possibly could have implicated Hillary Rodham Clinton) from grand jury review.

He has remained very active in Democratic circles: as special counsel for the House's 1983–1984 investigation of how Ronald Reagan's 1980 campaign came up with hundreds of pages of briefing material intended for use by President Carter in their forthcoming debate. He also served as the Clinton-Gore transition counsel for nominations and confirmations and later as a principal Clinton White House adviser for Supreme Court nominations. He represented Timothy Keating, Monica Lewinsky's immediate White House supervisor, during the Clinton administration's own time of troubles. More recently, Hamilton was in charge of vetting vice presidential candidates in 2000 for Al Gore and in 2004 for John Kerry.

Terry Lenzner, the Ervin Committee associate counsel whose investigatory methods regarding Bebe Rebozo were so extreme that even Sam Dash expressed expiration and concern, founded Investigative Group International, Inc., in 1984. In other words, he became a private eye for hire. IGI is a private investigative agency, much of whose primary work appears to have been directed against Republicans. He was alleged to have dug for dirt on staff members of Whitewater special prosecutor Ken Starr's staff—and was called before the grand jury that was investigating whether this impeded Starr's investigations. Starr's two-sentence press statement of February 24, 1998 said:

> *This office has received repeated press inquiries indicating that misinformation is being spread about personnel involved in this investigation. We are using traditional and appropriate techniques to find out who is responsible and whether their actions are intended to intimidate prosecutors and investigators, impede the work of the grand jury, or otherwise obstruct justice.*

IGI was one of a number of private-eye operations hired by the Clinton White House in its attempts to deal with—and squelch—the scandals that kept arising. Foremost among these were the numbers of women who claimed that they had been intimate with, or imposed upon by, the forty-second president (the famous "bimbo eruptions" that marked Clinton's career in Little Rock and Washington). San Francisco's Palladino & Sutherland agency was unleashed on Clinton mistress Gennifer Flowers, and Lenzner's IGI was sicced on Paula Jones, in an attempt to undermine her credibility by denigrating her intelligence and alleging that her sexual conduct was loose.

Ms. Jones was an Arkansas state employee whom Governor Clinton saw at a public function in a Little Rock hotel. He allegedly sent a state trooper to bring her to his hotel suite, where he exposed himself to her, and solicited oral sex from her. Based on Lenzner's activities, Clinton campaign guru James Carville sank the politics of personal destruction to a new low, when he famously said of Ms. Jones's charges that "this is exactly what happens when you drag a dollar bill through a trailer park." Asked under oath whether Hillary Clinton was an IGI client, Lenzner declined to answer on the grounds of lawyer-client privilege.

According to a *Washington Post* profile of Lenzner in March 1998:

> *Equally troubling to some has been the cloudy identity of some of IGI's employers. When IGI investigators were discovered researching Sen. Edward Kennedy's opponent in 1994, the Kennedy campaign first denied employing Lenzner, then admitted it when confronted by the* Boston Globe. *When no record of payments to or donationss by IGI turned up on Kennedy's campaign finance reports, it was finally discovered that Washington lawyer James Flug had hired IGI and been reimbursed by the campaign. Likewise, IGI investigators materialized in the 1994 gubernatorial race in Tennessee asking questions about Nashville Mayor Philip Bredesen, but refused to say whom they were working for.*
>
> *The exact relationship between Lenzner and the Clinton White House has been similarly unclear, although Lenzner has been working at least since 1994 for Clinton lawyers in the Whitewater and Paula Jones cases, did work for the Democratic Party in 1997 [sic].*

IGI bears an eerie and unsettling resemblance to Sandwedge, the separate campaign intelligence agency (far enough separated from the candidate's actual campaign organization to provide cover) that Jack Caulfield first proposed to John Dean in 1971.

A product of Exeter, Harvard, and Harvard Law, Lenzner has, in the course of a long career in Washington, found some devoted friends, many ardent enemies, and a vast middle ground of people who are, frankly, scared by him. The same 1998 profile in the *Washington Post* quoted one of his neighbors and longtime friends:

> *"Terry is a very, very complex man," says a Cleveland Park neighbor who claims long friendship. "He's a perfect Type A personality: smart, aggressive, obsessive and more than a little paranoid. He's got a sense of humor and unlike so many people in Washington he's not consumed by self-importance. But God help you—and I really mean that—if you're on the other side. He's got a dark side that's pretty scary."*

The profile provided another insight into the former Watergate staffer whose recent clients include both Clintons. "He's certainly not characterized by restraint," says one longtime acquaintance. Says another: "He's like a guy walking around with gasoline poured over him, looking for a match."

And these are quotes from his employees and friends.

Scott Armstrong, Bob Woodward's Yale classmate, who worked in Lenzner's group and later joined Woodward at the *Washington Post,* became the principal assistant in the research and writing of Woodward's second Watergate book, *The Final Days,* and later coauthor with Woodward of *The Brethren* (about the U.S. Supreme Court). Armstrong founded the National Security Archive in 1985, which has been accused of encouraging the leaking of classified material. Subsequently, he founded and remains executive director of the Information Trust. According to an article titled "The Leaker as Plumber," published in the *American Spectator* on July 9, 2007:

> *Its mission is the enabling of federal government leakers of classified information. Information Trust, according to Senate Intelligence Committee staff and Federal Bureau of Investigation officials, is believed to have played a critical role in the leaking of national security*

and intelligence data . . . about the CIA's secret prisons that housed al
Qaeda terrorists overseas. The organization also is believed to have
assisted in the leaking of information on the SWIFT financial moni-
toring system out of the Treasury Department.

These are serious accusations, which have been repeated elsewhere, but I have been unable to obtain independent verification. Armstrong certainly founded the National Security Archive as well as the Information Trust—and has participated in panel discussions defending publication of information about CIA overseas prisons and Treasury Department use of the SWIFT monitoring program.

WSPF STAFF ATTORNEYS

Harvard, as it has for four centuries, took care of its own: Special Prosecutor *Archibald Cox* returned to the law school to resume his teaching career. In 1975, he was awarded an honorary degree. Teddy Kennedy launched a full-scale effort to have Cox named to the First Circuit Court of Appeals in the late 1970s, but President Carter never even submitted Cox's name for Senate consideration. This slight undoubtedly fueled Kennedy's determination to run against the ingrate incumbent.

James Vorenberg and *Philip Heymann* also both returned to their Harvard Law School teaching careers. Vorenberg, whose laconic demeanor belied his razor-sharp mind, was appointed associate dean in 1977 and was then elevated to serve as dean of the law school from 1981 to 1989.

Heymann, who had advocated dragging everyone in the Nixon White House in for WSPF interviews, just to see what might be revealed, was one member of the Kennedy clan invited to join the Carter administration. He returned to Washington as assistant attorney general in charge of the Criminal Division in 1978. Eventually returning to the law school, he was associate dean (under Vorenberg) before returning to Washington in 1993 as deputy attorney general under President Bill Clinton. In Clintonian Washington, Heymann found himself unhappily wedged between the politically naive Janet Reno and the wily associate attorney general Webster Hubbell,

Hillary Clinton's former law partner at Little Rock's Rose Law Firm, and the First Couple's political watchdog in the Justice Department, who ended up going to jail for tax evasion. (Substantial amounts of money were arranged to take care of Hubbell's family, and high-paying "consultancies" with no visible responsibilities were arranged for him. But where Democrats are concerned, judges like John Sirica, those judicial firebrands determined to find the truth, seem to be few and far between.)

President Clinton's White House counsel at the time was Bernard W. Nussbaum, one of Hillary Rodham's colleagues on the House Judiciary Committee's impeachment inquiry staff. Vincent Foster, another of Mrs. Clinton's Rose Law Firm partners, joined the Clinton White House as associate counsel and handled a number of highly sensitive public and private legal matters for the First Family. Feeling overwhelmed, he apparently took his own life—leaving behind a plaintive note stating that in Washington, "Here ruining people is considered sport."

There's a widely known story about a phone call Phil Heymann made to Bernie Nussbaum during the two days following Foster's suicide, when federal law enforcement officials were barred from entering his White House office, while Clinton staff members removed sensitive files and scoured it for any possibly embarrassing evidence of misconduct (anyone alert for parallels will appreciate this John Dean in reverse play). "Are you hiding something from us, Bernie?" Heymann asked; knowing the answer, he warned that they were making "a terrible mistake." Not getting a satisfactory answer, Heymann—who had been prepared to ride roughshod over individual rights when he wanted to find out what had happened in the Nixon White House—simply turned tail. He quietly resigned, and returned to his comfortable ivory tower in Cambridge. He claimed to have left over personality differences with Reno and Hubbell—but he remained silent about his failure to do his job when confronted with what he appeared to consider an outright obstruction of justice by the Clinton White House.*

---

*Hillary Rodham Clinton's book confirms this delay, as well as the removal from Foster's office of "personal files containing work he had done for Bill and me when he was our attorney in Little Rock, including files that had to do with the land deal called Whitewater."

At least Phil Heymann got out of the Clinton administration with his own legal reputation largely intact. He was able to write any number of articles, including a September 1997 op-ed article published in *The New York Times*, criticizing any thought of applying to the Clinton White House a federal statute that prohibited political fund-raising solicitations on federal property. He wrote, "It remains a very bad idea to bend general standards of prosecution either to reach or avoid political figures." This from the man who seems to have bent the standard to the breaking point with Republicans during Watergate.

Henry Ruth, deputy special prosecutor under both Cox and Jaworski, and Jaworski's successor as special prosecutor, conducted the independent review for Attorney General Janet Reno of the U.S. Treasury report on its agents' conduct in the siege of the Branch Davidian compound in Waco, Texas, and the deaths that resulted. Attorney General Reno accepted full responsibility for this human tragedy and political embarrassment—and Ruth's investigation, which was neither thorough nor public, seemed willing to let it go at that.

James Neal, head of the WSPF's Watergate Task Force, returned as counsel to the 1982 Senate Abscam Committee, whose main focus was to deconstruct and criticize the FBI's 1982 undercover sting operation that resulted in the convictions of seven bribe-friendly members of Congress.*

Once again there was irony for those with eyes to see. While it was noble for senators to "view with alarm" any possible wrongdoing in presidential elections in which Republicans won, it was something else entirely when Democrats controlled the Congress, and their own colleagues were concerned. On Capitol Hill, the motto isn't "equal justice under law"; it's "there but for the grace of God go I." Exposing lawbreaking congressmen by actually videotaping them taking bribes was a practice that had to be squelched posthaste—and Jim Neal, the scourge of God

---

*In 1978 the FBI had set up a phony company—Abdul Enterprises, Ltd.—purporting to represent Middle Eastern business interests; videotapes captured agents posing (in full robes and accents) as representatives of a wealthy sheik who was willing to pay bribes for special services to, among other public officials, several congressmen and U.S. Senator Harrison Williams of New Jersey. It became popularly known as the "Abscam sting."

when Jimmy Hoffa and Richard Nixon were involved—was just the man to help do it.

Neal later defended Vice President Al Gore during the 1997–98 investigations of charges that Gore had used his White House office and phone to solicit campaign contributions, and that he had attended an illegal fund-raiser at the Buddhist Hsi Lai temple in Los Angeles. The offenses were serious, and Gore's defense—which hovered between "I didn't know and what I did know I don't remember" and "the dog ate my homework"—was ludicrous.

Nonetheless, Neal successfully persuaded Attorney General Janet Reno (admittedly not a very hard sell) against appointing the independent prosecutor called for by both Congress (which was now in Republican hands) and FBI director Louis Freeh. Neal was certainly in a position to describe firsthand the horrors and adverse impacts that might follow from such an appointment. As pressures from Congress mounted, Philip Heymann issued an op-ed bolt from Cambridge, decrying the intrusion of politics into the functioning of the independent counsel law. It is hard to believe that he actually had a straight face when he wrote, in April 1997, "There has never been anything quite like this in the history of the independent counsel statute."

Richard Ben-Veniste, Neal's successor as head of the Watergate Task Force, had declined to reveal his party affiliation during Watergate, righteously observing that he was "against crooks in both parties." Before too long, however, he emerged as one of the Democratic Party's most dependable and aggressive spear-carriers. He vigorously defended his (indicted and later convicted) Abscam clients who had been captured on camera actually taking cash from FBI agents posing as Arab sheiks seeking special services.

Later, he was minority counsel to the Senate Whitewater Committee—loudly complaining that the Republicans seemed intent on ascribing a sinister motive to every one of the Clintons' acts.

He also wrote an op-ed for *The New York Times* in late 1998, claiming that questioning President Clinton about the Monica Lewinsky affair constituted a perjury trap—somehow missing the irony that the same allegation might have been leveled against him in almost any of his Watergate grand jury questioning of prominent White House officials.

Ben-Veniste was widely criticized for alleged misbehavior while committee counsel during the Whitewater investigation. Published reports said that after blocking inquiries about Webster Hubbell's $500,000 contract with the Lippo Group, despite his lack of relevant expertise and the fact that no work was required of him, Ben-Veniste then turned around and defended Truman Arnold, the man he was supposedly investigating.

He also defended Clinton friend and DNC director Terry McAuliffe when he was

> *called as a witness in a Teamsters corruption trial. McAuliffe, a Washington lawyer, and "the top money man for the Democratic Party," was an unnamed player in the indictment of Teamsters political director Bill Hamilton, who prosecutors say illegally schemed with McAuliffe to swap union money for Democratic cash in a money-laundering scheme involving the DNC, the Teamsters, several White House aides, and the 1996 Clinton-Gore re-election campaign.*

Ben-Veniste was named one of the Democratic appointees to the 9/11 Commission, where his dual mission was to trash the Bush administration as having essentially been responsible for the attack, by not having acted earlier on fragmentary information, while preventing any effective review of the seriously contributory actions by cocommissioner (and Clinton friend from Yale days) Jamie Gorelick, who had replaced Phil Heymann as deputy attorney general, and aggressively enforced the Carter-era communication barrier between the CIA and the FBI. Gorelick was so committed and effective that the divide between the two organizations, which prevented them from sharing intelligence information, actually became known as the "Gorelick Wall."

Charles Ruff, who had been deputy head of the Campaign Contributions Task Force, heading investigations into virtually ever aspect of Republican fund-raising, became special prosecutor upon Henry Ruth's resignation in October 1974. After returning to private practice, he represented a number of prominent Democrats, including former Virginia governor Chuck Robb* and one of the senators involved in the Keating Five scandal.† He was also one of the team of lawyers for Anita Hill, who was Clarence Thomas's principal accuser during his 1991 confirmation hearings.

Ruff became counsel to President Clinton following Nussbaum's 1994 resignation, and acted as his chief lawyer during his 1997 Senate impeachment trial. He later was alleged to have presided over the destruction of thousands of e-mails from within the Clinton White House, sent from 1996 to 1998, which were required by law to have been maintained—a situation not dissimilar to that of the 18½ minute gap—but without the same dramatic reaction.

Stephen G. Breyer served a Supreme Court clerkship with Arthur Goldberg before joining his old Harvard Law School professor Archibald Cox as an assistant special prosecutor. In 1978, Teddy Kennedy made Breyer the special counsel of the Senate Judiciary Committee. In 1980, Jimmy Carter appointed him to the federal bench. In 1994, Bill Clinton named him to the Supreme Court. His brother, *Charles R. Breyer*, also served on the WSPF; after seventeen years in private practice, he was appointed to the U.S. District Court for the Northern District of California by President Clinton, in 1997.

House Judiciary Staff

Jerry Zeifman, who had been majority counsel for the full Judiciary Committee from 1961 through 1974 and wrote the rather astounding *Without*

---

*In 1991 three of Robb's aides resigned when it was disclosed they had come into possession of illegally recorded telephone conversations of then governor Douglas Wilder. News reports at the time indicated a grand jury was investigating whether Robb and his aides had conspired to distribute the contents of those wiretaps, but there were no indictments.

†Charles Keating, chairman of Lincoln Savings and Loan Association in Irvine, California, made campaign contributions in the late 1980s totaling $1.3 million to five senators in an attempt to influence federal reviews of his institution. A federal investigation followed, as well as an inquiry by the Senate Ethics Committee. Senators were widely criticized but no one was indicted.

Honor: The Crimes of Camelot and the Impeachment of President Nixon in 1995, has remained an avowed and vocal opponent of Hillary Rodham Clinton and a number of other Democrats, issuing a series of thunderbolt columns (which can be found by Googling "Jerry Zeifman"), including one dated August 16, 1999, claiming Hillary Clinton's 1974 Watergate "procedures were ethically flawed"; one dated January 30, 2006, claiming Senator Edward Kennedy had disgraced himself during confirmation hearings on Supreme Court Justice Samuel Alito; and one dated April 6, 2007, calling upon House Speaker Nancy Pelosi to resign for fostering "tyranny by the majority."

Renata Adler, one of Hillary's Yale classmates who also was recommended to John Doar by professor Burke Marshall, went on to a distinguished, if exceptionally liberal—and controversial—literary career, writing pieces for *The New York Times*, the *New Yorker*, the *Atlantic, Harper's,* the *New Republic, Vanity Fair,* and the *New York Review of Books.* She also has written at least eight books of her own, including one in 1999 titled *Gone: The Last Days of* The New Yorker, where she noted that she had once declined to review the autobiography of Watergate icon Judge John Sirica because he was "a corrupt, incompetent, and dishonest figure, with a close connection to Senator Joseph McCarthy and clear ties to organized crime."

All of which makes her 1976 article in *Atlantic Monthly*, "Searching for the Real Nixon," so fascinating. As noted previously, it not only raises intriguing questions about internal workings of the impeachment inquiry staff, but seems to suggest that subsequent disclosures about abuse of power by prior presidents substantially undercut any case for Richard Nixon's own impeachment.

Bernard Nussbaum, Hillary's senior on the impeachment inquiry staff, as has been previously noted, went on to become the first counsel to the president in Bill Clinton's administration. Further contact with the Clintons was apparently corrupting, because he was forced to resign following a *New York Times* editorial dated March 4, 1994, which observed:

> *It is, of course, long past time for Mr. Nussbaum to be dismissed. He seems to conceive of his being "the President's lawyer" as a license*

to meddle with the integrity of any federal agency. First, he and his staff tried to involve the Federal Bureau of Investigation in a politically inspired White House purge of employees of its travel office. When Vincent Foster, the deputy counsel, committed suicide, Mr. Nussbaum interfered with the investigation by the National Park Service and transferred secret files to Mr. Clinton's private lawyer.

Bill* and Hillary Clinton are, in many ways, the latest representatives of the Kennedy style of presidential politics, and the ultimate legatees of the Camelot Conspiracy. Bill Clinton credits his decision to enter politics to shaking hands with JFK in the Rose Garden when he was part of an American Legion Boys State delegation during high school. He modeled his life and presidency on his hero, and eagerly adopted the three distinguishing characteristics of Kennedy presidential politics: unlimited amounts of money; an unabashed view of women as purely sexual objects; and a cross between codependency and synergy with a compliant and supportive media. He has excelled in exactly the thing he was constantly detecting and denouncing in others—"the politics of personal destruction." (Itself a quintessentially Kennedy-style macho way of deflecting attention and criticism. Hillary Clinton's canard of a "vast right-wing conspiracy" showed that she was no less a master than her husband of this disingenuous reverse play.) With the Clintons, as with the Kennedys, it could be very costly, if not downright dangerous, to be their opponent.

Despite his exceptional intellect and undeniably roguish, raffish charm, Bill Clinton never really rose above the ranks of the JFK wannabes. His attempts were too obvious, and his flaws were too evident. It was close—but no cigar.

Rather, it is former first lady and 2008 presidential candidate Senator Hillary Rodham Clinton who has consistently demonstrated the greatest similarity of any politician of the last few decades to a Kennedy. But her

---

*While never an actual member of the impeachment inquiry staff, Hillary notes that Bill was offered a position by John Doar—his name being higher on Burke Marshall's list than hers was—but turned it down because of his intention to return to Arkansas to run for Congress.

affinity is not with the easy, witty charm of JFK, nor with the shaggy indecisiveness of Teddy. She favors the ideological intensity of Robert Kennedy.
She shares with him an intense and humorless personality, combined with
a long and unforgiving political memory and a talent for retribution. And,
thanks to her work for the House impeachment inquiry—where she obeyed
her instructions to suppress the Woodward report—she actually played her
own (and as yet largely unexplored) part in the Camelot Conspiracy.

P ower corrupts, a phenomenon well known to the Founding Fathers—and
properly feared by them. As a result, they designed a national government with checks and balances to keep each branch from consolidating too
much power—as well as a Bill of Rights to protect individuals from their
government. Watergate and its cover-up were bad enough, but actions of
Kennedy Clan Democrats who hijacked Watergate for their own political
purposes— breaching separation of power bulwarks, criminalizing politics, and denying their political opponents the equal protection of the laws
and the rudiments of due process—constituted far greater abuse. Every bit
as bad, their attitude and approach, particularly their emphasis on the
politics of personal destruction, are still practiced today by their Watergate-
trained alumni.

LIST OF APPENDICES

Appendix A: Frampton memo to Files of November 2, 1973, concerning "Interview with John Dean." From WSPF files at National Archives.

Appendix B: Undated, unattributed handwritten notes from WSPF file labeled "Dean Violations." From WSPF files at National Archives.

Appendix C: Carver memo to Cox of June 4, 1973, concerning "Post Watergate Trial Grand Jury Testimony." From WSPF files at National Archives.

Appendix D: Cox memo to Neal of June 14, 1973, asking for daily briefing of planned Watergate activities. From WSPF files at National Archives.

Appendix E: Cox memo to Silbert team of June 15, 1973, regarding Neal's involvement. From WSPF files at National Archives.

Appendix F: Glanzer memo to Silbert of June 12, 1973, recounting conversation with Charles Shaffer. From WSPF files at National Archives.

Appendix G: Silbert memo to Cox of June 5, 1973, concerning "News Media Publicity re Henry Petersen." From WSPF files at National Archives.

Appendix H: Vorenberg memo to File of June 14, 1973, concerning Senator Weicker. From WSPF files at National Archives.

Appendix I: Hand-typed memo dated March 26, 1973, entitled "John Dean III, From Liddy" with initials "JWMc" (James W. McCord). From WSPF files at National Archives.

Appendix J: Neal memo to Heymann of June 11, 1973, concerning "Robert Davis." From WSPF files at National Archives.

Appendix K: Heymann memo of June 18, 1973, concerning "Some Steps that Should be Taken in Watergate Prosecution." From WSPF files at National Archives.

Appendix L: WSPF Guidelines issued by Attorney General Elliot Richardson on May 18, 1973. *Watergate: Chronology of a Crisis.* Washington, D.C.: *Congressional Quarterly*, 1975, p. 97.

Appendix M: Titus statement of May 24, 1973, concerning status of Watergate. From WSPF files at National Archives.

Appendix N: Draft of Cox letter of May 29, 1973. From the Papers of Archibald Cox, Harvard Law School Library, Box 21, Folder 9.

Appendix O: Cox memo to Petersen of May 25, 1973, requesting copies of all communication with U.S. Attorney Titus. From WSPF files at National Archives.

Appendix P: HLS professor John Ely memo to Cox of May 31, 1973, concerning whether sitting president can be called before a grand jury. From the Papers of Archibald Cox, Harvard Law School, Box 22, Folder 10.

Appendix Q: Department of Justice Press Release of May 29, 1973, containing statement by Special Prosecutor Archibald Cox. From WSPF files at National Archives.

Appendix R: Heymann memo of July 24, 1973, concerning systematically calling all staff assistants in for interviews. From WSPF files at National Archives.

Appendix S: Lacovara memo to Ben-Veniste of February 6, 1974, concerning "Possible Charges Against William Bittman." From WSPF files at National Archives.

Appendix T: Neal memo of August 15, 1973, concerning "Plumbers Task Force Schedule." From WSPF files at National Archives.

Appendix U: Denny/Rient memo to files of November 15, 1973. From WSPF files at National Archives.

Appendix V: Neal memo of October 2, 1974, concerning "John Dean's Contacts and Information Imparted to the Original Prosecutors." From WSPF files at National Archives.

Appendix W: Frampton/Hecht memo of November 30, 1973, concerning "Dean Subpoena," along with Hecht memo of January 30, 1974, concerning "Provision of Copies of Dean's Documents to Dean." From WSPF files at National Archives.

Appendix X: Lacovara memo to Jaworski of September 13, 1974, concerning "Validity of Pardon of Former President Nixon" along with Jaworski memo to Ruth in response. From WSPF files at National Archives.

Appendix Y: Campaign Contributions Task Force introduction from "WSPF Report" of October 1974, pp. 71–72.

Appendix Z: McBride memo to Jaworski of August 19, 1974, concerning "Your Inquiry of Today." From WSPF files at National Archives.

APPENDIX A

"Sugar coating Dean's destruction of evidence" (See text p. 28.)

WATERGATE SPECIAL PROSECUTION FORCE   DEPARTMENT OF JUSTICE

Memorandum

TO   :   FILES   DATE: November 2, 1973

FROM   :   George Frampton

SUBJECT: Interview with John Dean

       In an interview this afternoon with John Dean,
I questioned Dean about the contents of Howard Hunt's
safe. Dean disclosed, for the first time, that he had
probably destroyed the "Hermes" notebook which Hunt has
claimed was located in Hunt's safe.

       Dean related that sometime in late January 1973
Dean discovered, in a file folder in Dean's office safe
containing the President's Estate Plan, two thin cloth-
bound notebooks with cardboard covers and lined pages,
containing some handwriting. Dean at that time recalled
that these had come from Hunt's safe. Dean did not look
at the contents and cannot recall what might have been
in them. He assumed it related to the Ellsberg break-in.
He shredded both notebooks in his shredder.

       At the same time, Dean also discovered a "pop-up"
address book containing some names, with each page
"x-ed out." Dean threw this into his waste basket.

APPENDIX B

"Beginning of a potentially long list" (See text p. 29.)

Item 22(e)

Dean Violations

Showing F.B.I. reports to outsiders

Embezzlement of the portion
of the $350,000 used to pay
Attorneys.

18 USC § 3

APPENDIX C

"Career prosecutors had moved quickly as Watergate cover-up collapsed;
the primary source for Deep Throat revelations" (See text p. 71.)

UNITED STATES GOVERNMENT

Memorandum

DEPARTMENT OF JUSTICE

TO : Archibald Cox, Special Assistant   DATE: June 4, 1973
to the Attorney General
Attn: Mr. Tom McBride

FROM : G. Allen Carver, Jr., Attorney   177-16-8
General Crimes Section
Criminal Division

SUBJECT: Post Watergate Trial
Grand Jury Testimony

The following list of summarized testimony and
that which remains to be summarized is provided in
response to your request. The list includes all
post-Watergate trial grand jury testimony that has
been received from the United States Attorney for
the District of Columbia.

Summarized

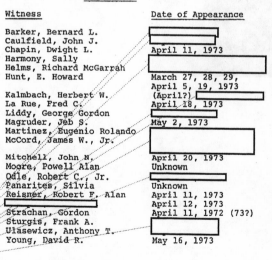

Witness	Date of Appearance
Barker, Bernard L.	
Caulfield, John J.	
Chapin, Dwight L.	April 11, 1973
Harmony, Sally	
Helms, Richard McGarrah	
Hunt, E. Howard	March 27, 28, 29, April 5, 19, 1973
Kalmbach, Herbert W.	(April?)
La Rue, Fred C.	April 18, 1973
Liddy, George Gordon	
Magruder, Jeb S.	May 2, 1973
Martinez, Eugenio Rolando	
McCord, James W., Jr.	
Mitchell, John N.	April 20, 1973
Moore, Powell Alan	Unknown
Odle, Robert C., Jr.	
Panarites, Silvia	Unknown
Reisner, Robert F. Alan	April 11, 1973 April 12, 1973
Strachan, Gordon	April 11, 1972 (73?)
Sturgis, Frank A.	
Ulasewicz, Anthony T.	
Young, David R.	May 16, 1973

FOIA(b)3 - Rule 6(e), Federal Rules of Criminal Procedure

-2-

Remains to be summarized

Witness	Date of Appearance
Barker, Bernard L.	
Caddy, Michael Douglas	
Ehrlichman, John	May 3, 9, 14, 1973
Gonzalez, Virgilio	
Haldeman, Harry Robbins	
Hunt, E. Howard	May 2, 1973
Kalmbach, Herbert W.	
Liddy, George Gordon	
Mardian, Robert C.	
Martinez, Eugenio Rolando	
Segretti, Donald H.	April 11, 1973
	April 27, May 16, 1973
Sturgis, Frank A.	April 24, 1973

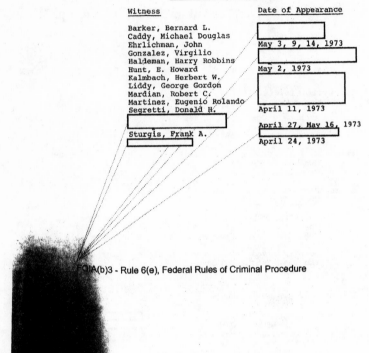

FOIA(b)3 - Rule 6(e), Federal Rules of Criminal Procedure

APPENDIX D

"Cox moves to head off imminent indictments" (See text p. 80.)

Form DJ-150
(Ed. 4-26-65)

ML Watergate Status   *Mr Neal*

UNITED STATES GOVERNMENT   DEPARTMENT OF JUSTICE

Memorandum

TO   :   James Neal   DATE: June 14, 1973

FROM   :   Archibald Cox

SUBJECT:

     As you are, for the time being, responsible for the so-called Watergate cover-up case and as sensitive matters on which I need to be advised in advance may continually arise, you are to advise me at least by the late afternoon of each day of the activities planned by you, Silbert, et al for the next succeeding day or days.

     I will take the time to discuss the planned activities with you in advance of such activities and expect to be advised by you of the purpose of such activities.

APPENDIX E

"Cox asserts control of career prosecutors" (See text p. 80.)

Form DJ-150
(Ed. 4-26-65)

UNITED STATES GOVERNMENT   DEPARTMENT OF JUSTICE

Memorandum

TO   :   Messrs. Neal, Silbert, Glanzer   DATE: June 15, 1973
           and Campbell

FROM   :   Archibald Cox
           Special Prosecutor
           Watergate Special Prosecution Force

SUBJECT:

        I am asking Jim Neal to be sure to sit in on all
interviews with potential defendants, prospective witnesses
and others who may be interviewed in investigating or
preparing for trial on anything growing out of the
Watergate incident. You must be sure this is done.

        It may be that we should designate some other new
member of the staff to be available for the lesser parts
of this. Jim is to decide when he takes part and when
someone sits in for him.

APPENDIX F

"Candid snapshot of Dean maneuvering to avoid grand jury appearance"
(See text p. 80.)

Form DJ-150
(Ed 4-26-65)

UNITED STATES GOVERNMENT

DEPARTMENT OF JUSTICE

Memorandum

TO : Mr. Earl J. Silbert
Principal Assistant U.S. Attorney

DATE: June 12, 1973

FROM : Seymour Glanzer
Assistant U.S. Attorney

SUBJECT:

   About 6:30 P.M. on Sunday, June 10, 1973, Charles
Shaffer called me at home. He wanted us to know that
Dean intended to assert his Fifth Admendment privilege.
I told him we understood that this was Shaffer's position.
But in light of Dean's public pronoucenents about wanting
to be heard and being desirous of cooperating we felt
compelled to call him before the grand jury to test this
position. Besides, we wanted the Senate Committee to know
that he had been given an opportunity to testify before
the grand jury.

   Then Shaffer asked me if a letter from Dean saying
that he intends to invoke his privilege would suffice.
I told him that this might have been satisfactory with
Professor Cox but that this proposal should have been
explored on Friday with Professor Cox. He said that he
might take the position that Dean's appearance was designed
to generate publicity and was futile because the prosecutors knew Dean intended to assert his privilege. I told
him that he should move to quash the subpoena on those
grounds before Judge Sirica. I told him arguments like
that had been raised in the past by attorneys predicting
what their clients would do and the Court had consistently
ruled that the witness must assert the privilege to specific
questions posed. He indicated that this was consistent
with his past experience elsewhere. However, he said he
might still move to quash.

   I asked him when Dean was going to testify before
the Senate and he said he was not sure. I asked him if
he turned over the Segretti tape to the Committee and he
said he had. But Shaffer did say he told the Committee
that we had requested it first and they indicated we could
have it afterwards. Meanwhile, Shaffer said he has a transcript for us. Shaffer also advised me that he turned over

- 2 -

Segretti's records (which had been given to Dean by O'Brien)
to the Committee. Shaffer said he could get copies for us.1/

Shaffer asked why we were not conferring immunity
on Dean. I told him that we were using that technique
sparingly. He indicated that he had heard from his "sources"
that we were immunizing people wholesale. I asked him to
back up that allegation with specifics. He said Colson.
I told him Colson had not been immunized.

Shaffer indicated he was quite irritated about our
dealings with Colson. He indicated Colson was the worst
of the bunch. I said that may be true but we had no evidence
to support his conclusion. He said Colson knew about the
bugging of the DNC beforehand. I said Dean had not made that
charge before nor had he ever supported such a conclusion.
He mentioned telephone conversations between Magruder and
Colson. I said Magruder and Colson had told us about one
such pre-June 17 conversation; that we had spoken to both
Magruder and Colson and there were no major discrepancies
between them.2/ He said then Magruder hasn't been truthful
yet. I said that both Colson and Magruder had come in and
talked and let us decide what their status was to be. I
hinted that Dean's displeasure with Colson might be attributed
to the fact that Colson has gone "public" also and hurts him
badly on several points.

Shaffer said he can't understand why we focused
on Dean. I said we had focused on Dean as well as others.
He wanted to know why we had this attitude about Dean since
he had in effect helped break the case. I said Colson and
Magruder claim they have. 3/ He said Dean had been candid
and I said we disagreed. He asked in what respect. I said
Dean had withheld the incriminating role he played with regard
to Walters. He said that he had mentioned Walter's name. I
said that added emphasis to my contention because that meant

1/ We had requested these records some time back
but never got around to buttoning it up.

2/ This is a February conversation. It was detailed
in Colson's June 1972 memo which was given to Dean. Dean told
Colson later we can't turn this over to Silbert because it
impeaches Magruder.

3/ So does McCord.

- 3 -

he had not forgotten the episode and still he had suppressed the details. Furthermore, I said the "executive clemency" offer from Dean that was relayed to McCord through Caulfield was another significant episode that Dean had withheld. Shaffer said the failure to disclose was inadvertent. He indicated he would like to continue "phase one." I said we can talk in Silbert's office after Dean's abbreviated appearance before the grand jury.

Subsequently, about midnight, Shaffer called and said he was going to move on Monday to quash the subpoena.

APPENDIX G

"Cox untroubled by character assassination of renowned career
prosecutor" (See text p. 84.)

TES GOV....NMENT   DEPARTMENT OF JUSTICE

Memorandum

TO   :   Honorable Archibald Cox   DATE: June 5, 1973
           Special Prosecutor

FROM :   Earl J. Silbert
           Principal Assistant
           United States Attorney

SUBJECT: News Media Publicity re Henry Petersen

        Recent news media publicity, particularly an
article in today's New York Times, indicates that
Henry Petersen is a subject of the investigation into
the Watergate coverup.

        This news media publicity is tremendously
disturbing. While, as you know, it is our belief
that Mr. Petersen is a necessary witness to the
obstruction of justice perpetrated by the White
House, particularly with respect to the conduct of
John Dean, there is absolutely no evidence known to
the grand jury investigation that Mr. Petersen participated in, contributed to, or knew of any coverup. It
would be totally unfair in my view and that of my
associates, Mr. Glanzer and Mr. Campbell, to permit
the totally misleading effects of this news media publicity to reflect adversely on a man whose long record
of public service has been characterized by integrity
and devotion to law enforcement.

cc: Henry E. Petersen

*It would not be
appropriate for me
to make a
statement on this
AC

note sent him a
note saying only that we
did not leak AC*

APPENDIX H

"Lowell Weicker—a friend indeed" (See text p. 97.)

UNITED STATES GOVERNMENT	DEPARTMENT OF JUSTICE

Memorandum

TO : The File   DATE: June 14, 1973

FROM : James Vorenberg

SUBJECT:

Bob Herrema in Senator Weicker's office called to say that
Senator Weicker and some members of his staff propose to go
see the FBI and sit with some agents while the agents go
through the files containing the 1500 requests and approxi-
mately 300,000 items in response that Wannell informed me
were involved in Weicker's letters to Ruckelshaus and Cox.

I said that I assumed that no action by us was required at
this time and Mr. Herrema said that was so although we would
probably be hearing from the FBI. I said that I did not know
how the FBI would react to the procedures Senator Weicker
proposed and since I did not know what was in the files I
did not know what our reaction would be to specific requests
although we were certainly anxious to cooperate.

APPENDIX I

"Dean to Liddy to McCord" (See text p. 104.)

March 26, 1973

JBJECT: JOHN DEAN III

From Liddy:

John Dean, Jeb Magruder, Gordon Liddy and John Mitchell in Feb 1972
met in Mitchell's office at the Department of Justice and held the
first formal discussion of bugging and other related operations.
This information came to me from several discussions before and after
the meeting, and came from Gordon Liddy. John Mitchell was then Attorney
General and was A/G until March 1, /as I understand it.

Liddy had planned for the meeting very carefully and had drafted out in
longhand budget figures for various items of expense, and had discussed
them and certain details of the overall operation with Jeb Magruder, so
Liddy told me. Magruder reportedly set up the meeting with Mitchell.

Liddy was at that time in an office on the 4th floor at 1701 Pennsylvania
Avenue, N.W., near Magruder's office. Subsequent to seeing the longhand
drafts, Liddy had a typed report on the subject on his desk during one
of these discussions and my impression was that he was planning to send
it, or take it, by hand, to someone in the White House. I do not know
to whom he took it.

The meeting was set up for one particular day, but was cancelled, and
reset for a day or so later. It was an afternoon meeting as I recall,
and my impression was, from what Liddy told me, that it lasted an hour
or more. He said that the discussion covered the pros and cons of various
bugging type operations. No decisions were made at the meeting, about
proceeding with the operation, but the impression Liddy had seem to be
that the operation would be approved.

A few days later Dean told Liddy that a way would have to be worked out
to undertake the operation without directly involving the Attorney General
so that he would have deniability about it at a future date. Dean told
Liddy at this time that the funding for the operation would subsequently
come to him through other than regular Committee for the Re-Election (CRP)
funding mechanisms so that there would be no record of it. This was not
further explained to me.

About 30 days after the February meeting in the A/G's office, Liddy told
me that the operation "had been approved" and that the funding for it
would be through shortly. My impression was that this word of the approval
came from Dean, although this was not specifically stated by Liddy. Dean
was Liddy's legal counterpart at the White House. Liddy was at this time
(February 1972) legal counsel for the Committee to Re-Elect the President.

Leads

1. Liddy's secretary in February 1972 was Sylvia Panarites. I would believe
that she may have typed some of the drafts referred to above and possibly
other correspondence in connection with the meeting with the Attorney General
and possibly for Dean from Liddy in connection thereo.

1

APPENDIX J

"Kennedy Clan Democrats all pulling together" (See text p. 112.)

(See text p. 112.)

JN/flc

PHIL HEYMANN   K   June 11, 1973

JIM NEAL

ROBERT DAVIS

    Carmine Belino of the Ervin Committee wishes also
to interview this man and I advised him you would let him
know when we plan to have Davis in town for our purposes.

    I think this is an arrangement in which we can
cooperate with the Committee without any danger to our
operation.

APPENDIX K

"Why Watergate indictments were postponed until after Ervin hearings" (See text p. 112.)

UNITED STATES GOVERNMENT   DEPARTMENT OF JUSTICE

Memorandum

TO   :   Messrs. Cox, Vorenberg,   DATE: June 18, 1973
              Neal, and Silbert

FROM   :   Phil Heymann

SUBJECT: Some Steps that Should be Taken
              in Watergate Prosecution

    1.   A list should be made of the dates and content of all
Presidential pronouncements on executive privilege or national
security privilege between June 1972 and May 1973. The timing
should be checked against what we know of the emerging break-
down of cover-up efforts.

    2.   One or two younger lawyers should be assigned full
time to read the entire transcripts of the Select Committee
and of all other Congressional hearings and produce a list of
charges and supporting evidence on this basis alone. The
result will be:

        a.   We will be sure to pick up any additional evidence
            generated on the Hill.

        b.   We will get a double check on our "charging" deci-
            sions as to people and crimes.

        c.   We will not be subject to the charge of having
            ignored an alternative investigative effort.

    3.   We must develop more fully the pay-off aspect of the
cover-up. The defendants are going to argue that this was a
"legal defense" fund of a perfectly proper sort. We haven't
even clarified the conceptual line at which such a fund becomes
an obstruction of justice, let alone target the necessary
evidence.

L °

4.   One person on the Watergate team should be asked to
maintain a "perjury" file both for possible later prosecution
and for bargaining purposes. Congressional committees are
already referring matters of possible perjury to us. The file
should list all likely instances by defendant and conflicting
statements.

5.   Some miscellaneous points:

a.   Can we corroborate Magruder's alleged conversation
with Haldeman in January?

b.   Sunday N.Y. Times, page 44, says Mitchell suspects
Colson involvement. How can we check this out?

c.   Three former special agents, now no longer with
FBI Headquarters, can tell us something about
Gray's role. How should we interview:

(i)   Robert Kunkel (Agt. in Charge, St. Louis).

(ii)   Charles Bates (assigned to San Francisco).

(iii)   Charles Bolz (at HUD or Transportation).

d.   How can we get Krogh to comment on Dean's allegation that Krogh said the Ellsberg break-in was
approved by President Nixon?

APPENDIX L

"An incredible usurpation of executive power by Kennedy's Judiciary Committee" (See text p. 125.)

Duties and Responsibilities of the Special Prosecutor

Following are guidelines relating to the special Watergate prosecutor issued by Attorney General-designate Elliot L. Richardson May 19:

THE SPECIAL PROSECUTOR

There will be appointed by the attorney general, within the Department of Justice, a special prosecutor to whom the attorney general shall delegate the authorities and provide the staff and other resources described below.

The special prosecutor shall have full authority for investigating and prosecuting offenses against the United States arising out of the unauthorized entry into Democratic National Committee headquarters at the Watergate, all offenses arising out of the 1972 presidential election for which the special prosecutor deems it necessary and appropriate to assume responsibility, allegations involving the President, members of the White House staff, or presidential appointees, and any other matters which he consents to have assigned to him by the attorney general.

In particular, the special prosecutor shall have full authority with respect to the above matters for:

• Conducting proceedings before grand juries and any other investigations he deems necessary.

• Reviewing all documentary evidence available from any source, as to which he shall have full access.

• Determining whether or not to contest the assertion of "executive privilege" or any other testimonial privilege.

• Determining whether or not application should be made to any federal court for a grant of immunity to any witness, consistently with applicable statutory requirements, or for warrants, subpoenas, or other court orders.

• Deciding whether or not to prosecute any individual, firm, corporation or group of individuals.

• Initiating and conducting prosecutions, framing indictments, filing informations, and handling all aspects of any cases within his jurisdiction (whether initiated before or after his assumption of duties), including any appeals.

• Coordinating and directing the activities of all Department of Justice personnel, including United States attorneys.

• Dealing with and appearing before congressional committees having jurisdiction over any aspect of the above matters and determining what documents, information, and assistance shall be provided to such committees.

In exercising this authority, the special prosecutor will have the greatest degree of independence that is consistent with the attorney general's statutory accountability for all matters falling within the jurisdiction of the Department of Justice. The attorney general will not countermand or interfere with the special prosecutor's decisions or actions. The special prosecutor will determine whether and to what extent he will inform or consult with the attorney general about the conduct of his duties and responsibilities. The special prosecutor will not be removed from his duties except for extraordinary improprieties on his part.

STAFF AND RESOURCE SUPPORT

Selection of Staff. The special prosecutor shall have full authority to organize, select, and hire his own staff of attorneys, investigators, and supporting personnel, on a full or part-time basis, in such numbers and with such qualifications as he may reasonably require. He may request the assistant attorneys general and other officers of the Department of Justice to assign such personnel and to provide such other assistance as he may reasonably require. All personnel in the Department of Justice, including United States attorneys, shall cooperate to the fullest extent possible with the special prosecutor.

Budget. The special prosecutor will be provided with such funds and facilities to carry out his responsibilities as he may reasonably require. He shall have the right to submit budget requests for funds, positions, and other assistance, and such requests shall receive the highest priority.

Designation and Responsibility. The personnel acting as the staff and assistants of the special prosecutor shall be known as the Watergate special prosecution force and shall be responsible only to the special prosecutor.

Continued Responsibilities of Assistant Attorney General, Criminal Division. Except for the specific investigative and prosecutorial duties assigned to the special prosecutor, the assistant attorney general in charge of the criminal division will continue to exercise all of the duties currently assigned to him.

Applicable Departmental Policies. Except as otherwise herein specified or as mutually agreed between the special prosecutor and the attorney general, the Watergate special prosecution force will be subject to the administrative regulations and policies of the Department of Justice.

Public Reports. The special prosecutor may from time to time make public such statements or reports as he deems appropriate and shall upon completion of his assignment submit a final report to the appropriate persons or entities of the Congress.

Duration of Assignment. The special prosecutor will carry out these responsibilities, with the full support of the Department of Justice, until such time as, in his judgment, he has completed them or until a date mutually agreed upon between the attorney general and himself.

APPENDIX M

"Prediction that Watergate indictments are imminent (before special prosecutor's arrival)" (See text p. 129.)

(See text p. 129.)

PRESS RELEASE

HAROLD H. TITUS, JR.
UNITED STATES ATTORNEY
FOR THE
DISTRICT OF COLUMBIA

May 24, 1973

I WISH TO MAKE AN ANNOUNCEMENT TODAY CONCERNING THE
WATERGATE CASE. AT MY REQUEST, THE PROSECUTORS I HAVE
ASSIGNED TO THIS CASE -- EARL J. SILBERT, MY PRINCIPAL
ASSISTANT, SEYMOUR GLANZER AND DONALD E. CAMPBELL -- HAVE
PRESENTED TO ME THEIR ASSESSMENT OF THE CURRENT STATUS OF
THEIR INVESTIGATION. AFTER REVIEWING THEIR PRESENTATION I
AM ABLE TO REPORT TO YOU THE FOLLOWING.

THE INVESTIGATION UNDERTAKEN BY MY PROSECUTIVE
TEAM IN CONJUNCTION WITH THE FEDERAL GRAND JURY IS SUBSTANTIALLY
COMPLETE. AS MANY OF YOU ARE BY NOW PROBABLY AWARE, THE
MAJOR BREAK-THROUGH IN THE INVESTIGATION REPORTED IN THE NEWS
MEDIA A LITTLE OVER A MONTH AGO WAS DIRECTLY ATTRIBUTABLE TO
THE CONTINUING EFFORTS OF THESE PROSECUTORS. IN THIS REGARD
THEY HAVE FOLLOWED A STRATEGY THEY FORMULATED PRIOR TO THE
RETURN OF THE FIRST INDICTMENT IN THIS CASE AND THE TRIAL OF
THE DEFENDANTS NAMED THEREIN. CONSISTENT WITH THEIR EFFORTS
AND THEIR STRATEGY, THE PROSECUTORS HAVE INTERVIEWED MOST OF
THE IMPORTANT WITNESSES AND POTENTIAL TARGET DEFENDANTS ON
ONE OR MORE OCCASIONS AND THE MAJORITY OF THEM HAVE APPEARED
BEFORE THE GRAND JURY. THE PROSECUTORS HAVE DEVELOPED AND
OUTLINED BEFORE THE GRAND JURY A COMPREHENSIVE AND COHERENT
THEORY OF PROSECUTION. ONE KEY MEMBER OF THE CRIMINAL

- 2 -

CONSPIRACY HAS ALREADY AGREED TO PLEAD GUILTY WITHOUT
IMMUNIZATION AND TO TESTIFY AS A PROSECUTION WITNESS AT
TRIAL. NEGOTIATIONS ARE PRESENTLY IN PROCESS TOWARDS
SECURING THIS OBJECTIVE AS TO OTHERS WHO HAVE ALSO ADMITTED
THEIR CULPABILITY. WHERE CONSISTENT WITH THE PUBLIC INTEREST,
JUSTICE AND SOUND LAW ENFORCEMENT, THIS OFFICE HAS SOUGHT
AND OBTAINED IMMUNITY FOR OTHER WITNESSES.

SOME WORK, OF COURSE, REMAINS TO BE DONE. FOR
IN THIS, AS IN EVERY CRIMINAL CASE, THE INVESTIGATION PRIOR
TO INDICTMENT MUST BE AS THOROUGH AS CIRCUMSTANCES PERMIT.
NEVERTHELESS, I HAVE BEEN ADVISED BY MR. SILBERT THAT IT IS
REALISTIC TO ANTICIPATE A COMPREHENSIVE INDICTMENT WITHIN
60 TO 90 DAYS, ASSUMING THE PRESENT PACE OF THE INVESTIGATION
AND PREPARATION CONTINUES WITHOUT INTERRUPTION. THE PROPOSED
INDICTMENT WOULD FOCUS ON THE OBSTRUCTION OF JUSTICE WHICH
OCCURRED AFTER THE WATERGATE ARREST ON JUNE 17, 1972, BUT WILL
INCLUDE CRIMINAL ACTIVITIES BEGINNING IN 1971, WHICH TOGETHER
WITH THE WATERGATE BREAK-IN, MOTIVATED THE MASSIVE OBSTRUCTION.

AS IS NOW WELL KNOWN PROFESSOR ARCHIBALD COX OF
HARVARD LAW SCHOOL, A FORMER SOLICITOR GENERAL OF THE
UNITED STATES, HAS BEEN APPOINTED AS THE SPECIAL PROSECUTOR
IN THIS CASE.

- 3 -

ON TUESDAY, MAY 22, AFTER SERIOUS CONSIDERATION
BETWEEN THE PROSECUTORS AND MYSELF, IT WAS DETERMINED THAT
IN ORDER FOR PROFESSOR COX TO BE FREE IN THE CHOICE OF HIS
STAFF, OUR OFFICE SHOULD WITHDRAW FROM THE ONGOING INVESTI-
GATION. ANOTHER IMPORTANT FACTOR INFLUENCING THIS DECISION
WAS THE UNCERTAINTY OF WITNESSES, POTENTIAL DEFENDANTS AND
THEIR RESPECTIVE ATTORNEYS, AS WELL AS THE PROSECUTORS
THEMSELVES, CONCERNING THE AUTHORITY OF THIS OFFICE TO MAKE
DECISIONS IN THE CASE.

IT WAS, OF COURSE, OUR INTENTION TO TRANSMIT
IMMEDIATELY TO PROFESSOR COX ALL FILES, RECORDS, TRANSCRIPTS
AND OTHER DOCUMENTS CONTAINED IN THE WATERGATE INVESTIGATION
FOR HIS REVIEW AND STUDY AND TO BE AVAILABLE AT HIS REQUEST
TO CONSULT WITH AND ASSIST HIM IN THE UNDERSTANDING AND
COMPREHENSION OF THE MANY COMPLEX AND INTRICATE ISSUES
INVOLVED IN THIS HIGHLY PUBLICIZED CASE.

THEREFORE, ON TUESDAY, I SCHEDULED A PRESS CONFERENCE
IN ORDER TO ANNOUNCE OUR DECISION. PRIOR TO THAT CONFERENCE,
HOWEVER, I RECEIVED A CALL FROM PROFESSOR COX REQUESTING
THAT WE MEET WITH HIM YESTERDAY IN ADVANCE OF ANY PUBLIC
ANNOUNCEMENT RELATIVE TO OUR CONTEMPLATED WITHDRAWAL FROM
THE CASE. I EXPRESSED TO PROFESSOR COX MY STRONG VIEW AS
TO THE PROPRIETY OF OUR ANTICIPATED COURSE OF CONDUCT AND
OUR FIRM INTENTION TO PROCEED WITH THE ANNOUNCEMENT.

- 4 -

HOWEVER, IN DEFERENCE TO HIS REQUEST WE AGREED
TO MEET WITH HIM. THAT MEETING TOOK PLACE IN THE DEPARTMENT
OF JUSTICE AT 3:00 P.M., AT WHICH TIME HE URGED US, IN
VIEW OF THE IMPORTANT WORK WE WERE DOING, THAT IT WAS IN
THE PUBLIC INTEREST THAT WE CARRY ON THE DEVELOPMENT OF
THE CASE.

AT THIS TIME, I WISH TO ADVISE YOU THAT WE WILL
ACCEDE TO PROFESSOR COX'S REQUEST AND WILL CONTINUE TO
CONDUCT THE INVESTIGATION.

APPENDIX N

"Proof positive of Cox effort to derail indictments" (See text p. 129)

~~approval~~ case without prior approval and will make prompt and full disclosure to me of your activities and what you have learned.

Some of what I am saying, especially the part about written assurance, may seem offensively rude. I do not mean to be rude. I am not insinuating that any of you is responsible for the Hirsch story or any other story. But no room can be left for any misunderstanding upon this point and I cannot forget that you chose to make a statement about the substance of the case last Thursday after I had explicitly disapproved.

Will each of you please advise me in writing whether you wish to continue working on the case on the above basis. I hope that you will continue to perform this public service - at least until my staff and I have mastered the case. But there is no room for conditions or limitations.

APPENDIX O

"Cox effort to learn extent of any Titus authority to bring
Watergate indictments" (See text p. 130.)

Mr. Henry E. Petersen   May 25, 1973
Assistant Attorney General
Criminal Division

Archibald Cox
Special Assistant Attorney General

      Will you please send me, as soon as possible,
any letters, memoranda, or other instructions or
suggestions from your office to U. S. Attorney Titus
concerning any aspect of the Watergate investigation,
however remote. Where the suggestions or instructions
were oral, I would like to have the date and time, any
contemporaneous memorandum, and any recollection you
or your assistants may have of anything not reduced
to writing.

      Sometime later we will have to run through all
this together, but I would like to get what I can in
writing as soon as possible.

APPENDIX P

"Early indication that Nixon is Cox's real target from the outset" (See text p. 133.)

Law School of Harvard University

Cambridge, Mass. 02138

May 31, 1973

CONFIDENTIAL

MEMORANDUM

TO: Archie Cox

FROM: John Ely

I've spent a couple of days rummaging about and wanted
to let you know what I've come up with. The question with which
I'd like to begin is whether the President enjoys some immunity
from being called before a grand jury. In the Boston Globe for
May 30, at p. 30, Alex Bickel states what I gather must be the
sort of argument on which those supporting such immunity must
rely, one generally emanating from the separation of powers:

> It is not a matter of law, but of assumed convention.
> The President, alone, is presumed to be immune to the
> judicial process.

But of course observing that there is a separation of powers does
not begin to disclose its contours: the question, here as everywhere, is what powers, privileges and immunities are distributed
in what ways. Alex appeals to some historically evolved and broadly assumed convention, perhaps thereby trying to move considerations

APPENDIX Q

"There's a new sheriff in town—a Kennedy Democrat"
(See text p. 134.)

 **Bepartment of Justice**

FOR IMMEDIATE RELEASE   SP
TUESDAY, MAY 29, 1973

       Special Prosecutor Archibald Cox issued the following
statement today:

       During the past week the press has carried extraordinary
statements about the theory or theories of a possible Watergate
prosecution and the evidence expected from one or more witnesses.

       All decisions about theories of investigation or prosecution,
the grant of immunity, the acceptance of pleas in return for testimony,
and the conduct of the investigation will be made by me. I have made
no such decisions, and authorized none. I have not had time to
review the results of the on-going investigation and have neither
endorsed nor disapproved any charges or theory of the case.

       The U.S. Attorney and his aides have been instructed to
refrain from any kind of statement, comment or speculation about
any aspect of the investigation. All officials in the Department of
Justice will be so instructed. No previous statement or comment
about any aspect of the investigation has been authorized by me.

OVER

- 2 -

I am well aware of the intense public interest in all aspects
of the investigation and will try to find ways to give the public all
the information consistent with a prosecutor's professional obligations
and a careful, thorough and fair investigation and, if indictments
are warranted, a fair trial of those accused.

I prepared this statement prior to Mr. Buzhardt's telephone
call. I gave him the substance of it then and later read it to him,
solely to confirm the accuracy of what I had said.

APPENDIX R

"Why not parade everyone before a grand jury—just to see
what they might know?" (See text p. 144.)

*Plann &
Coord.
check for copy*

PBH:bas

Bill Merrill and Jim Neal   July 24, 1973

Philip B. Heymann

    Have we ever tried to develop systematically a list of
all the staff assistants, special assistants, and other working
personnel associated with the principal figures in the Watergate
and Ellsberg matters? Secretaries don't talk, but eager young
men do, and I have the feeling that we keep coming upon new
ones. In particular, I wonder if we'vereever checked out either
Douglas Howlitt, who worked for a short period for Colson, or
Lewis Engman, now chairman of the Federal Trade Commission, but
formerly a close associate of Ehrlichman on the Domestic Council.

    What I am suggesting is that we should put someone to work
interviewing one or two people and getting a complete list of
names then we can go ahead to check who has been and who should
be interviewed.

cc: H. Ruth

cc:
Chron
Files

APPENDIX S

"Keep asking—again and again—why Bittman was never indicted" (See text p. 149.)

WATERGATE SPECIAL PROSECUTION FORCE   DEPARTMENT OF JUSTICE

Memorandum

TO   : Richard Ben-Veniste   DATE: February 6, 1974

FROM   : Philip A. Lacovara

SUBJECT: Possible Charges Against William Bittman

        In my opinion the facts as you state them would
provide a basis for including Bittman in the overall
Watergate conspiracy to obstruct justice. Even though
Bittman's role in the conspiracy is different from
those on the White House end, that is not at all
uncommon in a conspiracy case. The critical factor is
that Bittman joined with the other co-conspirators to
bring about a set of circumstances that constituted an
improper interference with the administration of
justice. In addition, the fact that his motive for
attempting to achieve those results -- the payment of
money to his client and to himself in return for his
client's silence about the criminal involvement of
others -- might have been different from the motive
of the White House/FCREP co-conspirators and does not
divorce him from the conspiracy. It is also relatively
common for the various members of a criminal conspiracy to have different motives for agreeing to
promote the same improper objective. That difference
in motives does not separate the common plan or
objective into separate conspiracies.

APPENDIX T

"Were others, equally guilty, also passed over?" (See text p. 157.)

$\mathcal{C}$ ⌐Strat

FM:aw

William Merrill   August 15, 1973
Philip Bakes

James F. Neal

Plumbers Task Force Schedule.

    I note that you have scheduled Baroody, Chenow and
Colson for office and/or grand jury appearances and you
plan to schedule [   ] and Ehrlichman.

    This task force has a limited interest in Baroody
and Chenow and of course we are vitally interested in
[   ], Colson and Ehrlichman. Indeed, [   ] committed
perjury before the grand jury and has admitted his perjury
to me and to Silbert and Glanzer. He told [   ] that his
perjury before the grand jury was the result of pressure.
(See my interview of [   ].)

    With respect to Baroody and Chenow I am asking that
George Frampton get with you and apprise you of the information we seek from these individuals.

    With respect to Colson and Ehrlichman, I urge that we
have a general meeting and agree on scheduling of these individuals at a time that both your task force and mine can
participate in a full interrogation covering all areas.

    With respect to [   ], I simply ask that you coordinate
his appearance with Rick Ben-Veniste and keep in mind that he
has committed perjury and that we will probably want to indict
him somewhere along the line.

cc. Mr. Cox ✓
    Mr. Ruth
    Mr. Ben-Veniste
    Mr. Frampton
    Mrs. Volner

APPENDIX U

"WSPF's own 'smoking gun'" (See text p. 158.)

File - Dean

WATERGATE SPECIAL PROSECUTION FORCE

DEPARTMENT OF JUSTICE

Memorandum

TO : Files

DATE: Nov. 15, 1973

FROM : Peter F. Rient ?FR
Judy Denny

SUBJECT: Meetings with Seymour Glanzer and Donald Campbell -
September 18 and October 10, 1973.

On September 18, and October 10, 1973, Peter F. Rient
and Judy Denny of the Special Prosecutor's Office interviewed
Assistant U. S. Attorneys Seymour Glanzer and Don Campbell
in Glanzer's office, concerning contacts after April 1, 1973,
between the original Watergate prosecutors and John Dean
and/or Dean's attorneys. During and after these interviews,
Glanzer and Campbell provided their handwritten notes taken
at their May 2 and 3 meetings with Dean. Other documents
referred to are Glanzer's May 31 memo to Cox and a September
6 memo to files from Rient and Denny re Silbert interview.

Except as otherwise stated, Glanzer and Campbell
both gave the following information.

1. Glanzer knew both Charles Shaffer and Tom Hogan
(Dean's attorneys). Glanzer and Shaffer are close friends
and have known each other since Shaffer worked in the Department of Justice. Glanzer knew Hogan when Hogan was a
law clerk for Judge Jones. The two attorneys for Dean came
to Glanzer's office on about April 2, 1972, saying they

- 2 -

represented Dean. They believed that a subpoena was

outstanding for Dean and they wanted to assure the prose-

cutors that Dean would be produced upon request without such

measures. (There was actually no subpoena at the time.)

Shaffer and Hogan primarily wanted to set up a modus

vivendi for Dean's cooperation. They were also interested

in knowing about and meeting Silbert, so Glanzer took them

to meet Silbert. Campbell was not present at the meeting.

The two attorneys repeated their stance to Silbert. [The

prosecutors at this time were becoming interested in Dean

because of leaks from McCord's discussions with Dash and

adverse publicity about Dean from the Gray hearings.] The

meeting ended with the prosecutors saying they would contact

Dean's attorneys. (Glanzer notes that Shaffer is a brilliant

and resourceful attorney.)

2. Late in the evening of April 5, Shaffer called

Glanzer at home, saying there was an emergency that he

needed to discuss immediately. The two met alone at Glanzer's

home. There was a mutual understanding that the discussion

was in confidence. Shaffer began by asking Glanzer how

far the prosecutors were willing to pursue the case. Glanzer

replied that there were no restraints and they would go

wherever the evidence led. Shaffer then expressed concern

that since he (Shaffer) was known as a friend of the Kennedys

- 3 -

and Glanzer was a Democrat, there might be accusations of
scheming against the Administration, but Glanzer told him
not to worry.

Shaffer asserted that Dean could "deliver Mitchell"
and made general references to the January and February
meetings with Liddy. Shaffer then stated that these discussions had to be off-the-record because the prosecutors'
chain of command led directly to Kleindienst who, as a friend
of Mitchell, might inform Mitchell. Shaffer even preferred
that Glanzer not talk to Silbert. (Shaffer also expressed
uncertainty about an attorney-client privilege, and there
was some discussion of work product privilege and executive
privilege.)

Shaffer acknowledged that Dean was in trouble although he stated that he had not debriefed Dean completely.
However, Shaffer thought Dean would make a valuable witness
and hoped to obtain immunity for him. There was also some
discussion of a potential plea. Glanzer responded that
such judgments couldn't be made on the disclosures thus
far and that he (Glanzer) would have to talk with Silbert
about it. Shaffer continued to ask if the prosecutors
would really take on the Administration and perhaps indict
Mitchell. Glanzer told Shaffer the prosecutors would go

FORCE

- 4 -

where the evidence led. Shaffer was satisfied with this.
Glanzer said Shaffer should debrief Dean and then tell
the story to the prosecutors off-the-record.

Shaffer also asserted in a more general way that
Dean could "deliver Magruder." He contended Dean's value
was greater than Magruder's because Dean had not perjured
himself as Magruder had. [Shaffer had told Bierbower
(Magruder's attorney) that Magruder had lied and told
Glanzer that Magruder's Grand Jury transcripts had been
floating around. (Magruder had taken the transcripts during
preparation for trial. Bierbower eventually returned them
to the prosecutors.)]

Glanzer attempted to reach Silbert and ask him to
come over to Glanzer's home that night, but was unable to
do so. Glanzer assured Shaffer that he (Shaffer) could deal
with Silbert the same as with Glanzer. A meeting was set
up for the following afternoon.

3. Before the afternoon meeting of April 6, Glanzer
told Silbert and Campbell about the substance of his meeting with Shaffer the night before.

At the April 6 meeting, between the prosecutors and
Shaffer and Hogan, Shaffer gave a well organized presentation aimed at "selling" his client and whetting the prosecutors' appetites. (It is Glanzer's opinion that the

Nov. 15, 1973

- 5 -

presentation was very general because Dean had come to
Shaffer only shortly before Shaffer came to the prosecutors and Shaffer had not yet learned all that Dean knew.)
Silbert said that Shaffer should make the presentation.
Shaffer offered Dean's cooperation in return for immunity,
stressing Dean's value and reliability. Silbert rejected
the idea at that point. Saying that he thought the prosecutors could be trusted, Shaffer offered to have Dean
tell his story directly to them as long as it was off-the-
record. Shaffer emphasized that Petersen and Kleindienst
should not be informed.

Shaffer talked only of Dean's knowledge regarding
Mitchell and Magruder. There was nothing said about
Ehrlichman, Haldeman, Colson, or Nixon.

Shaffer's disclosures confirmed much of McCord's
grand jury testimony. Up to this point, McCord had been
an unbelievable witness. He had answered questions at the
grand jury by reading from a prepared script and many of
the jurors disbelieved him. However, McCord had led the
prosecutors to Reisner and Harmony and he had first told the
prosecutors that Gemstone was the code word for the
clandestine operation involving the break-in and the wiretapping.

- 6 -

The meeting ended with Silbert saying he would contact Dean's attorneys about further meetings.

4. At 2:00 p.m. on April 8, the three prosecutors met at Shaffer's office with Dean, Shaffer and Hogan. Shaffer's office was picked to avoid publicity. The meeting was short because Dean was eventually called to a White House meeting (around 3:30) after receiving several calls from the White House.

Dean's disclosures were very diffused and of little substance and he hedged considerably because of the attorney-client privilege and the fact that the President had not been told everything yet. Dean said that it was "about time someone bit the bullet and I'm willing to." However, Dean wanted to tell Nixon first and he was afraid he couldn't get through Haldeman. (At some point Dean referred to Haldeman and Ehrlichman as the "Berlin Wall".)

(a) Substantive disclosures by Dean follow:

Dean told about the January and February meetings in Mitchell's office, but did not tell about the hiring of Liddy or of talking with Liddy before the January meeting. At the first meeting, Dean said, a million dollar plan was presented by Liddy with charts and codes which in part included electronic surveillance. After this meeting, Dean told Liddy to destroy the charts. At the February 4

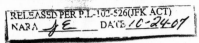
- 7 -

meeting, Dean arrived late. Liddy boasted that he
could hire the most sophisticated expert in electronics
for the job. Dean cut short the meeting by saying these
things shouldn't be discussed in the Attorney General's
office. Dean did not mention his subsequent meeting
with Haldeman at this time. He gave no information at
all about Haldeman or Ehrlichman.

Dean said he learned of the June 17 break-in and
McCord's arrest while returning from Manila. He did not
know McCord. He learned that one of the Cubans had an
envelope with Hunt's name on it, but saw no significance
in the fact at that time. Dean called Kleindienst, who
told him about the incident with Liddy at the Burning
Tree Country Club. Realizing Liddy must be involved,
Dean called and then met with Liddy on the 19th. Liddy
confessed and said it was Magruder who pressured him for
better information. Liddy also said he was a good soldier
and volunteered to go to any street corner to be shot.

Dean admitted cross examining Magruder for his
grand jury appearance and suggesting weaknesses in
Magruder's testimony. Magruder told Dean that Porter
would back up Magruder on his story about the purpose for
which the money was given to Liddy. Dean did not mention
LaRue, Parkinson, O'Brien, or Mardian in connection with
the cover story.

CIAL PROSECUTION

DATE: NOV. 13

- 8 -

Dean admitted that he, Mitchell and Magruder
met in Becker's office shortly before Magruder's third
grand jury appearance, at which time there was a discussion about altering Magruder's diary, and they agreed
to say the meetings in Mitchell's office had concerned
election laws.

Dean denied that he lied to the FBI about Hunt's
office.

Glanzer and Campbell both think Dean mentioned
Kalmbach. (Campbell thinks this was on April 9 instead
of April 8.) When money for Hunt's requests was needed
(not spelled out as hush money), Dean said Mitchell said
"activate Kalmbach." Dean only knew Kalmbach's bag man
as "Tony." Dean also mentioned the $350,000 cash fund
at the White House designated for polling. Dean mentioned
Caulfield and Sandwedge being the predecessor to the Liddy
plan.

Dean was concerned because he thought Liddy was
talking to the prosecutors, as there was a rumor circulating
to that effect. Glanzer and Campbell say they were responsible for helping spread this rumor. Dean said he
thought Liddy could corroborate him on some aspects of his
testimony.

- 9 -

(b)   Other Matters.

The prosecutors were led to Kalmbach by Segretti
and by Flug who had examined some of Kalmbach's bank
records. They talked to Petersen about Kalmbach at their
meeting on the 14th.

'No notes were taken at this meeting and no memos
were made. In order to preserve feelings of mutual trust,
Glanzer would from time to time tell Shaffer who was
appearing before the grand jury and how leads to those
persons came from a source other than Dean. Reisner and
Powell Moore are two witnesses that Glanzer remembers
telling Shaffer about.

5. On the evening of April 9, the three prosecutors
continued their meeting with Dean and his attorneys. Dean
began to get more specific.

(a)   Substantive disclosures by Dean follow:

Dean said that Magruder had been looking for a lawyer to handle CRP intelligence gathering activities and
first wanted Fielding, Dean's assistant. Dean persuaded
Fielding not to accept and then Krogh recommended Liddy.
Dean took Liddy to meet Mitchell on November 24. Liddy
was mostly interested in the salary and his being directly
responsible to Mitchell, and although an agenda prepared
for the meeting mentioned electronic surveillance, the sub-

- 10 -

ject wasn't discussed. The prosecutors asked for,
but never received, a copy of this agenda. (Dean gave
it to the Senate Select Committee.) Dean took Liddy to
meet Magruder in December.

Dean never acknowledged a cover-up or conspiracy
or paying the defendants for silence until after he was
fired (April 30, 1973). Dean did tell about Hunt's money
requests through O'Brien and about meeting Kalmbach outside
the Hay Adams on Mitchell's instructions. He also knew
about money arrangements being made by Parkinson, O'Brien,
and LaRue. Dean was definitely minimizing his own role.

Dean explained in more detail what was discussed
at the January 27 and February 4 meetings, and stated that
the plans for interceptions of communications, surveillance,
prostitution, goon squad, etc. were intended to obviate
disruptions similar to those at the 1968 Democratic Convention. Mitchell listened politely, puffing on his pipe,
but concluded that Liddy's plan "wasn't quite what he had
in mind" and that he wanted something more restricted.
(Dean notes that Mitchell was like a father to him.) After
the February 4 meeting, Dean told Haldeman about the meetings and Haldeman replied that the White House should not
be involved.

- 11 -

It was at the meeting in Arthur Becker's office that Dean told Mitchell he (Dean) would be a good witness for Mitchell about Mitchell's role at the meetings because he could say Mitchell did not expressly approve Liddy's plans. At this meeting Dean wanted his name erased from Magruder's diary entries, but Magruder said it would be detected by the FBI.

Dean talked with Ehrlichman after he talked with Liddy on June 19th. Dean says he was called to Ehrlichman' office and told to clean out Hunt's safe. Colson was there and had supposedly received a call from Hunt concerning the embarrassing contents of the safe. (Colson doesn't corroborate.) In Hunt's safe were bogus cables which indicated that Kennedy was responsible for Diem's assassinatio. Meanwhile, the FBI began calling for the contents of the safe. Dean spoke to Ehrlichman about turning the contents over and Ehrlichman told him to "deep six" it. Dean was troubled by this order and mentioned it to Fielding. There was a delay of several days. Then Dean reminded Ehrlichman that disposing of the evidence was stupid because so many people knew about the contents' existence. Ehrlichman agreed but suggested eliminating the politically dangerous material when he (Dean) made the turnover. Dean turned over all the material to the agents except for the politically explosive stuff which he gave to L. Patrick Gray personally.

15, 1973

- 12 -

Now Dean was in a position to say truthfully he turned
over everything from Hunt's safe to the FBI.

At the meeting on the 19th, Ehrlichman also told
Dean to call Liddy to tell Hunt to leave the country.
Later Dean convinced Ehrlichman that this was crazy. The
order was rescinded, but it was too late.

Glanzer and Campbell agree that Dean's receiving
FBI 302 reports was not mentioned on the 8th or 9th of
April. Glanzer says it was mentioned on the 15th of April.

At some time either in 1972 or 1973, Dean mentioned
to Haldeman a request for money from Hunt through O'Brien.
Haldeman said to go see Mitchell.

Dean said that at some time Parkinson and LaRue
had come to Dean's office with a sheet of paper with money
requests from Hunt on it, but Dean never said that the
money was for Hunt's silence.

Dean mentioned the McCord letter complaining about
a CIA defense being contemplated. Ehrlichman told Dean
to "stroke" McCord. Also Bittman visited Colson and discussed clemency. Again the response by Ehrlichman and
Haldeman was that Colson should "stroke" Bittman, but make
no promises.

Dean mentioned the LaCosta meetings without giving
any details.

- 13 -

Dean asserted that he had been told by Magruder that Liddy and Sloan had stolen money from CRP.

Dean spent quite a bit of time talking about his recent relationships with Magruder and Mitchell. Dean said Magruder was becoming nervous and was phoning everyone. One conversation between Magruder and Dean at Camp David was taped by Dean. Dean stated that Mitchell was going to "stonewall it." Dean was scheduled to meet with Mitchell the next day and Glanzer suggested that Dean be wired by the prosecutors. Shaffer objected, but said he might do it himself.

Campbell remembers that Dean told of the March 21 meeting where Dean attempted to tell the President about the situation, but that the President didn't understand. Dean would not divulge his exact words because of attorney-client privilege and executive privilege.

Dean said Howard and Strachan had given him $15,900 to hold in his safe, but didn't relate this to either the $22,000 or the $350,000.

(b)   Other Matters.

After the prosecutors had heard Magruder, they began to understand more of what Dean had told them. Realizing that they could use Magruder as a witness against Mitchell, their emphasis with Dean turned to Haldeman and Ehrlichman.

- 14 -

6. Glanzer knows no more about Shaffer's April
10 phone call to Silbert than what is in the May 31 memo
to Cox.

7. Shaffer came to the Courthouse late on the evening of April 12 and saw Glanzer and Silbert. Shaffer said
Dean had "nibbled" on the $15,900 that Howard and Strachan
had given him, having taken about $4,000 for his honeymoon
and put a check in the safe. Shaffer wanted the prosecutors
to know this fact before they heard from Strachan. [Strachan
had not yet corrected his grand jury testimony and the prosecutors had told him to get an attorney before he came back
to the grand jury.] Shaffer also said he had been told by
Dean that Haldeman and Higby had coached Strachan before
Strachan's grand jury appearance.

8. Shaffer and Glanzer had three telephone conversations and one meeting on April 14th. Glanzer cannot remember
who called who the first time, but in any event Shaffer came
to Glanzer's home as a result of the call. This was probably
in the early morning. Glanzer brought up the subject of a
guilty plea for Dean and Shaffer was not unreceptive. (At
this point, the prosecutors had begun to think of Dean as
a defendant rather than as a witness, and felt that Dean
or his attorney should be so advised.)

In the early evening on the 14th, Glanzer called
Shaffer from the Department of Justice while meeting with

--CUTION FORCE

- 15 -

Titus and Petersen. Later in the evening, Glanzer called
Shaffer to inform Shaffer of the prosecutors' disclosures
to Kleindienst. Shaffer thought this was a breach of
their agreement, but Glanzer explained that telling
Kleindienst was necessary if the President were to be
notified as Dean wished.

9. On the afternoon of the 15th, Silbert and
Glanzer met with Dean and Shaffer. (Campbell was unable to
attend.) [Glanzer remembers Petersen instructing them to
obtain more evidence on the case, but remembers no specific
emphasis on facts concerning Haldeman and Ehrlichman.]

Dean told about himself, Mitchell, Magruder, LaRue
and perhaps Mardian and Parkinson concocting a story about
how much money went to Liddy. Magruder then testified to
this story. Dean learned from Petersen that Silbert and
the grand jury suspected that Magruder was lying, but had
no evidence to prove it. Dean relayed this fact to Mitchell.

General Cushman's name came up and perhaps Walters'
also. Dean said something about a memo from Cushman with
his (Dean's) name on it and that Ehrlichman was responsible.
Neither Cushman nor Walters were mentioned in connection
with an obstruction of justice.

Glanzer thinks Dean discussed receiving 302's from
Gray "to keep abreast of the news leaks." Dean did not

- 16 -

mention that he had previously requested 302's from
Petersen and Kleindienst and been turned down. Dean
did not say to whom the reports were shown.

Dean made a memo of his April 10 meeting with
Mitchell and remarked that Mitchell said he was going to
"stone wall it". The prosecutors asked for, but never
received, a copy of the memo.

Glanzer (having heard of Greenspun elsewhere) asked
Dean if he knew about Greenspun. Dean replied that Kalmbach
was asked by Colson in California to get information about
Muskie from Greenspun.

Dean mentioned McPhee's romancing of Judge Richey
in the rose garden, the $200,000 Vesco contribution involving
Don Nixon and the ITT scandal, indicating that Watergate
was just the tip of the iceberg of corrupt activities. The
climax of this series of disclosures by Dean was the revela-
tion that Hunt and Liddy had broken into Ellsberg's psychiatrist's office in 1971.

Glanzer doesn't recall that Dean mentioned Segretti.

10. Glanzer phoned Shaffer on April 19 to confirm
that Shaffer and Dean understood that Dean had been given
no commitment of immunity. Petersen had requested confirmation of this fact after being asked by the President
about Dean's status.

- 17 -

11. On the evening of April 23, Shaffer met
with Silbert and Glanzer. Glanzer says that by this
time, the discussions had turned into a political game.
Dean was bargaining with the Senate for immunity and the
prosecutor's attempts at agreeing on a plea were in vain.
Shaffer suggested a plea to misprison of a felony (never a
firm offer), but then rejected this when it was determined
that it was a felony and the possible sentence was too long.

12. On April 29, Shaffer called Glanzer at home
to discuss the Vesco case. (It was not unusual for Shaffer
to call Glanzer to discuss things generally.) Shaffer told
Glanzer that Dean would either be a witness in the case or
would not testify. Shaffer also told Glanzer that Colson
would have information about Haldeman and Ehrlichman.

After April 15, the situation was in a state of
flux. The appointment of Cox and the preparation for the
Senate hearings changed the outlook from all sides.

13. By the end of April, Dean had become much more
antagonistic toward Haldeman and Ehrlichman in his discussions with the prosecutors and also in public, issuing
the "scapegoat" statement. Before that, the impression
he gave of Haldeman was of a "great devoted public servant,"
clean and hard working. He had been restrained in his
praise of Ehrlichman.

DEPARTMENT ~~ ~

- 18 -

14. On May 2, Silbert, Glanzer, and Campbell met
with Dean and Shaffer at Shaffer's office. At this
meeting the note taking prohibition was waived. Initially,
there were procedural discussions about listening to Dean
tell about Presidential involvement, including the problem
of executive privilege and attorney-client privilege.
The prosecutors decided to listen to whatever Dean had
to say.

Dean played for the prosecutors a copy of the
Colson-Hunt dictabelt. Dean said he had played the tape
for Haldeman and Ehrlichman at Camp David on November 15
at a meeting about Chapin's future and for Mitchell in
New York also on the 15th. 1/

a. Substantive disclosures made by Dean follow:

Dean told of seeing Haldeman after the February 4
meeting and Haldeman relaying this to Ehrlichman. 2/

Dean says the White House put pressure on his
secretary, Jane Thomas, to provide information against
him (Dean).

1/ Campbell's notes indicate the tape was made between the
election and November 15. Glanzer's notes indicate that on
the tape Hunt emphasized that commitments had been made to all
the defendants, that the stakes were high and things must not
break for foolish reasons. Both sets of notes indicate
November 25 was the deadline for resolution of the problem.
Glanzer's notes go into some more detail about the contents
of the tape.

2/ Both Campbell's and Glanzer's notes show that Haldeman
did not want the White House involved. Glanzer's notes show
that Haldeman recounted his and Dean's conversation in front
of Mitchell also.

- 19 -

Operation Sandwedge, according to Dean, was an
elaborate plan with overt and covert operations including
illegal electronic surveillance. 3/ The written proposal
was sent to Ehrlichman whose copy should still be at the
White House even though Caulfield took all of his files
with him when he left. Anne Dawson could corroborate
Dean on this. (There was a budget for Sandwedge.)

Dean said Colson called Caulfield to do a "bag
job" on Brookings, but Dean did not mention a fire.

Dean knew that "Tony" (Ulasewicz), Caulfield's
friend did various discrete jobs for the White House,
e.g., pricing boats and picking out the "Sequoia".

Before June 17, 1972, Gemstone summaries went to
Strachan. After the 17th, Strachan told Dean that
Haldeman had instructed him (Strachan) to pull all intelligence material. All "proceeds" from Watergate wiretaps
were destroyed. Haldeman's files included memos of
meetings of Haldeman, Strachan and Kalmbach about financing.

Dean taped an interview he had with Segretti and played
the tape on November 10 or 11, 1972, for Haldeman and
Ehrlichman at Haldeman's villa in Key Biscayne.

Segretti wrote the letter insinuating sexual
deviations in Jackson and Humphrey. Segretti had a network

3/ Campbell's notes show that Ehrlichman and Mitchell said
"No" to the proposal because Caulfield was not the right man

- 20 -

of 50 operatives and kept records of all the people and movements. Segretti obtained bogus stationery from a Cuban printer (through Hunt).

When asked for corroboration for some of his information, Dean suggested Tod Hullin, Higby and diaries of Ehrlichman and Haldeman. He said Colson could corroborate the meeting on June 19th where Ehrlichman gave the order to tell Hunt to leave the country. (Dean became hostile to Colson when Colson did not corroborate.)

Sometime shortly after the break-in, Hunt was in his White House office. Colson was somewhat shaken when he realized that at the same time a newsman was talking with Hallett next door.

Pat Boggs of the Secret Service told Ehrlichman about the Hunt check found on one of the Miami men.

In July of 1972, Dean met with Haldeman and Ehrlichman at San Clemente to discuss the Watergate situation.

On September 2, 1972, Dean met with Haldeman and Ehrlichman at the Newporter Inn and told them everything he had learned about Watergate.

At Camp David on November 15, Dean told Haldeman that part of the $350,000 White House cash fund had to be released. The money was thereafter released. Howard and Strachan turned over the balance of $22,000 to Dean.

- 21 -

After the break-in, Mitchell, Mardian, LaRue and
Dean discussed raising money for the defendants. Kalmbach
was mentioned and Mitchell told Dean to get Ehrlichman's
approval. After asking Ehrlichman, Dean met Kalmbach
at the Mayflower and explained to Kalmbach that Mitchell,
Haldeman and Ehrlichman all felt the defendants needed to
be paid. Dean said LaRue would be in contact with Kalmbach
for details. Kalmbach asked Dean to have Caulfield call
him (Kalmbach). Stans turned over $80,000 to LaRue about
this time.

Later Dean met Kalmbach in Lafayette park. Kalmbach
had money with him (some from LaRue, some raised through
his own efforts) and asked for delivery instructions.
Kalmbach also wanted Dean to convey a message to Haldeman
and Ehrlichman that he (Kalmbach) was opposed to delivering
this money. (Dean says Kalmbach frequently handled tasks
like this, e.g., $200-400,000 delivered to Wallace's
opponent in the gubernatorial race.)

Dean said Kathleen Chenow would be a good witness to
Hunt's and Liddy's White House activities. Krogh and Young
would know about the Ellsberg matter.

Dean said he was told by Liddy on June 19th that
it was Magruder who pushed him into going back into the DNC.

- 22 -

At the Republican Convention MacGregor was pestering Dean for a briefing on Watergate. Ehrlichman advised Dean to "stroke" MacGregor, but not tell him anything.

On February 10-11, 1973, at LaCosta, California, Haldeman, Ehrlichman, Moore and Dean met to review the White House handling of the Senate hearings. The question of the defendant's continued silence was also raised. Moore was sent to New York to get Mitchell to raise money to replace the $350,000 White House fund. Moore took the message to Mitchell but was rebuffed.

On March 12, 1973, O'Brien told Dean that he (O'Brien) had met Hunt on March 9 and that Shapiro had had a similar meeting with Hunt. Hunt threatened to tell all the "seamy" things he had done for the White House if $72,000 for legal fees and $50,000 for living expenses was not paid to him.

Dean said that Gray was wrong to call him (Dean) a liar.

At a meeting in Haldeman's office between Haldeman, Ehrlichman, Dean and Mitchell, Ehrlichman asked Mitchell about Hunt's money problem. Mitchell replied that he didn't think it was a problem any more.

Dean says Haldeman and O'Brien knew each other because O'Brien had been an advance man in the 1960 campaign.

- 23 -

Segretti's diaries 4/ show violations of § 612 and possibly § 241 and § 242.

Dean says LaRue was working on some deal with Tom Pappas. 5/

b. Procedural matters:

The meeting broke up in the early hours of the 3rd and was resumed again that night.

15. On May 3, Dean began focusing on Presidential involvement, thus changing dramatically from his previous stance. Glanzer and Campbell agree with Silbert's account of Dean's statements about the President. (See Rient and Denny memo to files dated September 6, 1973 re Silbert interview.) Glanzer and Campbell say, however, that Dean told them that Krogh told him about the instructions for the Ellsberg break-in coming from the Oval office at the

---

4/ Glanzer's notes add that O'Brien was the one who brought the diaries in.

5/ Campbell's notes indicate the following items were also discussed: the August 29, 1972, Presidential announcement of Dean's investigation (Glanzer puts this on May 3rd) and the President's urging on April 17, 1973 that no White House aides receive immunity. Glanzer's notes add that (1) Strachan's testimony was worked on by Haldeman and Higby, (2) Sloan came to Ehrlichman about the pressure being applied to him (Sloan), and (3) that Dean thought Mitchell had already committed perjury. Glanzer's and Campbell's notes both indicate that it was June 21 that Ehrlichman gave Dean the order to "deep six" material from Hunt's safe.

- 24 -

time of Krogh's deposition (i.e., August 1972), not
during the Gray hearings. Dean also said that Mitchell
knew of the Ellsberg break-in shortly after June 17.

Among the procedural matters discussed were the
question of whether Dean would go to the grand jury as a
witness (this was left undecided) and the possible filing
by Shaffer of an interpleader concerning documents which
Shaffer said would destroy the President. Dean was
somewhat concerned about being arrested for turning over
the documents since he never had control of them. The
prosecutors asked that the interpleader not be filed till
the following Monday.

a. Substantive disclosures by Dean follow:

Ehrlichman and the President convinced Hoover
to tap certain newsmen and White House personnel in 1969.
(For details of other surveillance, see memo for Glanzer
to Cox, May 31, 1973, p. 13) 6/

Months before Dean's March 21 conversation with
Nixon, Dean had discussed the cover-up with Dick Moore.
Although Moore suggested going to Nixon then, Dean did not
do so. Sometime after March 21, Dean met with Nixon when
Moore was present.

b. Other matters:

6/ Glanzer's notes add that [   ] was a victim of 7c
a tap.

- 25 -

Around May 3, Glanzer advised Dean to go to his
"Camp David", collect his thoughts, put them down
coherently and provide documents and witnesses to corroborate
them. 7/

16. On Friday night, May 4, Shaffer told the prosecutors that Dean would not go to the grand jury the next
day. Shaffer agreed that on the question of executive
privilege, the prosecutors would prevail before Sirica.

17. Glanzer's evening conversations on May 12 with
Dean and Shaffer were accurately related in Glanzer's May 31
memo to Cox. Dean and Shaffer were together.

18. Miscellaneous

Bob Bennett first told the prosecutors of Hunt
being asked to leave the country.

Walters and McCord first told the prosecutors about
the attempts to use the CIA.

7/ Glanzer's notes indicate that the following items were
also discussed on May 3. (1) After the September indictments,
Nixon complimented Dean, saying "Bob has been keeping me
informed." (2) In March 1973 during Gray hearings, Dean
mentioned Hunt's threat to Nixon and the million dollar
conversation took place, (3) on Friday March 23, 1973,
Ehrlichman talked with Kleindienst about the grand jury,
(4) when Greenspun was mentioned in front of Haldeman,
Haldeman jumped up and said he didn't want to hear about
it.

- 26 -

Dean first told the prosecutors about money being
paid to the defendants.

McCord and Caulfield first told of the clemency offer
to McCord.

O'Brien came to the prosecutors voluntarily. In
fact they saw him only after many days of his persisting in
attempting to meet with them. O'Brien's story was very
disjointed. The prosecutors did not use Dean's leads in
questioning O'Brien, but instead used notes O'Brien made
for a meeting with Ehrlichman (obtained from Ehrlichman).

Glanzer originally wanted to give Dean immunity
because of his value as a witness, but was persuaded by
Silbert and Campbell that Dean should not be granted immunity.
In hindsight, Glanzer thinks this was a good decision.

Glanzer thinks that the prosecutors' effect was
neutralized by the appointment of a special prosecutor
and the Senate Committee coming into being, and that they
began to lose control over the case.

APPENDIX V

"Proof positive WSPF worried about Dean's changed testimony"
(See text p. 163.)

WATERGATE SPECIAL PROSECUTION FORCE   DEPARTMENT OF JUSTICE

Memorandum

TO   : Larry Iason   DATE: October 2, 1974

FROM   : Jim Neal

SUBJECT: John Dean's Contacts and Information Imparted
          to the Original Prosecutors

   Larry, I need for you to prepare today while we are
picking the jury, a summary day-by-day of the information
imparted by Dean to Silbert, Glanzer, et al. It should
start with April 18 through May 25, 1973. I don't need
extensive information, just the development. We need to
show, if it's a fact, that Dean was giving the prosecutors
information in a chronological manner, rather than as an
"escalation" to higher-ups in order to get immunity as
implied in the memorandum from Silbert to Cox dated May 31,
1973. In other words, that he did start with
pre-break-in period for two reasons: First, because it
appeared to be the focal point of the investigation at that
time; and second, because in early April he admittedly hoped
to avoid an investigation into the cover-up, not only for
himself but for others. He states, however, that as the
meetings progressed and as they continued to probe, it became impossible to explain what happened pre-June 17 without explaining the matters that happened thereafter, and that
his revelations proceeded on a chronological basis.

   Dean states, further, that he advised Shaffer in his
early meetings with him that he wanted to tell the story
of Watergate. It was Shaffer's idea that Shaffer seek
immunity for Dean. Dean agreed that that would be fine but
he continued on the course of commitment to tell the story
with immunity if he could get it, or without immunity if he
could not.

   Larry, we need to be prepared either on direct of Dean
or re-direct or in rebuttal to support this story and I need
you to analyze the original prosecutors' notes, Silbert's
diary, and the above-mentioned memorandum for the factual
support therein. (The Silbert to Cox memorandum of May 31
is in my cabinet in the notebook labeled "Silbert Pros.
Memos.)

APPENDIX W

" 'Deep sixing' Dean's purloined files" (See text p. 170.)

WATERGATE SPECIAL PROSECUTION FORCE   DEPARTMENT OF JUSTICE

Memorandum

TO : Henry Ruth   Jay Horowitz   DATE: November 30, 1973
       Tom McBride   Rich Davis
       William Merrill   Peter Kriendler
       Joseph Connolly

FROM :
       George Frampton GTF
       Henry Hecht HH GTF

SUBJECT: Dean Subpoena

     John Dean has asked that we give him a subpoena covering material in his possession relevant to our investigations.

     The attached draft of a subpoena will be served on Dean on Monday, unless you have any changes or additions in the language covering your area.

     Please let Henry Hecht or George Frampton know about any changes by noon on Monday.

     Thanks.

DRAFT: Subpoena to John Dean

All documents, memoranda, papers, and other
writings and all tapes and other electronic and/or
mechanical recordings and reproductions relating to:

1) The break-in and wire tapping of the Democratic
National Committee Headquarters at Watergate in May and
June 1972 and subsequent attempts to conceal and cover-
up the identit~~y~~ies of ~~any~~ individual~~s~~ with ~~any~~ knowledge *concerning this matter*
~~of the break-in and wiretapping.~~

2) The establishment and activities of the White
House Special Investigations Unit (so called "Plumbers"
group) and ~~its members~~ *persons connected with the Unit*;

3) Activities by the staff of the White House
and/or Committee to Re-Elect the President to obtain
political intelligence information relating to the 1972
Presidential campaign and/or to conduct campaign espionage
or sabotage in connection with that campaign;

4) Activities by the staff of the White House
and/or Committee to Re-Elect the President to influence
the actions of other federal agencies, offices, or
officials;

RELEASED PER P.L. 102-526(JFK ACT)
NARA _4E_ DATE _10-24-07_

5) Activities by the staff of the White House
or others in connection with the conduct or settle-
ment of Government anti-trust cases involving the
International Telephone and Telegraph Company;

6) Activities by the staff of the White House,
the Committee to Re-Elect the President, the Finance
Committee to Re-Elect the President, or others
relating to the solicitation, receipt, reporting,
or use of campaign contributions in the 1972 campaign,
and/or ~~the existence of~~ any connection between ~~such~~ *the above*
activities
~~contribution~~s and the influencing of action by any
Government agency, office, or official;

7) Wiretapping or other electronic eavesdropping
done at the direction of members of the White House
staff or the President.

WATERGATE SPECIA ', PROSECUTION FORCE   DEPARTMENT OF JUSTICE

Memorandum   *15. 11*

TO   : Philip Lacovara   DATE: January 30, 1974
        Henry Ruth

FROM : Henry L. Hecht

SUBJECT: Provision of Copies of Dean's Documents to Dean

        Following conversations with McBride and Lacovara,
I telephoned Dean concerning his request for copies
of the documents he furnished this Office pursuant to
a Grand Jury subpoena. I explained that it was my
understanding that his attorney, Charles Shaffer,
agreed that it was in Dean's interest not to have
copies so that he would not be subject to discovery
by civil litigants.

        For the present, Dean said he would not request
copies of the documents. I will provide Dean with
copies of the inventories of documents received to
date.

cc:
    Chron
    File
    Hecht
    McBride

APPENDIX X

"Brilliant legal argument of how a regulation trumps a
President's constitutional prerogative" (See text p. 190.)
"Brilliant legal argument debunked" (See text p. 191.)

WATERGATE SPECIAL PROSECUTION FORCE   DEPARTMENT OF JUSTICE

Memorandum

15.42

TO : Leon Jaworski   DATE: September 13, 1!
      Special Prosecutor

FROM : Philip A. Lacovara
       Counsel to the Special
       Prosecutor

SUBJECT: Validity of Pardon of Former President Nixon

     Earlier this week you asked me to have prepared a memorandum
dealing with the validity of the "full, free and absolute pardon"
granted to former President Nixon by President Ford on September
8, 1974. I have asked Robert L. Palmer of my staff to prepare
such a memorandum and, despite the short deadline I gave him, has
produced what I consider a comprehensive and substantial legal
memorandum on this subject. A copy of his full memorandum is
attached.

     Mr. Palmer concludes that, as I had initially advised you,
it is well settled that the Presidential pardon power may be
exercised at any time after a federal offense is committed, even
before any criminal proceedings are instituted. He explains,
however, as I orally indicated to you on September 11, that there
is a substantial argument supporting the proposition that the
pardon in this case was invalid. The basic reason for this conclusion is that the President explicitly assented to regulations
issued by the Attorney General which, by their terms, declare
that the President will not exercise his "constitutional powers"
to interfere with the "independence" given to the Special Prosecutor for exercising "full authority for investigating and
prosecuting" Watergate-related offenses and particularly allegations concerning the President. The regulations to which the
President expressly assented also explicitly assign to the Special
Prosecutor full authority for "deciding whether or not to prosecute any individual." The argument is a straightforward one:
despite the President's inherent constitutional powers to control all law enforcement decisions, whether by directing that an
investigation not proceed, directing that an indictment be dismissed, or granting a pre-conviction pardon, the President has
voluntarily bound himself not to exercise these "constitutional
powers" if their exercise would interfere with the independent
judgment of the Special Prosecutor to decide whom to prosecute.

The argument analyzed by Mr. Palmer is a substantial one
that -- as a legal matter -- could be asserted in good faith.
You may feel constrained not to advance such an argument because
of a more restrictive understanding of what "constitutional
powers" the President was agreeing not to exercise. My understanding of the circumstances which led to the inclusion of that
Presidential commitment in our charter, however, leads me to
believe that no such restrictive interpretation was intended.
I do not suggest, of course, that you or the President (then Mr.
Nixon) or Acting Attorney General Bork or anyone else expressly
focused on the pardon question. It seems to me, though, that
the commitment embodied in the regulations can reasonably be
understood as extending as broadly as necessary to avoid the
danger for which it was committed: to guarantee that the President would not be able to undercut the discretionary judgment
the country felt had to be reposed in an independent Special
Prosecutor. I see no compelling reason why the broad terms of
this commitment should be confined to a breach not to exercise
one kind of constitutional power (the power to direct and if
necessary dismiss subordinate officials) while leaving open the
ability to achieve precisely the same effect by the exercise of
another constitutional power, such as the power to grand a pre-
prosecution pardon.

Mr. Palmer's analysis could be challenged on two other
bases, however. First, it could be argued that the cases on
which he relies and on which we depended in United States v.
Nixon are not truly apt here. Those cases involved contentions
by an individual that his rights had been prejudiced because a
government agency had violated its own regulations in taking
action adverse to him. In the present context, a conclusion
that President Ford's action constituted a breach of the regulations would not necessarily render invalid the action taken.
Here the interests of a third party, Mr. Nixon, are involved,
and the breach of a commitment not to exercise the pardon power
in favor of a third person prior to conviction might not
invalidate that exercise. This situation is sui generis, and
I conclude that there is a significant possibility that a court
would conclude that President Ford's action was effective vis-
a-vis Mr. Nixon even if it constituted a violation of the regulations governing the relationship between the White House and
the Special Prosecutor.

A second possible counter to the Palmer thesis would involve principles of estoppel. The essence of such an argument
would be that this Office had substantial notice of President

Ford's inclination or intention to grant a pre-prosecution
pardon to Mr. Nixon. Whether or not any representations were
made to the White House about the desirability of acting upon
such an intention prior to indictment the courts might well
hold that it was incumbent upon us to assert actively an ob-
jection to that possible course and to apprise the President
of its possible contravention of outstanding regulations. To
some extent this argument would be neutralized by the absence
of one of the traditional ingredients in an estoppel, namely
reliance by the other party. While President Ford undoubtedly
changed his position, it is hard to conceive of any way in which
Mr. Nixon has changed his position to his detriment in reliance
upon any failure on our part to object to the proposed pardon.
He has not admitted his guilt publicly nor has he agreed to
yield any of his rights in return for the pardon. Therefore,
in terms of legal rights and obligations, the invalidation of
the pardon would simply restore the status quo ante.

I do not see any legal basis to an argument that President
Ford was not bound by these regulations, to the extent that
they may be construed as applying to the exercise of the pardon
power. It is an elementary principle that laws, including
government regulations, are not confined to named individuals
but apply to categories or offices. That is, the regulations
issued by Acting Attorney General Bork are fully binding (until
validly revoked or amended) upon Attorney General Saxbe,
irrespective of whether Mr. Saxbe had any role in their promul-
gation. Quite simply, the regulations bind the office, irrespective of the incumbent. By the same token these regulations contain a commitment from Richard Nixon, not as an individual, but
as President, not to interfere with the independence of the
Special Prosecutor's Office. Whether or not there might be the
same need for such a guarantee under the new Administration, it
is clear to me that President Ford is bound by these regulations
at least to the extent that he cannot legally dismiss you or
limit your jurisdiction in the exercise of his "constitutional
powers" except after obtaining the consensus of the committee of
eight. It follows that if the regulations would have bound
President Nixon from aborting a prosecution of John Mitchell,
for example, by issuing a pre-prosecution pardon, President Ford
is and was equally bound not to use a similar mechanism to pre-
empt your responsibility for deciding whether to prosecute
Richard Nixon.

Legally, the issuance of a pardon does not prevent the
return of an indictment. A pardon is in effect an affirmative

defense, or "plea in bar," which must be asserted by the
defendant. This procedure, among other things, gives the
defendant an option to stand instead upon a not-guilty plea
in an effort to secure an acquittal of the charges rather than
to rely on a pardon, which technically presupposes guilt. In
addition, this mechanism allows the prosecution to contest the
effect of the pardon, such as by contending that it was invalid,
that any conditions to it have not been satisfied, or that it
is not applicable to the charges in question. I recommend that
you not request or sign an indictment against Mr. Nixon if both
of the following conditions are clear in your judgment: (1) Mr
Nixon would assert the pardon rather than seek exoneration at a
trial, and (2) you have decided not to challenge the effectiveness of the pardon. While it would be technically lawful to do
so, I believe it would be unwarranted under these circumstances
although an argument could be advanced that the grand jury was
entitled to lodge for the record its formal accusation despite
Mr. Nixon's ability to avoid a trial. If you do ascertain that
Mr. Nixon would avail himself of an opportunity to litigate the
allegations against him or if you conclude that a challenge to
the pardon, although by no means inevitably successful, would
nevertheless be fair and appropriate, then an indictment could
be returned.

Attachment

cc: Mr. Ruth
    Mr. Palmer
    Files

"Brilliant legal argument of how a regulation trumps a
President's constitutional prerogative" (See text p. 190.)
"Brilliant legal argument debunked" (See text p. 191.)

WATERGATE SPECIAL PROSECUTION FORCE   DEPARTMENT OF JUSTICE

Memorandum

TO   : Henry S. Ruth, Jr.   DATE: Sept. 14, 197

 FROM : Leon Jaworski

SUBJECT:

I observe that Phil Lacovara sent you a copy
of his memorandum to me of date September 13, 1974,
"Subject: Validity of Pardon of Former President
Nixon" to which he attached copy of a memo from
Robert Palmer to him.

I would have difficulty ever asserting that I
considered the regulations to preclude the President
from exercising his constitutional power under
Article 2, Section 2.

My inquiry to Phil was really directed at the
question of defects in procedure -- wording of the
pardon -- its all-encompassing aspects, etc., which
this memorandum ignores. It is my judgment that no
court -- certainly not the Supreme Court -- would
hold that the President abdicated his pardon power by
agreeing to our charter -- but I am interested in your
views.

APPENDIX Y

"Doublespeak designed to obfuscate prosecutorial abuse" (See text p. 194.)

CAMPAIGN CONTRIBUTIONS

Investigations of 1972 Campaign Financing and Related Matters

Beginning in June 1973, the Campaign Contributions task force systematically examined the campaign finances of major 1972 Republican and Democratic Presidential candidates. This examination included the investigation of several hundred separate transactions, including corporate and labor union contributions, recipients' non-reporting of contributions and expenditures, and alleged *quid pro quo* relationships between contributions and Government actions.

The task force began its inquiries on the basis of the following major sources of information:

1. A list of persons who had made large contributions to President Nixon's reelection campaign before April 7, 1972—the effective date of a new campaign law which required that contributions be reported publicly. The existence of this list, which was kept by the President's secretary, was initially disclosed in a civil suit brought by Common Cause against the Finance Committee to Re-Elect the President (FCRP). WSPF later obtained the list from the White House.

2. Reports of pre-April 7 contributions to several Democratic candidates, which the candidates had made public.

3. Reports of post-April 7 contributions to candidates of both parties which had been filed with the General Accounting Office pursuant to the new law.

4. Referrals from the Internal Revenue Service.

5. Information obtained in the Watergate investigation about the sources and disposition of campaign funds used in the Watergate break-in and cover-up.

6. Newspaper articles, letters from citizens (many of them anonymous), and similar sources.

A variety of investigative methods were used. The prosecutors interviewed major Republican and Democratic fundraisers, including Herbert Kalmbach of FCRP, who cooperated with the office under an agreement involving his guilty plea to two charges (described elsewhere in this section). Agents of the FBI and IRS examined the campaign financial records of the major Presidential candidates and those Congressional candidates whose campaign finances, for various reasons, became relevant to matters directly within the jurisdiction of the Special Prosecutor. The prosecutors sent letters to about 50 known contributors asking them to telephone the office and answer certain questions. Many contributors were interviewed in person in WSPF's offices. FBI agents interviewed hundreds of employees and financial officers of corporations and unions and examined bank and corporate records; IRS agents took similar steps in cases that seemed to involve possible tax violations. In some cases, particularly when there was a suspicion of an explicit *quid pro quo* relationship between contributions and Government actions, WSPF attorneys conducted interviews of contributors, fundraisers, and Government officials. Witnesses were also called before the grand jury, especially when it appeared that attempts were being made to obstruct an investigation.

APPENDIX Z

"Governor Reagan could run for President in 1976; we're investigating him, too" (See text p. 206.)

WATERGATE SPECIAL PROSECUTION FORCE   DEPARTMENT OF JUSTICE

Memorandum   *10.11*

TO :   Leon Jaworski   DATE: August 19, 1974

FROM : Thomas F. McBride

SUBJECT: Your Inquiry of Today

      Attached is a memo from Chuck Ruff containing the information developed in the "Town House" investigation.

      The only other information of any possible consequence relates to Reagan. In 1970 Ross Perot, head of a large Dallas-based computer firm, was solicited by Kalmbach for a contribution to the 1970 mid-term congressional campaigns. He was also solicited for contributions to Reagan's 1970 gubernatorial campaign. According to Kalmbach, Perot did not ultimately contribute to the congressional races. He may, however, have contributed to the Reagan campaign. In May, 1970 Perot asked Kalmbach to set up meetings with Reagan and with Harry Dent, John Ehrlichman and possibly other administration figures. Perot says the purpose of these meetings was to complain about certain policies and actions of the Social Security Administration in requiring approval of contracts between medicare insurers (private insurance companies) and Perot's computer firm. In the case of Reagan the particular issue was the substitution of one private carrier (with whom Perot had computer contracts) by another (with whom Perot was not a subcontractor) as medicare carrier in several California counties. Perot did meet with Reagan and later (perhaps through Reagan's intervention) with HEW Secretary Finch and Undersecretary Veneman. Perot did not get the relief or remedy he sought. We have not, as yet, learned whether Perot did, in fact, contribute to Reagan's 1970 campaign.

cc:
File
Chron
Circ
Task Force File No._____
McBride
Ruth

2

It should be noted that any Kalmbach fund-raising activities for Reagan were cleared by either Haldeman, Ehrlichman or both.

NOTES

INTRODUCTION

4   **"I had been through"**   Nixon, Richard M. *RN: The Memoirs of Richard Nixon*. New York: Grosset & Dunlap, 1978, p. 277.

CHAPTER 1: TWO SUMMER NIGHTS: THE BRIDGE AT CHAPPAQUIDDICK AND THE WATERGATE BREAK-IN

10   **"The senator was silent"**   Damore, Leo. *Senatorial Privilege: The Chappaquiddick Cover-up*. Washington, D.C.: Regnery Gateway, 1998, p. 81.

CHAPTER 2: WATERGATE: WHAT REALLY HAPPENED—AND WHY

20   **"McGovern was obviously running"**   Magruder, Jeb Stuart. *An American Life: One Man's Road to Watergate*. New York: Atheneum, 1974, p. 202.

Chapter 4: Kennedy Politics: Long Memories and Sharp Knives

39   **"They play hard. They"**   Matthews, Christopher. *Kennedy & Nixon: The Rivalry That Shaped Postwar America.* New York: Simon & Schuster, 1996, p. 51.

40   **"Running liquor during Prohibition"**   Talbot, David. *Brothers: The Hidden History of the Kennedy Years.* New York: Free Press, 2007, p. 129.

43   **"Personally he felt Hoffa"**   Navasky, Victor S. *Kennedy Justice.* New York: Atheneum, 1971, p. 407.

44   **"Does the Justice Department"**   Ibid., p. 425.

47   **JFK also knew how**   Bartlett, Charles. "Kennedy's Reply to Texan Related." *The New York Times,* November 5, 1961. But see Lasky, Victor. "Bartlett's Unfamiliar Quotations," *Human Events,* January 5, 1962.

49   **As far as macho**   Clymer, Adam. *Edward M. Kennedy: A Biography.* New York: William Morrow, 1999, p. 138.

50   **As if to leave**   Quoted in Ibid., p. 133.

50   **"Having had the experience"**   Clymer, *Edward M. Kennedy,* p. 133.

Chapter 5: John Dean's Cover-up Collapses

58   **"A few days later"**   Dash, Samuel. *Chief Counsel: Inside the Ervin Committee—The Untold Story of Watergate.* New York: Random House, 1976, pp. 26–27.

64   **"For his attorney Dean"**   en-Veniste, Richard, and George Frampton, Jr. *Stonewall: The Real Story of the Watergate Prosecution.* New York: Simon & Schuster, 1977, pp. 101–2.

64   **"Shaffer played a critical"**   Ibid., p. 104.

67   **"This advice to start"**   Dash, *Chief Counsel,* p. 25.

CHAPTER 6: THE CAMELOT CONSPIRACY COMMENCES

74   **"At the time of"**   Dash, Samuel. *Chief Counsel: Inside the Ervin Committee—The Untold Story of Watergate.* New York: Random House, 1976, p. 107.

76   **"Dean's testimony before the"**   Ben-Veniste, Richard, and George Frampton, Jr. *Stonewall: The Real Story of the Watergate Prosecution.* New York: Simon & Schuster, 1977, p. 63.

CHAPTER 7: OBSTRUCTING JUSTICE: POSTPONING DEAN'S INDICTMENT

78   **Sam Dash's book seems**   Dash, Samuel. *Chief Counsel: Inside the Ervin Committee—The Untold Story of Watergate.* New York: Random House, 1976, pp. 71–73.

79   **"Neal arrived at Room"**   Doyle, James. *Not Above the Law: The Battles of Watergate Prosecutors Cox and Jaworski.* New York: William Morrow, 1977, p. 32.

CHAPTER 8: THE PIOUS FRAUD OF THE ERVIN COMMITTEE

92   **"I opposed the first"**   Ervin, Sam, Jr. *The Whole Truth: The Watergate Conspiracy.* New York: Random House, 1980, p. 21.

92   **"What the public did"**   Stans, Maurice H. *The Terrors of Justice.* New York: Everest House, 1978, pp. 285–86.

95   **"Coincidentally I received the"**   Dash, Samuel. *Chief Counsel: Inside the Ervin Committee—The Untold Story of Watergate.* New York: Random House, 1976, pp. 24–25.

96   **"The success of the"**   *Congressional Quarterly,* April 14, 1973, pp. 1–2.

98   **"It was my plan"**   Ibid., p. 88.

CHAPTER 9: FIRST BLOOD: JOHN DEAN TESTIFIES

105   **"He [Dash] wasn't out to"**   Dean, John. *Blind Ambition.* New York: Simon & Schuster, 1976, p. 290.

106   **"I limited my questioning"**   Dash, Samuel. *Chief Counsel: Inside the Ervin Committee—The Untold Story of Watergate.* New York: Random House, 1976, p. 164.

CHAPTER 10: THE ERVIN COMMITTEE PIONEERS
THE POLITICS OF PERSONAL DESTRUCTION

113   **"Ervin himself played a"**   Stans, Maurice H. *The Terrors of Justice.* New York: Everest House, 1978, p. 267.

115   **There is a passage**   Watergate Special Prosecution Force. *Report.* Washington, D.C.: October 1975, p. 72.

116   **John Dean's riveting public**   Burnham, David. *Above the Law: Secret Deals, Political Fixes, and Other Misadventures of the U.S. Department of Justice.* New York: Scribner, 1996, p. 372.

116   **"The memo, personally typed"**   Thomasson, Dan. "Team of FBI Agents used by President Johnson as Political Operatives at the 1964 Democratic Convention," A Scripps Howard Special Report, August 15, 1973.

118   **"According to Bellino, this"**   Dash, Samuel. *Chief Counsel: Inside the Ervin Committee—The Untold Story of Watergate.* New York: Random House, 1976, pp. 230–31.

119   **"I suspected that his"**   Ibid., p. 241.

CHAPTER 11: THE WATERGATE SPECIAL PROSECUTOR
AND THE TERRORS OF PROSECUTORIAL ABUSE

123   **"Our concern is based"**   *In Re Sealed Case* 838 F.2d 476 (1988).

125   **"Now Kennedy and Flug"**   Clymer, Adam. *Edward M. Kennedy: A Biography.* New York: William Morrow, 1999, pp. 200–201.

126   **"Cox, a Harvard Law"**   *Boston Globe.* May 26, 1973, p. 4.

128   **"The meeting lasted two"**   Doyle, James. *Not Above the Law: The Battles of Watergate Prosecutors Cox and Jaworski.* New York: William Morrow, 1977, p. 52.

132   **By now the message**   Ibid., pp. 49–51.

CHAPTER 12: COX'S ARMY OF IVY LEAGUERS

135   **The Watergate Special Prosecution**   Doyle, James. *Not Above the Law: The Battles of Watergate Prosecutors Cox and Jaworski.* New York: William Morrow, 1977, pp. 59–60.

135   **Pommerening estimated that the**   Ibid.

136   **Some of the ninety**   Ben-Veniste, Richard, and George Frampton, Jr. *Stonewall: The Real Story of the Watergate Prosecution.* New York: Simon & Schuster, 1977, p. 41.

137   **In 1973, while meeting**   Black, Conrad. *The Invincible Quest: The Life of Richard Milhous Nixon.* Toronto: McClelland & Stewart, 2007, p. 866.

138   **"The special prosecutor, Vorenberg"**   Doyle, *Not Above the Law,* p. 61.

143   **"Despite the homage repeatedly"**   Burnham, David. *Above the Law: Secret Deals, Political Fixes, and Other Misadventures of the U.S. Department of Justice.* New York: Scribner, 1996, p. 361, quoting William J. Campbell, "Eliminate the Grand Jury," *Journal of Criminal Law and Criminology,* vol. 64, no. 2 (June 1973): 178.

143   **"Would this license to"**   Burnham, Ibid., p. 362, quoting Stuart Taylor, Jr. "Taking Issue: Enough of the Grand Jury Charade." *Legal Times.* May 18, 1992, p. 23.

146   **At least American citizens**   Jaworski, Leon. *The Right and the Power: The Prosecution of Watergate.* New York: Reader's Digest Press, 1977, p. 151.

CHAPTER 13: FRIENDS IN HIGH PLACES: THE STRANGE AND UNUSUAL HANDLING OF WILLIAM O. BITTMAN, ESQ.

152   **"Bittman particularly became the"**   Doyle, James. *Not Above the Law: The Battles of Watergate Prosecutors Cox and Jaworski.* New York: William Morrow, 1977, pp. 303–4.

Chapter 15: The Media Invents a "Massacre"

166   **According to my understanding**   Doyle, James. *Not Above the Law: The Battles of Watergate Prosecutors Cox and Jaworski.* New York: William Morrow, 1977, pp. 154–56.

Chapter 16: Impeaching a President: The House Judiciary Committee Joins the Camelot Conspiracy

175   **"In view of the"**   Adler, Renata. "Searching for the Real Nixon." *Atlantic Monthly,* December, 1976, p. 78.

Chapter 17: The Liberal Media: Long-term Enablers of the Kennedy Clan

178   **When Kennedy was in**   Burnham, David. *Above the Law: Secret Deals, Political Fixes, and Other Misadventures of the U.S. Department of Justice.* New York: Scribner, 1996, p. 356.

178   **"Some years later, with"**   Ibid., pp. 356–58.

179   **In fact, there hadn't**   Doyle, James. *Not Above the Law: The Battles of Watergate Prosecutors Cox and Jaworski.* New York: William Morrow, 1977, p. 69.

180   **Sam Dash admitted that**   Dash, Samuel. *Chief Counsel: Inside the Ervin Committee—The Untold Story of Watergate.* New York: Random House, 1976, p. 24.

180   **Senator Weicker, who had**   Weicker, Lowell P., Jr., with Barry Sussman. *Maverick: A Life in Politics.* Boston: Little, Brown, 1995, pp. 57–58.

181   **Daniel Shorr, who was**   Dean, John. *Blind Ambition.* New York: Simon & Schuster, 1976, p. 325.

181   **"George Clifford, who has"**   Doyle, *Not Above the Law,* p. 70.

182   **"James Polk, then of"**   Ibid., pp. 70–71.

183   **One might assume that**   Ibid., p. 74.

183   **"We had breakfast, luncheons"**   Ibid.

184   **"Lewis would frequently fly"**   Ibid., pp. 362–63.

Chapter 18: Stage One of the Camelot Conspiracy: Destroying the President

187   **"Loyalists of Massachusetts Senator"**   "Winners and Losers," *Time*, August 26, 1974.

187   **"1973 saw a seemingly"**   Witcover, Jules. *Marathon: The Pursuit of the Presidency, 1972–1976.* New York: Viking, 1977, pp. 119–20

Chapter 19: Stage Two of the Camelot Conspiracy: Crippling the Republican Money Machine

194   **"Beginning in June 1973"**   Watergate Special Prosecution Force. *Report.* Washington, D.C.: October 1975, pp. 71–72.

200   **"turned out to be"**   Stans, Maurice H. *The Terrors of Justice.* New York: Everest House, 1978, pp. 20–21.

Chapter 20: Stage Three of the Camelot Conspiracy: Eviscerating Potential Opponents

203   **"Finally, he was tainted"**   White, Theodore H. *America in Search of Itself: The Making of the President, 1956–1980.* New York: Harper & Row, 1982, pp. 336–37.

Chapter 21: The Weakest Link: Teddy Kennedy Self-Destructs

211   **"The Kennedy campaign was"**   White, Theodore H. *America in Search of Itself: The Making of a President, 1956–1980.* New York: Harper & Row, 1982, p. 275.

Chapter 22: The Camelot Conspirators Today: From Edward M. Kennedy to Hillary R. Clinton

221   **"Equally troubling to some"**   Ringle, Ken. *Washington Post,* March 1998, p. C1.

224 **Hillary Rodham Clinton's book** Clinton, Hillary Rodham. *Living History.* New York: Simon & Schuster, 2003, pp. 177–78.

227 **"called as a witness"** Hopsicker, Daniel. Barry and the Boys: The CIA, the Mob and America. Chapter 29: "Who Is Richard Ben-Veniste?" New York: High Times Press, 2001.

BIBLIOGRAPHY

All the President's Men (movie). Burbank, CA: Warner Bros., 1976.

Anderson, Martin. *Revolution.* New York: Harcourt Brace Jovanovich, 1988.

Andrew, John A., III. *Power to Destroy: The Political Uses of the IRS from Kennedy to Nixon.* Chicago: Ivan R. Dee, 2002.

Ben-Veniste, Richard, and George Frampton, Jr. *Stonewall: The Real Story of the Watergate Prosecution.* New York: Simon & Schuster, 1977.

Black, Conrad. *The Invincible Quest: The Life of Richard Milhous Nixon.* Toronto: McClelland Stewart, 2007.

Bly, Nellie. *The Kennedy Men: Three Generations of Sex, Scandal, and Secrets.* New York: Kensington Publishing, 1996.

Bradlee, Ben. *A Good Life: Newspapering and Other Adventures.* New York: Simon & Schuster, 1995.

Burnham, David. *Above the Law: Secret Deals, Political Fixes, and Other Misadventures of the U.S. Department of Justice.* New York: Scribner, 1996.

Clinton, Hillary Rodham. *Living History.* New York: Simon & Schuster, 2003.

Clymer, Adam. *Edward M. Kennedy: A Biography.* New York: William Morrow, 1999.

Colodny, Len, and Robert Gettlin. *Silent Coup: The Removal of a President.* New York: St. Martin's Press, 1991.

Colson, Charles W. *Born Again*. Lincoln, VA: Chosen Books, 1976.

Dallek, Robert. *An Unfinished Life: John F. Kennedy, 1917–1963*. Boston: Little, Brown, 2003.

Damore, Leo. *Senatorial Privilege: The Chappaquiddick Cover-up*. Washington, D.C.: Regnery Gateway, 1998.

Dash, Samuel. *Chief Counsel: Inside the Ervin Committee—The Untold Story of Watergate*. New York: Random House, 1976.

Dean, John. *Blind Ambition*. New York: Simon & Schuster, 1976.

Doyle, James. *Not Above the Law: The Battles of Watergate Prosecutors Cox and Jaworski*. New York: William Morrow, 1977.

Ehrlichman, John. *Witness to Power: The Nixon Years*. New York: Simon & Schuster, 1982.

Elliott, Charles, Jr. *Whittier College: The First Century on the Poet Campus*. Redondo Beach, CA: Legends Press, 1986.

Ervin, Sam, Jr. *The Whole Truth: The Watergate Conspiracy*. New York: Random House, 1980.

Gergen, David. *Eyewitness to Power: The Essence of Leadership, Nixon to Clinton*. New York: Simon & Schuster, 2000.

Gormley, Ken. *Archibald Cox: Conscience of a Nation*. Boston: Addison-Wesley, 1997.

Halberstam, David. *The Best and the Brightest*. New York: Random House, 1972.

Haldeman, H. R. *The Haldeman Diaries: Inside the Nixon White House*. New York: G. P. Putnam's Sons, 1994.

———, with Joseph DiMona. *The Ends of Power*. New York: Times Books, 1978.

Hersh, Seymour. *The Dark Side of Camelot*. Boston: Little, Brown, 1997.

Hoff, Joan, and Dwight Ink. *The Nixon Presidency*. Washington, D.C.: Center for the Study of the Presidency, 1996.

Hopsicker, Daniel. *Barry and the Boys: The CIA, the Mob and America's Secret History*. New York: High Times Press, 2001.

Hougan, Jim. *Secret Agenda: Watergate, Deep Throat, and the CIA*. New York: Random House, 1984.

Jaworski, Leon. *The Right and the Power: The Prosecution of Watergate*. New York: Reader's Digest Press, 1977.

Kessler, Ronald. *The Sins of the Father: Joseph P. Kennedy and the Dynasty He Founded.* New York: Warner Books, 1996.

Labovitz, John R. *Presidential Impeachment.* New Haven, CT: Yale University Press, 1978.

Lasky, Victor. *It Didn't Start With Watergate.* New York: The Dial Press, 1977.

————. *Robert F. Kennedy: The Myth and the Man.* New York: Trident Press, 1968.

————. *JFK: The Man and the Myth.* New York: Macmillan, 1963.

Levin, Murray B. *Kennedy Campaigning: The System and the Style as Practiced by Senator Edward Kennedy.* Boston: Beacon Press, 1966.

Levin, Murray B., and T. A. Repak. *Edward Kennedy: The Myth of Leadership.* New York: Houghton Mifflin, 1980.

Liddy, G. Gordon. *Will: The Autobiography of G. Gordon Liddy.* New York: St. Martin's Press, 1980.

McCord, James W., Jr. *A Piece of Tape: The Watergate Story: Fact and Fiction.* Rockville, MD: Washington Media Services, 1974.

McGinnis, Joe. *The Last Brother: The Rise and Fall of Teddy Kennedy.* New York: Simon & Schuster, 1993.

Magruder, Jeb Stuart. *An American Life: One Man's Road to Watergate.* New York: Atheneum, 1974.

Matthews, Christopher. *Kennedy & Nixon: The Rivalry That Shaped Postwar America.* New York: Simon & Schuster, 1996.

Mollenhoff, Clark R. *Game Plan for Disaster: An Ombudsman's Report on the Nixon Years.* New York: Norton, 1976.

Navasky, Victor S. *Kennedy Justice.* New York: Atheneum, 1971.

Nixon, Richard M. *In the Arena: A Memoir of Victory, Defeat, and Renewal.* New York: Simon & Schuster, 1990.

————. *RN: The Memoirs of Richard Nixon.* New York: Grosset & Dunlap, 1978.

Novak, Robert D. *The Prince of Darkness: 50 Years Reporting in Washington.* New York: Crown, 2007.

Olsen, Jack. *The Bridge at Chappaquiddick.* Boston: Little, Brown, 1970.

Posner, Richard A. *An Affair of State: The Investigation, Impeachment, and Trial of President Clinton.* Cambridge, MA: Harvard University Press, 1999.

Price, Raymond. *With Nixon*. New York: Viking, 1977.

Safire, William. *Before the Fall: An Inside View of the Pre-Watergate White House*. New York: Doubleday, 1975.

Schlesinger, Arthur M., Jr. *Robert Kennedy and His Times*. Boston: Little, Brown, 1979.

Sirica, John J. *To Set the Record Straight: The Break-in, the Tapes, the Conspirators, the Pardon*. New York: W.W. Norton, 1979.

Stans, Maurice H. *The Terrors of Justice*. New York: Everest House, 1978.

Talbot, David. *Brothers: The Hidden History of the Kennedy Years*. New York: Free Press, 2007.

Thomas, Evan. *Robert Kennedy: His Life*. New York: Simon & Schuster, 2000.

Thompson, Fred D. *At That Point in Time: The Inside Story of the Senate Watergate Committee*. New York: Quadrangle/New York Times Book Company, 1975.

Transcripts of Eight Recorded Presidential Conversations. House Judiciary Committee: May–June, 1974.

Watergate: Chronology of a Crisis. Washington, D.C.: Congressional Quarterly, 1975.

Watergate Special Prosecution Force. Final Report. Washington, D.C.: Government Printing Office, June 1977.

———. *Report*. Washington, D.C.: Government Printing Office, October 1975.

Weicker, Lowell P., Jr., with Barry Sussman. *Maverick: A Life in Politics*. Boston: Little, Brown, 1995.

White, Theodore H. *America in Search of Itself: The Making of the President, 1956–1980*. New York: Harper & Row, 1982.

———. *Breach of Faith: The Fall of Richard Nixon*. New York: Atheneum, 1975.

———. *The Making of the President 1968*. New York: Atheneum, 1969.

———. *The Making of the President 1960*. New York: Atheneum, 1961.

White House. *Submission of Recorded Presidential Conversations*. Washington, D.C.: April 30, 1974.

Wills, Garry. *The Kennedy Imprisonment: A Meditation on Power*. Boston: Little, Brown, 1981.

Woodward, Bob. *The Secret Man: The Story of Watergate's Deep Throat.* New York: Simon & Schuster, 2005.

Woodward, Bob, and Carl Bernstein. *The Final Days.* New York: Simon & Schuster, 1976.

———. *All the President's Men.* New York: Simon & Schuster, 1974.

Woodward, C. Vann, ed. *Responses of the Presidents to Charges of Misconduct.* New York: Delacorte Press, 1974.

Zeifman, Jerry. *Without Honor: Crimes of Camelot and the Impeachment of President Nixa.* New York: Thunder's Mouth Press, 1995.

INDEX

Abscam sting, 225–26
Adler, Renata, 173, 175, 229
Agnew, Spiro, 202–3
Albert, Carl, 169
Alch, Gerald, 154–57
Alito, Samuel, 218, 219
All the President's Men (Woodward and
    Bernstein), 72
Alsop, Joseph, 46
American Ship Building Company, 199
American Spectator, 222–23
Anderson, Jack, 146, 181–82
Andreas, Duane, 195
Armstrong, Scott, 95, 117, 222
Arnold, Truman, 227
Ashland Oil, 199
Associated Milk Producers, 199, 203
Atlantic Monthly, 173, 229

Baker, Bobby, 147
Baker, Howard, 93–94
Baldwin, Alfred, 16
Barker, Bernard L., 15
Bartlett, Charles, 47
Bellino, Carmine, 32, 66, 112, 117,
    118, 218
    as chief investigator to Ervin Committee,
      68, 95

on Get Hoffa Squad, 43
    wiretapping for Bobby Kennedy by, 21
Ben-Veniste, Richard, 76, 106, 145–46,
    226–27
    background, 140
    and Bittman, 154
    McCord's claims against, 156
    on Shaffer-Dean relationship, 64–65
Bernstein, Carl, 33, 72
Bierbower, James, 71
Bittman, William O.
    connection to Kennedys, 147–48
    and Hunt memo to Colson, 148,
      150–51
    investigatory files and documents on,
      148–50, App. S
    involvement in cover-up, 148
    McCord accusations against, 154–57
    memos recommending prosecution of,
      151–52
    not indicted, 152–53
Blakey, G. Robert, 39
Bork, Robert, 6, 168, 217, 219
Boston Globe, 126–27, 130
Boyle, James, 15
Bradlee, Ben, 39, 47, 177–78, 179, 180–81
break-ins
    Ellsberg break-in, 22, 30
    Watergate (*See* Watergate)

Brethren, The (Woodward and Armstrong), 222

Breyer, Charles R., 228

Breyer, Stephen G., 228

Brothers (Talbot), 40

Buckley, William F., Jr., 137

bugging

  Liddy's bugging plans, meetings on, 23–24

  by Lyndon Johnson, 21

  by Robert Kennedy, 20–21

Burger, Warren E., 66, 126

Burnham, David, 143, 178, 179–80

Bush, George H. W., 217

Buzhardt, Fred, 84, 165

Byrd, Robert, 34–35

Camelot Conspiracy

  changing story of Dean, 73–76, 99, 104–5

  concurrent Ervin Committee and WSPF investigation, 88–90

  crippling Republican fund-raising apparatus, 192–201

  current activities of conspirators, 216–31

  Dean as double agent for, 69–72

  Dean-Shaffer-Kennedy connection, 70

  delay in issuing indictments, 73, 78–81, 86–88, 128–30

  destroying Nixon, 185–92

  and House Judiciary Committee's impeachment inquiry, 172, 173–76

  leaks to the press, 72–73

  neutralizing Richardson and Peterson, 82–85, 124–25

  and not indicting Bittman, 153

  potential Kennedy opponents investigated by WSPF, 202–8

  removal and silencing of federal prosecutors, 79–82, 85

  results achieved by, 214–15

Campaign Contributions Task Force, 193–201

  achievements of, 199–200

  report of, 194–99, App. Y

campaign intelligence, 20

Campbell, Donald, 70, 80–81

Denny/Rient memo summarizing meetings with, 158–63, App. U

"cancer on the presidency" speech, 54–55

Capone, Al, 42

Carswell, G. Harrold, 65, 66, 217, 218–19

Carter, Jimmy, 210–11

Carville, James, 221

Caulfield, Jack, 21–22

CBS, 81

Chancellor, John, 168–69

Chappaquiddick, 1, 8–15, 51

Chattanooga Times, 47

Clinton, Bill, 6, 189, 220–21, 230

Clinton, Hillary Rodham, 173, 174–75, 230–31

Clymer, Adam, 50, 124

Colson, Chuck, 26, 148

Committee to Re-Elect the President (CRP)

  defense costs of burglars paid by, 52, 60

  establishment of, 19

  Liddy's hiring, 22–23

  Magruder running, 19–20, 22

  Mitchell in charge of, 24

Congressional Quarterly, 96–97

Connally, John, 202–3

Connolly, Joseph J., 140–41

Cox, Archibald, 125–34, 146, 223

  See also Watergate Special Prosecution Task Force (WSPF)

  actions in week prior to being sworn in, 127–30

  appointment as special prosecutor, 125

  background, 138

  delays indictments, 128–30

  Ely's memo regarding Nixon appearing before grand jury, 133, App. P

  first public statement of, 134, App. Q

  Flug's briefing of, 132–33

  holds news conference on tapes, 167

  on indictments, 86–87

  leak saying Petersen under investigation, 84, App. G

  meets with Nieman Fellows, 130–31

  memos regarding Neal's role, 80, App. D, App. E

  powers as special prosecutor, 125–26, App. L

  and press, 179, 180, 183

prosecutorial memo submitted to, 78
rejects Stennis Compromise, 165–67
swearing in of, 126–27
and Titus and U.S. attorney's office,
     128–30, App. N, App. O
Crimmins, Jack, 9, 12
CRP. *See* Committee to Re-Elect the
     President (CRP)
Cushing, Richard Cardinal, 37

Dallas Morning News, 47
Dash, Sam, 67–68, 94, 112, 180
     See also Ervin Committee
     on Ervin Committee documents locked
          away, 116
     game plan of, 98–99
     on goal of Ervin Committee, 96–97
     hearings run by, 97
     McCord's revelations and subsequent
          press conference, 59–60
     pre-sentencing meeting with Sirica, 57, 59
     on Rebozo investigation, 118, 119
     Segretti as first target of, 67–68, 95–96
     and sentencing of burglars, 57–58
     views on Dean, 74–75
Davis, Richard J., 140
Dealey, Ted, 47
Dean, John W. III, 100–110, 148
     background, 101
     campaign intelligence operations set up
          by, 20, 21
     "cancer on the presidency" speech, 54–55
     changing stories of, 73–76, 99, 104–5,
          158–63
     collapse of cover-up, 52–62
     counsel to the president, 102–4
     criminal violations of, 27–29, App. B
     Dash-Dean-Shaffer meetings, 96, 105–6
     dealings with Gray, 28, 34, 35
     destruction of evidence, 28, App. A
     as double agent, 70
     early career of, 101–2
     embezzlement, 29
     enters plea, 164–65
     fails to create report, 56–57, 61–62
     fails to testify at grand jury, 75, 79
     FBI files received by, 28
     firing of, 74

first meeting with Nixon, 54–55
and Haldeman, 104–5
handling of Watergate by, 26–27
hiring of Liddy, 22–23
and Hunt's safe, 28
implicates Nixon, 74, 75, 106–7
indictment of, 73
joins Nixon administration, 102
on Kennedy's being behind hearings, 31
meetings on Liddy's plans, 23–24
meeting with Liddy after Watergate
     arrests, 25–26
misuse of government information, 28
plea agreement, 78
preventing White House disclosures
     about Watergate, 29–30
seeks immunity, 71, 73–76, 105
Shaffer as attorney, 35, 62, 64–65, 80
shares confidential White House files
     with U.S. attorney's office, 71–72
subornation of perjury, 27–28
witness tampering, 28–29
Deep Throat, 72
Democrats. *See* Kennedy Clan Democrats
Denny, Judith Ann, 141
     memo summarizing meetings with
          Glanzner and Campbell, 158–63,
          App. U
Des Moines Register, 180
dirty tricks
     Nixon as target of, 20
     by Segretti, 66–67
Doar, John, 171, 173–74
Dole, Bob, 205–6
Dorsen, David, 94
Doyle, James, 79, 128–29, 130, 132, 198
     background, 139
     on collusion between WSPF and press,
          181–82, 184
     on decision not to prosecute Bittman,
          152–53
     on staffing of WSPF, 138–39
     on Stennis Compromise, 166
Duffy, LaVern, 66, 95

Eastland, James, 32, 124
Education of a Public Man, The (Hum-
     phrey), 5

Ehrlichman, John D.
  counsel to the president, 62
  implicated by Dean, 74
  indictment of, 78
  Nixon announces resignation of, 76
  unaware of Dean's criminal involvement,
    53, 56, 60–61
Ellsberg, Daniel, 22
Ellsberg break-in, 22, 30
Ely, John Hart, 133, App. P
Enemy Within, The (Kennedy), 41
Ervin, Sam, 33–34, 92, 93, 112
Ervin Committee
  cooperation with WSPF, 111–13
  coordinated inaction of, 120–21
  Dash-Dean-Shaffer meetings, 105–6
  Dash's game plan for, 98–99
  Dean's testimony before, 106–9
  defeat of amendments related to,
    91–93
  documents dumped by, 116
  establishment of, 34, 91–93
  excesses in investigation of Rebozo,
    117–19
  goal of, 96–97
  hearings run by Dash, 97
  immunity sought by Dean, 74–75, 105
  lack of bipartisan perspective, 115–17
  members, 93–94
  perjury file, 112, 113
  preceding WSPF, 88–90
  Segretti and dirty tricks as focus of,
    67–68, 95–96, 98
  staffing, 94–95
  treatment of witnesses appearing before,
    113–14
  Weicker's role, 97–98
Exner, Judith, 44

Face the Nation, 81
FBI
  Dean's receipt of files and case
    information of, 28
  misdeeds at presidential behest,
    116–17
Feldbaum, Carl B., 139
Felt, Mark, 72
Fielding, Fred, 22, 103

Fielding, Lewis, Dr., 22
Final Days, The (Woodward), 222
Fleming, Ian, 39–40
Flowers, Gennifer, 221
Flug, James, 32, 66, 67–68, 124,
    218–19
  briefs Cox and staff, 132–33
  guidelines for powers of special
    prosecutor, 125, App. L
Ford, Eddie, 38
Ford, Gerald, 210
  appearance before House Judiciary
    Committee, 191
  pardons Nixon, 189
  sworn in, 186
  WSPF investigation of, 204
Fortune, 36
Foster, Vincent, 6, 219–20, 224
Frampton, George T., Jr., 141, 154
Freeh, Louis, 226

Galbraith, John Kenneth, 13
Game Plan for Disaster: An Omudsman's
    Report on the Nixon Years (Mollen-
    hoff), 180
Gargan, Joe, 9, 10, 11
Gemstone, 25
Get Hoffa Squad, 43, 63, 64
Get Nixon Squad, 82, 125, 126, 137, 183,
    188
Geyelin, Philip, 183–84
Giancana, Sam, 44
Gideon's Trumpet (Lewis), 179
Glanzer, Seymour, 70, 79–81, 158
  Denny/Rient memo summarizing
    meetings with, 158–63, App. U
  on Shaffer's attempts to put off Dean's
    grand jury appearance, 80, App. F
Goldman, Gerald, 141
Gone: The Last Days of The New Yorker
    (Adler), 229
Gonzalez, Virgilio R., 15, 16
Goodwin, Richard, 13
Gore, Al, 6, 226
Gorelick, Jamie, 227
grand jury
  abuse of process by WSPF, 143–46
  Dean's failure to testify, 75, 79

leaks of testimony, 146
post-Watergate trial grand jury
    testimony, 70–71, App. C
and Roadmap, 172
Gray, L. Patrick, 28
FBI director nomination and
    withdrawal, 34–35
Greenfield, Meg, 183–84
Griswold, Erwin, 127
Gulf Oil, 205
Gurney, Edward, 32–33, 94
Gwirtzman, Milton, 13

Halberstam, David, 3
Haldeman, H. R. (Harry Robbins)
assigning Dean to set up campaign
    intelligence operations, 20, 21
Dean's supposed meeting with, 104–5
implicated by Dean, 74
indictment of, 78
Nixon announces resignation of, 76
unaware of Dean's criminal involvement,
    56, 60–61
Hamilton, James, 94, 219–20
Hand, Learned, 144
Hardball, 218
Hart, George, 198
Haynsworth, Clement, 65, 217, 218–19
Heymann, Philip, 130, 223–25
background, 138
Flug's briefing of, 132–33
memo on Ervin Committee proceedings,
    112, App. K
urging interviews of Nixon's staff,
    144–45, App. R
Hill, Anita, 6, 218
Hoffa, Jimmy, 41–44, 147
Hogan & Hartson, 148, 150
Hoover, J. Edgar, 63
House Judiciary Committee, 171–76
approves Articles of Impeachment,
    172–73
Ford appears before, 191
prolonging impeachment process, 172,
    174
receives Roadmap from Judge Sirica, 172
Zeifman on strategies and goals of,
    173–75

Hubbell, Webster, 223–24, 227
Hughes, Howard, 117–18
Humphrey, Hubert, 4–5, 38, 207
Hunt, E. Howard, 15, 147, 148
in address book of burglars, 17
guilty plea of, 52
sentencing of, 58
White House safe, 28

Iason, Lawrence, II, 141
impeachment, 172–73
independent prosecutor, 123. *See also*
    special prosecutor
indictments
for cover-up, 73, 78, 172
Dean's, 73
delay in issuing, 73, 78–81, 86–88,
    128–30
Magruder's, 73
Information Trust, 222–23
Inouye, Daniel, 93
Investigative Group International (IGI),
    220–22

Jackson, Robert H., 86, 122–23, 142
Jackson, Scoop, 207
Jaworski, Leon, 67, 170, 207
deciding whether to indict and prosecute
    Nixon, 187–89
and Nixon pardon, 189, 191, App. X
and press, 183–84
"John Dean's Memory: A Case Study"
    (Neisser), 107–8
Johnson, Andrew, 185
Johnson, Lyndon B., 3, 137, 147–48
bugging used by, 21
FBI misdeeds at behest of, 116–17
Jones, Paula, 221

Kalmbach, Herbert, 196, 199
Keating Five scandal, 228
Kennedy, Edward, 146, 216–18
and Chappaquiddick, 1, 8–15, 51
creation of Get Nixon Squad, 125, 126
defeat of Ervin Committee amend-
    ments, 92

Kennedy, Edward (*cont.*)
  drinking of, 50
  fails to run in 1976, 210
  interviewed by Mudd, 212–14
  investigations by subcommittee of, 66–67
  1980 campaign, 211–14
  opposes Bork nomination, 217
  opposing Nixon's Supreme Court nominations, 65–66
  as potential presidential candidate in 1972, 50–51
  press coverage of, 50, 212–14
  as progenitor of Watergate investigations, 32, 33–34
  reaction to Ford's pardon, 191–92
  runs for Senate, 45–46
  sexual conduct of, 49–50
  and special prosecutor's appointment and powers, 125–26
  wins Senate whip positions, 50
  youth and education of, 48–49
Kennedy, Ethel, 127
Kennedy, Joe, Jr., 37
Kennedy, John F., 1–3
  assassination of, 2, 3
  money used in campaigns of, 37–39
  New Frontier presidency of, 2–3
  and press, 46–48, 177–78
  sexual relationships and affairs of, 44, 45
Kennedy, Joseph P., Sr., 2, 46
  as ambassador, 36–37
  Mafia connections, 40
  wealth of, used in JFK's political campaigns, 37–39
Kennedy, Robert, 3–4, 45, 46, 49
  assassination of, 4
  assigning Shaffer to Warren Commission, 63–64
  Bobby Baker case, 147–48
  bugging used by, 20–21
  crusade against Hoffa, 41–44
  relationship with the press, 48, 178
Kennedy Clan Democrats
  See also Camelot Conspiracy
  and 1980 campaign, 211–12
  liberal media and, 177–84
  loyalties of, following Kennedy assassinations, 3–4

slash and burn politics practiced by, 4–5, 6–7
Kennedy Justice (Navasky), 43
King, Martin Luther, Jr., 21
Kissinger, Henry, 127
Kleindienst, Richard, 28, 30, 76, 111
Kopechne, Mary Jo, 10–11, 14
Kreindler, Peter M., 139
Krogh, Bud, 22

Lackritz, Marc, 94, 117
Lacovara, Philip A., 139
  and Nixon pardon, 190–91, App. X
LaRosa, Ray, 10
LaRue, Fred, 24, 79
"The Leaker as Plumber," 222–23
leaks
  Deep Throat, 72
  of grand jury testimony, 146
  on lack of IRS cooperation in Rebozo case, 119
  Petersen under investigation, 84
  Silbert's transition memo leaked to CBS, 81
  by U.S. attorney's office, 72–73, 81
  and WSPF, 179–83
Lenzner, Terry, 32, 94, 117, 118–19, 220–22
Lerner, Max, 48
Lewis, Anthony, 131, 166, 179–80, 183–84
Liddy, G. Gordon, 15
  Dean's hiring of, 22–23
  found guilty at trial, 52
  intel operations plans of, 23–24, 104
  meeting with Dean after Watergate arrests, 25–26
  relationship with Magruder, 24–25
  sentencing of, 58
Lieberman, Joe, 219
Living History (Clinton), 175
Lodge, Henry Cabot, 37
Long, Russell, 50
Los Angeles Times, 130

Maas, Peter, 37
McAuliffe, Terry, 227
McBride, Thomas F., 140, 194, 198, 207

McClellan Rackets Committee, 41
McCord, James, 15
  on Dean telling Liddy not to discuss
      plans in presence of Mitchell, 104,
      App. I
  letter to Sirica alleging cover-up, 32,
      53, 58
  revelations of, 59
  second letter to Sirica, 154–57
  trial and conviction of, 52–53
McGovern, George, 20, 207
Macmillan, Harold, 45
McNamara, Robert, 13
Mafia, 40–44
  Hoffa crusade of Robert Kennedy,
      41–44
  and Kennedy family connections,
      40–41
Magruder, Jeb Stuart
  Dean's subornation of perjury with
      regards to testimony of, 27–28
  Gemstone, 25
  indictment of, 73
  meetings on Liddy's plans, 23–24
  negotiations with prosecutors, 71
  plea agreement, 78, 79
  relationship with Liddy, 24–25
  set up and running of CPR, 19–20, 22
Mansfield, Mike, 33
Markham, Paul, 9–10, 11
Marshall, Burke, 12, 13, 173
Martinez, Eugenio R., 15
Matthews, Chris, 39, 218
Maverick: A Life in Politics (Weicker), 72
media. See news media
Merrill, William H., 140
Metzenbaum, Howard, 218
Miller, Arthur, 94
Mills, Wilbur, 207
Milwaukee Journal, 131
Mitchell, John, 114
  indictment of, 78
  and meetings on Liddy's plans,
      23–24
  takes charge of CRP, 24
Mollenhoff, Clark, 180
Montoya, Joseph, 93
Mudd, Roger, 212–14
Muskie, Edmund, 207

Navasky, Victor, 43, 44, 179
Neal, James, 63, 78–80, 84, 153, 225–26
  background, 140
  on cooperation between WSPF and Ervin
      Committee, 112, App. J
  and co-opting of federal prosecutors,
      79–81
  lists persons for interview and/or grand
      jury summons, 145
  memo concerning Dean's contacts with
      original prosecutors, 163, App. V
  memo regarding interview of unindicted
      perjurer, 157, App. T
Neisser, Ulric, 107–8
Ness, Eliot, 42
New Frontier, 2–3
news media
  See also specific outlets
  coverage of and relationship to JFK,
      46–48, 177–78
  coverage of Ted Kennedy, 50, 212–14
  on Cox firing, 183
  liberal partisanship and advocacy by,
      177–84
  on potential candidacy of Ted Kennedy,
      186–87
  Robert Kennedy's relationship to, 48,
      178
  on Saturday Night Massacre, 168–69
Newsweek, 50, 178
New York Times, The, 48, 50, 79, 127, 130,
      131, 166, 178, 179, 225, 226,
      229–30
  on Chappaquiddick, 13
  on Ervin Committee hearings, 97
  Lenzner memo and IRS cover-up, 119,
      120
  reports Petersen under investigation, 84
Nieman, Agnes Wahl, 130–31
Nieman Foundation, 131
9/11 Commission, 227
Nixon, Richard
  on 1960 campaign, 4
  addresses America for first time on
      Watergate, 76–77
  Dean's "cancer on the presidency"
      warning, 54–55
  dirty tricks targeting, 20
  dislike of Ivy Leaguers, 137–38

Nixon, Richard (*cont.*)
  first reaction to bugging of DNC, 21
  implicated by Dean, 74, 75, 106–7
  meetings with counselors on Watergate,
    53–56
  1968 election, 4
  1972 election, 1
  orders Richardson to fire Cox, 167
  precedent for defense at Senate trial,
    185–86
  resignation of, 186
  and Stennis Compromise, 165–67, 169
  unaware of Dean's criminal involvement,
    53, 56, 59, 60–61
  willingness to disclose facts about
    Watergate, 29–30
  withdraws Gray's nomination for FBI
    director, 35
*Not Above the Law: The Battles of Watergate
  Prosecutors Cox and Jaworski: A
  Behind-the-Scenes Account* (Doyle),
  139
Nussbaum, Bernard, 173–74, 224, 229–30

O'Brien, Larry, 24
O'Donnell, Kenny, 3
Oliver, Spencer, 24
O'Neill, Tip, 38

Palladino & Sutherland, 221
pardons
  by Clinton, 189
  Ford pardons Nixon, 189
  WSPF analysis of, 189–91, App. X
Pearson, Drew, 46
Pentagon Papers, 22
Petersen, Henry, 28, 30, 72, 79
  lawyer-client privilege issue, 84
  leak claiming investigation of, 84,
    App. G
  neutralized by WSPF, 82, 83–85
Plumbers, 22
Pommerening, Glen, 135, 136
Powers, Samuel, 185–86
presidential elections
  of 1960, 4
  of 1968, 4

of 1972, 1
of 1976, 210–11
of 1980, 214
press. *See* news media
prosecutorial abuse, 122–23

Reagan, Ronald, 137, 214
  WSPF investigation of, 206–7, App. Z
Rebozo, Charles Gregory (Bebe), 117–19
Reno, Janet, 223–24, 225, 226
*Report of the Watergate Special Prosecution
  Force on Campaign Contributions,
  Investigation of 1972 Campaign
  Financing and Related Matters,*
  194–99, App. Y
*Responses of the Presidents to Charges of
  Misconduct . . .* (Woodward, ed.),
  174–75
Reynolds v. Sims, 179–80
Richardson, Elliot, 76, 81, 84
  agrees to Cox as special prosecutor, 125
  attorney general, 124, 126
  background, 123–24
  neutralized by WSPF, 82–83, 124–25
  resignation of, 167–68
Richmond Times-Dispatch, 48
Rient, Peter F., 158–63, App. U
Risner, Robinson, 137
Roadmap, 172
Robb, Chuck, 227–28
Roberts, John, 219
Rockefeller, Nelson, 204–5
Roosevelt, Eleanor, 37–38
Roosevelt, Franklin, 2
Roosevelt, Teddy, 2
Rose, H. Chapman, 185–86
Rotunda, Ron, 94
Ruby, Jack, 63
Ruckelshaus, William, 168
Ruff, Charles, 140, 196, 198, 201, 205–6,
  227–28
Ruth, Henry, 82, 119, 139, 198, 225

St. Clair, James, 186
St. Louis Dispatch, 127
Sandwedge, 22
Saturday Night Massacre, 164

Schlesinger, Arthur, Jr., 3, 13
Schorr, Daniel, 181
"Searching for the Real Nixon" (Adler), 173, 229
Segretti, Donald, 33, 66–68, 95–96
Select Committee on Presidential Campaign Activities. *See* Ervin Committee
Senate Judiciary Committee, 32, 124, 126
Shaffer, Charles, 35, 162, 219
  background of, 63–65
  Dash-Dean-Shaffer meetings, 96, 105–6
  as Dean's attorney, 35, 62, 64–65, 71, 80
  on Warren Commission, 63–64
Sheppard, Roy, 204–5
Sheridan, Walter, 43
Silberman, Laurence, 123, 142
Silbert, Earl, 70
  on Dean's changing story, 75–76
  on immunity for Dean, 74–75
  removal and silencing of, by WSPF, 79–82, 85
  transition memo leaked to CBS, 81
Sinatra, Frank, 40
Sirica, John, 15, 29, 146, 153
  McCord's first letter to, 32, 53, 58
  McCord's second letter to, 154–57
  presentencing meeting with Dash, 57, 59
  sentencing by, 58–59
Smith, Merriman, 46
Sorenson, Ted, 13, 169
special prosecutor, 6, 123
  See also Cox, Archibald; Watergate Special Prosecution Force
  Cox appointed as, 125
  duties and responsibilities of, 125–26, App. L
Stans, Maurice, 30, 92–93, 113–14, 200–1
Starr, Kenneth, 220
Steinbrenner, George, 199
Stennis, John, 166
Stennis Compromise, 165–67, 169
Stevenson, Adlai, 39
Stonewall: The Real Story of Watergate Prosecution (Ben-Veniste), 145
Strachan, Gordon, 25

Sturgis, Frank, 15
Sullivan, J. J., 185–86
Sullivan, William, 116
Sweig case, 57
Swindler and Berlin v. US, 219–20

Talbot, David, 40
Talmadge, Herman, 93
tapes of Nixon office conversations
  "cancer on the presidency" speech, 54–55
  Dean on Kennedy being behind hearings, 31
  Dean's allegations providing legal basis for obtaining, 110
  18½-minute gap in, 186
  impact of, 109–10
Taylor, Stuart, 143–44
"Team of FBI Agents Used by President Johnson as Political Operatives at the 1964 Democratic Convention," 116–17
Terrors of Justice, The (Stans), 200–1
Thomas, Clarence, 6, 217–18, 219
Thompson, Fred, 95, 112
Time, 45, 50, 186–87
Titus, Harold, 81, 128–30
  on status of Watergate, 129, App. M
To Set the Record Straight: The Break-in, the Tapes, the Conspirators, the Pardon (Sirica), 59
Townhouse Project, 196–97
Truman, Harry, 38
Tuck, Dick, 20
Tunney, John, 34–35

U.S. v. Remington, 144

Vesco case, 114, 201
Vidal, Gore, 41
Vietnam War, 137
Volner, Jill Wine, 141
Vorenberg, James, 112, 130, 187–88, 223
  background, 138
  on expanding scope of inquiry by WSPF, 87–88

Vorenberg, James (*cont.*)
  Flug's briefing of, 132–33
  on timing of anticipated indictments, 86
  staffing of WSPF, 83, 85–86, 135–36
  on Weicker, 97, App. H

Wagner, Helga, 11
Warren Commission, 63–64
Washington Post, 33, 60, 130, 180
  Deep Throat leaks to, 72
  on Lenzner, 221, 222
  on prosecutors threatening to resign,
    128
Washington Star, 130
Watergate
  first break-in, 24, 25
  post-Watergate trial grand jury testimony,
    70–71, App. C
  second break-in and arrests, 15–18, 25
  trial and sentencing of burglars, 52–53
  unraveling of cover-up, 52–62
Watergate Committee. *See* Ervin
    Committee
Watergate Special Prosecution Force
    (WSPF)
  allowing Ervin Committee to precede
    investigation by, 88–90
  analysis of Nixon pardon, 189–91,
    App. X
  and Bittman, 148–54
  Campaign Contributions Task Force,
    193–201, App. Y
  cooperation with Ervin Committee,
    111–13
  co-opting federal prosecutors, 79–82,
    85
  cover-up indictments, 172
  Cox's memos regarding Neal's role, 80,
    App. D, App. E
  deciding whether to indict and prosecute
    Nixon, 187–89
  Denny/Rient memo on Dean's changing
    story, 158–63, App. U

  disavows Stennis Compromise, 165–67
  expanding scope of inquiry, 87–88
  grand jury process abuses of, 143–46
  interviews of Nixon secretaries, 186
  investigations conducted by, 142–43
  leaks to and cooperation with press,
    179–83
  Peterson neutralized by, 83–85
  potential Kennedy opponents investi-
    gated by, 202–8
  Richardson neutralized by, 82–83,
    124–25
  and Roadmap, 172
  staffing, 83, 85–86, 135–42
  subpoena for Dean's files, 170, App. W
  Vorenberg's staffing of, 85–86
  Watergate Task Force, 142
  on when to expect indictments, 86–87
Weicker, Lowell, 72, 94, 97–98, 111–12,
    180–81, 219
Weitz, Alan, 94–95
White, Theodore H., 203, 211–12
"White House horrors," 71–72
The Whole Truth: The Watergate Conspiracy
    (Ervin), 92
Wiggins, Charles, 175
Wills, Frank, 16
Witcover, Jules, 187
Without Honor: Crimes of Camelot and the
    Impeachment of President Nixon
    (Zeifman), 173–75, 228–29
Woodward, Bob, 33, 201, 222
  information leaked to, 72
  off-the-record help for Dash, 180
Woodward, C. Vann, 174
Wright, Charles Alan, 165
WSPF. *See* Watergate Special Prosecution
    Force (WSPF)

Young, David, 22

Zeifman, Jerry, 173–76, 228–29